New Marketing Strategies

Evolving Flexible Processes to Fit Market Circumstance

Ian Chaston

SAGE Publications
London • Thousand Oaks • New Delhi

© Ian Chaston 1999

First published 1999

All rights reserved. No part of this publication may be
reproduced, stored in a retrieval system, transmitted or
utilized in any form or by any means, electronic, mechanical,
photocopying, recording or otherwise, without permission
in writing from the Publishers.

SAGE Publications Ltd
6 Bonhill Street
London EC2A 4PU

SAGE Publications Inc.
2455 Teller Road
Thousand Oaks, California 91320

SAGE Publications India Pvt Ltd
32, M-Block Market
Greater Kailash – I
New Delhi 110 048

British Library Cataloguing in Publication data

A catalogue record for this book is
available from the British Library

ISBN 0-7619-6201-8
ISBN 0-7619-6202-6 (pbk)

Library of Congress catalog record available
Typeset by M Rules
Printed in Great Britain by Biddles Ltd, Guildford, Surrey

UNIVERSITY OF HERTFORDSHIRE
LIBRARY, HERTFORD CAMPUS,
HERTFORD, SG13 8QF

CONTROL
285983

CLASS
658.802 CHA

COLLECTION/LOAN STATUS
HERT MAIN STANDARD

ITEM
44 0475301 4

44 0475301 4

New Marketing Strategies

WITHDRAWN

Contents

Preface

America's overwhelming economic success in the period immediately follow-ing the Second World War was accompanied by their business schools moving to the forefront in evolving theoretical paradigms for use in the effective management of organizations. In the world of marketing, individuals such as D.J. McCarthy and P. Kotler presented, in the first editions of their market-ing management texts, clear agendas for defining the components which comprise the marketing process.

The emergence of the new tiger nations from the Pacific Rim in the 1970s had a significant impact on management thinking around the world. Individuals such as R.M. Cyert, J.G. March and H. Mintzberg raised ques-tions about whether theories espoused and taught in Western nation business schools concerning the superiority of adopting a strategic management approach (which they referred to as 'classicist thinking') were relevant to organizations seeking to survive in a increasingly competitive and turbulent world.

During the 1980s some academics, through their studies of buyer–seller behaviour in industrial markets, began to identify alternative marketing models based on achievement of performance goals by avoiding confronta-tional competition and, instead, adopting a philosophy of building collaborative relationships within their industrial sector. Concurrently, as the expansion of the service sector was recognized as a characteristic of devel-oped nation economies, other academics began to propose that the transactionalist orientation which underpins many marketing management concepts should be replaced with paradigms concerned with building long-term customer loyalty.

Another added complication which emerged in the latter part of the twen-tieth century was the recognition of the importance of concepts such as 'total quality management', 'just in time' and 'process re-engineering'. The very dis-turbing aspect of many of these new areas of management thinking was that although they involved activities that encompassed building closer relation-ships with customers at all levels within the supply chain, marketers frequently found that the responsibility for process implementation was often vested with other departments within their organization such as Procurement, Manufacturing or Human Resource Management (HRM).

The intention of proposing the concept of Flexi-Marketing is to release the marketer from rigid adherence to prescriptive, standard managerial approaches. Instead it is suggested that the individual draw upon both intu-itive and logical styles of thinking to evolve marketing practices based upon both responding appropriately to market circumstance and exploiting those internal competences which form the basis of the organization's identified competitive advantage.

The objectives of this text are to introduce the reader to the implications of a more flexible approach to the development of marketing strategies by examining how differences in markets and corporate styles, when linked to the alternatives of adopting a transactional, relationship, entrepreneurial and/or network-based orientation, may influence the marketing process. The reader should note that this text does not adopt the extreme position taken by some theorists who propose we should now totally reject any approach based upon the principles of strategic marketing. My view is that traditional, transactional marketing still has relevance in today's world. Furthermore, this school of marketing has contributed some excellent models of management which can continue to provide theoretical foundations for use in the evolution of new concepts more suited to respond effectively to different and/or changing market scenarios.

Chapter 1 reviews how a new understanding of market situations has contributed towards evolving alternative marketing philosophies. Chapter 2 discusses why internal organizational competences can have a considerable influence on strategy and performance. Chapter 3 examines the nature of variations in market systems. In Chapters 4 and 5, it is shown how, by linking together external and internal market circumstances, organizations can evolve and select appropriate strategies for surviving in the face of ever-increasing competitive pressures.

The importance of understanding and responding to customer behaviour is presented in Chapter 6. A large number of accepted theories of marketing are grounded in the management of tangible, consumer goods products. Hence Chapters 7 and 8 examine how marketing philosophies may need to be revised to satisfy customer needs more appropriately in business-to-business markets and service markets respectively.

Chapter 9 reviews the critical role of new products in an organization's product portfolio and examines techniques for optimizing the innovation management process. Chapters 10 and 11 cover management of the promotion, price and distribution elements of the marketing mix.

The final chapter then examines the increasingly important role of international marketing and reviews the competences that may be required by organizations seeking to exploit further the opportunities available within global markets both now and well into the next millennium.

It is assumed that readers of the text, either as students and/or as practitioners, have already received some grounding in the basic principles of marketing management. The purpose of this text is to build on this knowledge, thereby helping the reader to comprehend how, by adopting a more flexible perspective in responding to the influence of differences in both internal and external market environments, one is more likely to optimise the future performance of organizations.

1 Marketing – an Evolving Philosophy

The success enjoyed by American firms such as Ford and General Motors has been a strong influencer of the strategic (or 'Classicist') school of management thinking. Not surprisingly, therefore, as marketing emerged as a distinct management discipline in the second half of the twentieth century, many academics drew upon strategic management concepts to create the first ever theoretical models of marketing process.

Over the last two decades, however, alternative approaches to management such as those tabled by the 'Processualists', Evolutionists' and 'Systemicists' have stimulated debate over the advisability of a rigid adherence to classic strategic management theories in the context of optimizing the performance of firms in today's turbulent trading environments. Observations of industrial and service sector organizations have, for example, raised questions about assuming that buyer–seller behaviour should continue be treated in textbooks as an essentially transactional process. Debate over this issue has led to the emergence of the concept known as 'relationship marketing'. Supporters of this concept believe it offers a more likely route by which to build long-term customer loyalty. Other researchers, especially those studying smaller firms, have noted variance between classic theories and practice in the case of highly innovative organizations. This has caused them to posit a concept known as 'entrepreneurial marketing'.

The risk of new, alternative perspectives is that some writers may be so strongly committed to their opinions, that they may cease to accept that the traditional concepts of marketing as practised by fast-moving consumer goods companies are still probably applicable in many market sectors. Hence, given the variety of trading circumstances facing organizations, perhaps the wisest course is to accept that transactional, relationship and/or entrepreneurial marketing all offer opportunities for firms to optimize performance. Thus it is proposed that adopting a more flexible approach to matching marketing processes to market circumstance will offer the most effective path through which to ensure 'ownership of the future'.

Alternative Management Perspectives

As the dominant trading nation for most of the twentieth century, it is under-standable that the USA, over the last 100 years, has become the primary source of many of the new theories of management. America's initial success in world markets was based upon the principle of exploiting the scale benefits of mass production to supply low-priced, standardized goods such as auto-mobiles, refrigerators and televisions.

Alfred Sloan, who rescued General Motors during the 1920s recession, held the view that the secret of successful management is grounded in the con-cept of applying rational planning to achieve the single-minded goal of maximizing profits. To help formalize this theory, Sloan and his supporters from within the academic community, such as Alfred Chandler and Igor Ansoff, have drawn upon the conceptual rules of business established by the economist Adam Smith (author of *The Wealth of Nations*) and the militaristic principles of the Greek and Roman empires. Described as a 'Classicist' approach to business, the principles of rational planning models as a way of optimizing organizational performance have subsequently become the foun-dation stone upon which the syllabi of many business schools around the world have been constructed (Whittington 1993).

America's loss of market share to the new economic tiger nations of Japan and Taiwan in the latter years of the twentieth century caused a rad-ical re-examination of the management principles being taught in Western nation business schools. Some researchers have focused their efforts on seeking to understand the nature of Pacific Rim managerial practices in the context of assessing how such nations are utilizing Classicist managerial philosophies. Their conclusions are that within Pacific Rim organizations, success can often be attributed to a Classicist approach to planning linked to a 'work ethic' commitment. Thus, for example, companies such as Daewoo are seen as users of a traditional Fordist manufacturing approach to achieve a level of employee productivity which greatly exceeds that of workers executing similar tasks in most European or American automobile plants.

Other Western researchers such as H. Mintzberg have adopted the view that there is a need to place greater emphasis on observing actual manage-ment practices when seeking to evolve new theoretical paradigms. From such perspectives, alternative schools of management thought have begun to emerge. Mintzberg (1989), for example, has questioned the basic premise of Classicist management theory that strategy formation is a controlled, con-scious process undertaken by humans acting as rational, economic thinkers. He, and other individuals such as R.M.Cyert, J.G. March and H.A. Simon, believe the rational, economic being is a figment of mythology rarely found outside of textbooks. Their view of the manager is of an individual who is reluctant to embark on unlimited searches for information and instead is more likely to form an opinion on the basis of the first satisfactory option that is presented for consideration. These academics would also argue that, as members of an organization, managers survive by being willing to accept compromise in return for achieving acceptance of an opinion. Known as the 'Processual' approach to management, this school of theorists downgrades the importance of rational analysis and instead perceives management as creating strategies through selecting those routines which within the organization can be identified as contributing to success.

Another perspective, which again questions the ability of senior managers to act as rational planners, is that of the 'Evolutionists'. This school of thought, strongly promoted by Bruce Henderson, founder of the Boston Consulting Group, believes the destiny of the firm is determined by 'the laws of the commercial jungle'. Hence in the real world, whichever plan is adopted by managers, ultimately the winner will be the organization most suited to surviving in the face of prevailing market conditions. The Evolutionists' view of strategic planning is to urge the manager to accept that markets control destiny and to give emphasis to selecting industrial sectors which are compatible with the identified capabilities of the organization.

In contrast to the Processualist and Evolutionist approaches to management, the 'Systemic' school of management supports the idea of organizations placing faith in a structured planning process through which to evolve a strategy compatible with the external environment in which the firm is required to operate. Although this is clearly a philosophy which in part is compatible with the Classicists' view of the world, the Systemicists feel that the actual behaviour of organizations is to a large degree determined by specific sociological contexts. This implies that decision-makers are strongly influenced by the social networks of which they are a part. Thus in examining alternative approaches for developing an effective planning philosophy, the systemicist will seek to comprehend the social roots from which the organization has emerged. Whitley (1991), for example, has studied the forms of business across the Pacific Rim and identified the influence of state, family and market structures. In South Korea, the country's strong centralist orientation has led to the emergence of the vast conglomerates known as *chaebols*. This can be contrasted with another equally successful world player, Taiwan, which is an example of a trading nation based around loosely linked, highly entrepreneurial, family businesses.

One approach to these alternative schools of thought is to recognize that they are driven by two key variables, namely breadth of objectives associated with the crafting of plans, and the degree to which the planning process is formalized within the organization. As illustrated in Figure 1.1, the Classicist and Evolutionary management models usually operate with a low number of business objectives directed towards achieving the classic economist's goal of profit maximization. The Systemic and Processual schools of management perceive organizations which, although also aspiring to achieve clear financial goals, in addition extend their objectives across other sociological issues such as a commitment to their employees and the adoption of a role as custodian of world environments.

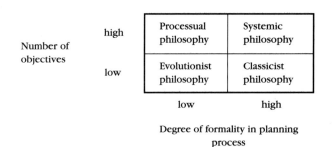

Figure 1.1   **Alternative managerial philosophies**

In terms of the degree to which management of the future is a highly formalized activity, within organizations with a Classicist or Systemic orientation planning is a highly structured, carefully regimented activity. This can be contrasted with companies with a Processual or Evolutionary orientation in which managers adopt a less routinized, less formalized planning philosophy.

The Birth of Marketing Theory

After the Second World War, as Europe and many areas of the Pacific Rim struggled to rebuild their war-devastated economies, the American GI returned home to a nation eager to adopt the mantle of being the leading economic power for the balance of the twentieth century. The expertise and wealth accumulated by acting as the manufacturing hub for the Allied Powers' military materials during the war was immediately directed towards the creation of what subsequently has become known as the 'American Dream'.

The post-war growth of the American economy, fuelled by rapidly rising consumer spending power, provided the platform for the subsequent global expansion of firms such as Coca Cola, McDonalds and Levi Strauss. Some management theorists seeking to understand the success of such firms concluded that performance could be linked to the adoption of a marketing orientated business philosophy. This approach to management is based on the concept that financial goals can best be achieved by first determining the needs of the customer and then satisfying these by providing appropriate products and/or services. Marketing, by reducing risk and improving understanding of customer needs, was presented as superior to the more traditional industrial model of constructing a plant to produce products and then seeking sufficient customers to purchase all available output.

The founding fathers of twentieth-century marketing such as D.J. McCarthy and P. Kotler were clearly influenced by the Classicist view of management. As a consequence and to this day, many standard textbooks (e.g. Kotler 1997) present marketing as a sequential, logical process designed to provide answers to three questions:

1   Where are we now?
2   Where are we going?
3   How are we going to get there?

To undertake this type of analysis, the marketer is advised to adopt a framework of the type shown in Figure 1.2. The entry point to the process is to execute a detailed study of both the internal and external environments confronting the organization. This knowledge then permits definition of future performance goals, the strategy by which to achieve these goals, and the elements of the plan necessary for underpinning adopted strategy. Delivery of the plan is achieved by utilizing the McCarthy '4Ps' variables of Product, Price, Promotion and Place. Concurrent with implementation of the plan is the creation of a feedback and control system which provides the manager with the knowledge necessary to monitor effectively actual versus planned performance.

In this Classicist view of the world, the marketer is assigned the task of acting as the interface between the market and the organization. As shown in Figure 1.3, the role is that of matching the resources available within the firm to opportunities evident within the external environment of which the organization is a part. The proven durability of this concept is demonstrated by

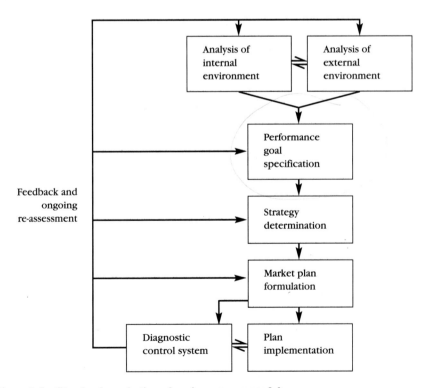

Figure 1.2   **Standard marketing planning process model**

Figure 1.3   **The Classicist view of the marketing role**

the fact that it is the rationale underpinning the brand management organizational structure which is still in use today within successful fast-moving consumer goods ('f.m.c.g.') organizations such as Unilever, Procter and Gamble and General Foods.

Marketing – a Troubled Adolescence

The basic theories of marketing were initially evolved through studies of the battle for market share between major brands in US consumer, tangible goods markets such as detergents and coffee. Researchers seeking to validate the benefits of classicist theories of marketing management in other situations such as industrial and/or service markets, however, have often encountered severe difficulties in locating evidence that classicist marketing concepts are widely accepted by managers within these latter industrial sectors.

Initially the apparent absence of a strategic market orientation was often attributed to the inadequacies of managers who failed to appreciate the benefits of a structured, formalized approach to marketing centred on a department responsible for orchestrating the customer satisfaction process. In the Nordic countries, however, a 'grounded theory' approach of avoiding preconceived hypotheses of management process, observing actual events and seeking convergence in practice has led to identification of alternative marketing models. Pioneering work by the Industrial Marketing and Procurement (IMP) Group proved that firms in many industrial markets, instead of seeking to build market share through emphasis on intense competition with other brands, are often orientated towards the concept of inter-firm co-operation as a path by which to build long-term relationships based upon trust and commitment.

Writers such as Nystrom (1990) assert that the Classicist school of marketing is based upon the economic theory of the firm in which well-defined products are made available in a market where both supplier and customer are fully informed about the relative merits of competing offerings. He argues that classicist marketing is founded on the assumption that access to information permits the customers to make a rational choice based upon a comparison of benefits offered by competing firms. Furthermore, he feels that classicist marketing incorrectly assumes buyers are passive, reactive users who are not interested in any form of interaction with the supplier.

Studies of the marketing process in service sectors such as finance and retailing have also revealed situations where customers do not exhibit strong transactionally orientated buying behaviour. This situation has thereby permitted supplier firms to exploit opportunities for building long-term relationships based on working in close partnership with purchasers.

In manufacturing environments, a move towards closer customer–supplier relationships has been given added weight by the managerial philosophies of Total Quality Management (TQM) and Just In Time (JIT). TQM is an organizational commitment to fulfilling the customer's expectations over product and/or service quality. Clearly a large Original Equipment Manufacturer (or OEM) such as IBM or Xerox can only fulfil customer expectations if their suppliers are also dedicated to the delivery of high-quality components. For this to be achieved, both the suppliers and the OEM have to move away from the traditional, price-based, confrontational negotiation style towards a relationship-orientated style based upon respect for each other's contribution to achieving the mutual goal of optimizing product quality.

JIT is a concept based upon reducing finished goods and work-in-progress by moving away from the traditional concept of long production runs of single items determined by an economic order quantity (EOQ) formula towards a highly responsive, batch-type manufacturing system based on matching production schedules to recently received customer orders. For firms such as Hewlett Packard JIT has significantly reduced inventory levels and concurrently enhanced the firm's image as being able to offer a rapid, flexible response to changing customer needs. However, as for TQM, for JIT to be successful the OEM must create a close working relationship with suppliers in order to implement concepts such as same-day delivery, willingness to come on to the shop floor to manage restocking of component bins and automated invoice generation using Electronic Data Interchange (EDI) systems.

During the 1970s and 1980s, there was a massive expansion in companies dedicated to the provision of services in sectors as diverse as finance, fast food and management consultancy. Marketers hired by these organizations encountered significant problems when attempting to apply classical concepts such as influencing customer demand through application of the '4Ps'. The conclusion of both practitioners and academics was that because of features such as the intangible nature of goods, difficulty in separating production from consumption and the heterogeneous nature of customer need, effective service marketing would require the evolution of new paradigms.

As with the marketer in industrial markets, many service marketing theorists focused on the fact that firms who were placing emphasis on single transactions should in fact be attempting to build long-term relationships with customers. A strong impetus to this alternative philosophy was provided by Reichfeld and Sasser (1990) who demonstrated that a transaction

orientation could result in focusing excessive resources on attracting new customers when in fact the real benefits of marketing come from programmes
directed at retaining existing customers (or in their terminology ensuring
achievement of 'zero defections').

Relationship versus Transactional Marketing

As a result of studies of the marketing processes employed by both industrial
and service firms, a new school of thought has emerged which examines how
the firm can orchestrate internal resources and processes to create and sustain
customer loyalty. Collectively this new orientation, which has both American
(Berry 1982) and Nordic (Gummesson 1987) roots, is known as Relationship
Marketing. Supporters of this new form of marketing argue that in order to
survive in markets which have become more competitive and more turbulent,
organizations must move away from managing transactions and instead focus
on building long-lasting customer relationships (Webster 1992).

Advocates of relationship marketing will typically support their views
through a comparison of process of the type shown in Table 1.1.

Table 1.1   *Contrasting marketing philosophies*

Transactional marketing	Relationship marketing
Orientation towards single purchase	Orientation towards repeat sales
Limited direct customer/supplier contact	Close, frequent customer/supplier contact
Focus on product benefits	Focus on value to customer
Emphasis on near-term performance	Emphasis on long-term performance
Limited level of customer service	High level of customer service
Goal of customer satisfaction	Goal of 'delighting the customer'
Quality a manufacturing responsibility	Quality a total organization responsibility

Some disciples of the 'new marketing' have suggested that traditional concepts based around the approach of focusing resources on the '4Ps', which
may have been appropriate in North American consumer branded goods
markets of the 1950s and 1960s, are no longer relevant in today's world.
Gronroos (1994: 253), for example, proposes that 'the usefulness of the 4Ps as
a general theory for practical purposes is, to say the least, highly questionable'. A somewhat less extreme position, however, has been proposed by
Nevin (1994) who feels firms should adopt a segmentation philosophy ranging from building strong relationships with key customers through to
continuing to utilize the traditional '4Ps' approach for those customers seeking a standardized, generic product proposition. A similarly balanced view is
presented by Anderson and Narus (1991) who recommend that firms weigh
both customer orientation towards closer relationships and the cost/benefit
implications of sustaining close relationships when selecting the most appropriate strategy to suit prevailing market conditions.

Entrepreneurial Marketing

Another area of academic debate, again reflecting dissatisfaction with the traditional transactional '4Ps' approach to marketing, is that smaller firms exhibit a somewhat different approach to the management of customers. This has occurred because academics (e.g. Carson et al. 1995) have questioned whether many of the classic large-firm marketing theories can be transferred into the small-firm sector.

By moving away from hypothesis testing based on the American business school style of thinking and instead observing actual management practices, these researchers are beginning to evolve a somewhat different perspective of what might constitute effective marketing practices within the smaller firm (Carson et al. 1995). This latter type of research has prompted these writers to conclude that marketing within the smaller firm can often be viewed as an integral part of managing entrepreneurial activities.

The justification for proposing that small firms adopt an entrepreneurial marketing philosophy is that they face specific constraints which set them apart from larger organizations. Birley (1982) has suggested that these constraints include (a) goals not based on analysis of opportunity, but determined by the actions which appeal to the owner/manager, and (b) a lack of resources and/or knowledge which precludes decision-making based on the classic strategic marketing approach of analysing markets, selecting a long-term growth strategy and optimal management of a detailed plan. Carson (1985) subsequently identified two further constraints – lack of general management expertise and limited customer base, which can also be expected to influence the marketing processes employed by the owner/manager.

An Alternative Model of Marketing Philosophies

A potential hazard with emerging theories of management is that polarization of opinions may cause academics to reject alternative perspectives and, at the extreme, begin to claim firms can only succeed by adopting their prescriptive solution. Fortunately, the competent marketing practitioner is usually able to identify which theories tend to exhibit the 'emperor's new clothes syndrome', and are capable of adopting those concepts which are best suited to managing prevailing market circumstances. Furthermore, observation of such individuals would suggest that they often create effective hybrid management practices which are based on selecting from various available theories those elements of management practice most likely to contribute to enhancing overall performance of their organization.

In the case of relationship marketing, Jackson (1985) argued that the philosophy may not be relevant to all situations. To her, transactional marketing is probably more appropriate in those cases in which the customer has a short time horizon, and switching suppliers is a low-cost activity. Thus a customer seeking a standard specification microchip can purchase this item from a number of manufacturers and the purchase decision will be heavily influenced by which supplier is offering what are perceived as the best terms and conditions at time of order placement. In contrast, where the customer has a long time horizon and the costs of switching are high, then the purchase decision will involve a careful search for a supplier who is prepared to invest time and money to build a strong, lasting relationship with the customer. An example of this latter type of situation would be an automobile manufacturer seeking to purchase a 'state of the art', robotic car assembly line, who will carefully review the project bid specifications and commitment to partnership exhibited by potential suppliers of robotic machine tools.

If one accepts Jackson's perspective, then the debate between transactional versus relationship marketing is one of choice; namely, in virtually every industrial and/or service sector situation there are price-oriented customers who respond well to a transactional marketing philosophy whereas there are other purchasers with whom a strong long-term relationship can be created. The objective, under these circumstances, for marketers is to select the marketing philosophy for their organization which is most suited to their firm's internal capabilities and/or the nature of the product proposition they desire to offer to the market.

The same proposal on internal capability and nature of product offering can be made in the context of an entrepreneurial versus a non-entrepreneurial marketing orientation. Some firms are best suited to manufacturing standardized goods at a competitive price. Other firms are extremely competent at managing 'leading-edge' technology, and clearly this skill can best be exploited by adopting an entrepreneurial orientation of regularly launching new, innovative products.

If one accepts the perspective that both transactional versus relationship, and entrepreneurial versus conservative, marketing are not mutually exclusive concepts, then this permits consideration of hybrid management models. The latter approach seems eminently more likely to be of greater benefit to the evolution of new theories of marketing than the trait of exhibiting an unchanging allegiance to a single, purist philosophy. Acceptance of alternative views of the world then permits the suggestion that all of the following approaches to marketing are equally valid choices:

1 Conservative-transactional style firms who operate in markets where the customer is seeking standard specification goods or services at a competitive price and has little interest in building a close relationship with suppliers (e.g. double glazing firms bidding on Local Government replacement window contracts).

2 Conservative-relationship style firms who operate in markets where the customer is seeking standard specification goods or services but is willing to work closely with suppliers to optimize quality and/or obtain mutual

benefits from creating an effective purchase and delivery system. (e.g. engineering firms supplying components to OEMs who operate JIT/TQM manufacturing philosophies).

3   Entrepreneurial-transactional style firms who operate in markets where customers are seeking innovative products or services which can be procured without forming a close relationship with suppliers (e.g. software houses using direct mail to market low-cost, customized spreadsheet packages which solve sector-specific management accounting problems).

4   Entrepreneurial-relationship style firms who operate in markets where customers work in partnership with suppliers to develop innovative new products or services (e.g. producers of low-volume, customized microprocessors used by specialist machine tool manufacturers).

One way of presenting these alternative market positions is to assume there are two dimensions influencing marketing strategy, namely closeness to customer and level of entrepreneurial activity. By using these two dimensions, it is possible to create a matrix of the type shown in Figure 1.4 to visualise the four alternative marking styles that might offer alternative strategic choices to a firm.

The possible existence of alternative hybrid marketing styles stimulated initiation of a research project to examine whether differences in style can be measured and whether style influences the overall performance of the firm. Miller (1983) has proposed that entrepreneurial style encompasses the elements of risk-taking, innovation and proactiveness. Covin and Slevin (1988) applied this definition to evolve and validate a tool which uses statements of managerial process to measure the degree to which respondent firms exhibit an entrepreneurial style.

Although a review of the literature provides a number of different descriptions of the characteristics exhibited by relationship-orientated organizations, no appropriate scale appears to exist which can be used as a research tool. Anderson and Narus (1991) have suggested that marketing strategy can be considered as a continuum ranging from transactional through to a

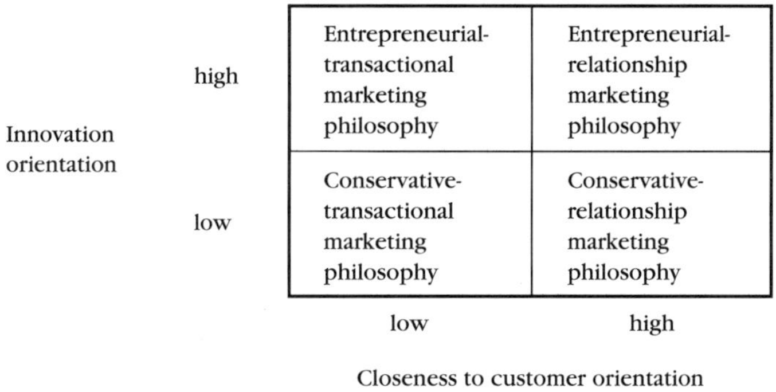

		low	high
Innovation orientation	high	Entrepreneurial-transactional marketing philosophy	Entrepreneurial-relationship marketing philosophy
	low	Conservative-transactional marketing philosophy	Conservative-relationship marketing philosophy

Closeness to customer orientation

Figure 1.4   **Alternative marketing philosophies**

relationship orientation. By adopting the same research design as in the Covin/Slevin study, it may be possible to determine a firm's position on a strategic continuum by seeking owners'/managers' level of agreement with descriptive statements concerning management of customer relations.

Gummesson's (1987) and Gronroos's (1994) relationship (1994) models permitted the generation of 20 descriptive statements which were reviewed in focus group meetings with manufacturing firms. From this list the following six statements were found to differentiate most clearly between firms which operate in markets in which the customer is seeking standard components at a competitive price and those in which the customer seeks to build a close working relationship with suppliers:

1   Revenue is primarily generated from repeat sales from customers with whom the firm has developed long-term, close personal relationships.
2   In-depth understanding of customer needs is achieved through building close working relationships over a number of years.
3   New and improved products are developed by working in close partnership with customers.
4   The firm's quality standards are specifically tailored to meet the individual customer's needs.
5   Staff are strongly committed to meeting the needs of others both inside and outside the organization.
6   Staff at all levels within the firm interact with customers in seeking solutions to identified problems.

SME (Small and Medium-size Enterprise) sector UK manufacturing firms were asked to respond to statements concerning entrepreneurial relationship style. Firms were classified into the four styles of conservative-transactional, conservative-relationship, entrepreneurial-transactional and entrepreneurial-relationship marketing style according to whether their entrepreneurial and relationship scores were above or below the mean value for these two indices.

Summary statistics for the performance of the four marketing styles are shown in Table 1.2. It can been seen from these data that the entrepreneurial-transactional firms have the highest overall sales growth rate, entrepreneurial-relationship and conservative-relationship firms have slightly lower, but similar, growth rates, and conservative-transactional firms have the lowest growth rate.

Table 1.2   *Summary statistics by style of management*

Style	Number	Mean growth	SD growth
Entrepreneurial-transactional	22	5.71	0.644
Entrepreneurial-relationship	31	5.06	1.202
Conservative-relationship	23	5.09	0.811
Conservative-transactional	28	3.59	1.803

The results of this study do appear to support the possible existence of four different marketing styles which reflect a merger of the concepts of relationship and entrepreneurial marketing. In terms of commenting upon which is the most appropriate style for small UK manufacturing firms, on the basis of the significantly lower average sales revenue reported for conservative-transactional style firms, it does appear that this is the least appealing strategic option. This is in contrast with entrepreneurial-transactional, conservative-relationship or entrepreneurial-relationship marketing styles, all of which, on average, achieve higher revenue growth.

The results of the study should not, however, be used to make prescriptive recommendations about which is the best style for a firm to adopt. It is clearly very necessary to recognize that market circumstances and/or the orientation of the management will influence this decision. For example, a firm may operate in a market where customers are essentially transactionally orientated and/or the benefits of moving closer to the customer are greatly outweighed by the costs a firm would encounter in implementing such actions. Alternatively if the personal aspirations of management are to develop radically innovative new products, then building extremely close links with customers might limit the firm's ability to become a leading-edge supplier of technology because the pace of innovation might be constrained by the conservative nature of the average customer in their industrial sector.

Features of Alternative Marketing Philosophies

The very different nature of the alternative marketing philosophies' styles described in Figure 1.4, suggest that the following operational orientations will be needed to drive the marketing process within these four types of firm:

Conservative-transactional orientated firms
- price/quality/value product combination superior to that of competition.
- standardized products
- excellence in managing production and distribution logistics
- information system designed to rapidly identify manufacturing and/or logistic errors

Conservative-relationship orientated firms
- product/service combination which delivers complete customer-specific solution
- product solution based on standard specification for industrial sector
- obsession with finding even more effective solutions to customer problems
- information systems which rapidly identify errors in solution provision
- culture of all employees committed to working closely with counterparts within the customer organization

Entrepreneurial-transactional orientated firms
- product offering outstanding superior performance versus competition
- orientation towards even more innovation and extending the performance boundaries of existing products
- excellence in entrepreneurial activity by all members of the workforce
- culture of employees always challenging current methods of operation

Entrepreneurial-relationship orientated firms
- product contributes to ensuring customer output delivers superior performance relative to their competitors
- orientation towards assisting customers achieve even more innovation and extending the boundaries of their existing products
- excellence in joint entrepreneurial activity between employees and their counterparts in the customer organization
- culture of employees always working with their counterparts in the customer organization jointly to challenge current operations within both organizations

Into Adulthood

At the end of the 1970s, marketing as a management discipline in the Western world entered a period of crisis. Academics, having noted the failure of many firms to embrace classical strategic marketing, began to express doubts about the future prospects for the survival of their subject. Practitioners were finding the introduction of TQM and/or customer care programmes had often resulted in many of their traditional responsibilities for understanding and satisfying customer needs being shared with other departments such as manufacturing and distribution. Furthermore, in some firms, new departments were created to manage the functions of corporate communications and/or internal marketing.

Some people were so disturbed by these trends that conferences were held to ponder the proposition that 'the end of marketing is nigh'. Thankfully after a lengthy period of debate, the wiser heads among both academics and practitioners have prevailed. Their conclusion is that marketing is not coming to the end of its useful life, but instead that a new alternative vision is beginning to emerge. The basic tenets of the new vision are that variation in circumstance across areas such as markets, customer behaviours, process technologies and organizational competencies are combining to require marketing to move away from a single, purist managerial concept towards a multi-faceted approach in which strategic decisions are influenced by whether the organization has adopted a transactional, relationship and/or entrepreneurial orientation to manage process.

The concept of a multi-faceted approach to marketing should not be interpreted as a proposal that marketers should reject all aspects of classic strategic marketing thinking. In highly transactional markets where customers seek standardized goods (e.g. many of the fast-moving consumer goods markets such as coffee, health and beauty aids (HbAs) or detergents) then many of the basic principles of marketing as practised for many years by the multi-national branded goods companies will probably remain totally relevant for the foreseeable future. Instead what is being proposed is the philosophy of 'Flexi-Marketing' where the marketer first determines the nature of customer need and then selects a marketing style most suited to prevailing circumstances.

Thus, for example, if market research reveals customer satisfaction can best be achieved through a new, innovative benefit solution then perhaps an entrepreneurial marketing orientation would be the most effective route through which to build brand share. Alternatively, if customers exhibit a homogeneous need for a standard product then classic strategic marketing centred around promotion and price may be the best approach.

An alternative way of explaining recent events is to view marketing during the period 1945–85 as being at a 'caterpillar stage' of management – eating, growing and expanding in size. For a few years in the late 1980s, the species ceased to move forward because it had entered the pupal stage. Hopefully the transformation is now almost complete, resulting in marketers adopting a much more flexible approach. Assuming this can occur, then as we progress into the next millennium the species will emerge as a colourful and vibrant butterfly.

References

Anderson, J.C. and Narus, J.A. (1991) 'Partnering as a focused market strategy', *California Management Review*, Spring: 95–113.

Berry, L.L. (1982) 'Relationship marketing', in L.L., Berry, G.L. Shostack, and G.D. Upah (eds), *Emerging Perspectives on Service Marketing*, Chicago: American Marketing Association, pp. 25–8.

Birley, S. (1982) 'Corporate strategy and the small firm', *Journal of General Management*, 8(2): 82–6.

Carson, D.J. (1985) 'The evolution of marketing in small firms', *European Journal of Marketing*, 19(5): 7–16.

Carson, D.J., Cromie, S., Mcgowan, P. and Hill, J. (1995) *Marketing and Entrepreneurship in SMEs*, London: Prentice Hall.

Covin, J.G. and Slevin, D.P. (1988) 'The influence of organizational structure on the utility of an entrepreneurial top management style', *Journal of Management Studies*, 25: 217–37.

Gronroos, C. (1994) 'From marketing mix to relationship marketing', *Journal of Academic Marketing Science*, 23(4): 252–4.

Gummesson, E. (1987) 'The new marketing – developing long-term interactive relationships', *Long Range Planning*, 20(4): 10–20.

Jackson, B.B. (1985) *Winning and Keeping Industrial Customers: The Dynamics of Customer Relationships*, Lexington, MA: D.C. Heath.

Kotler, P. (1997) *Marketing Management: Analysis, Planning, Implementation and Control* (9th edn), Upper Saddle River, NJ: Prentice Hall.

Miller, D. (1983) 'The correlates of enterpreneurship in three types of firm', *Management Science*, 29: 770–91.

Mintzberg, H. (1989) 'Strategy formation: schools of thought', in J. Fredickson (ed.), *Perspectives on Strategic Management*, San Francisco: Ballinger.

Nevin, J.R. (1994) 'Relationship marketing and distribution channels: exploring fundamental issues', *Journal of Academic Marketing Science*, 23(4): 334–7.

Nystrom, H. (1990) *Technological and Market Innovation: Strategy for Product and Company Development*, Chichester: Wiley and Sons.

Reichfeld, F.F. and Sasser, W. (1990) 'Zero defections: quality comes to services', *Harvard Business Review*, September–October: 301–7.

Webster, F.E. (1992) 'The changing role of marketing in the organization', *Journal of Marketing*, 56 (October): 1–17.

Whitley, R.D. (1991) 'The social construction of business systems in South East Asia', *Organization Studies*, 11(1): 1–28.

Whittington, R. (1993) *What is Strategy and Does it Matter?* London: Thomson Business Press.

2 Internal Competences

The concept of mass marketing is rooted in a philosophy of seeking to fulfil customer need by the provision of standardized, low-cost goods produced through exploitation of the economies of scale offered by mass production. In the 1970s, as Western nations awoke to the competitive threat emerging from the success of Pacific Rim firms in world markets, both academics and management consultants sought to comprehend why the 'new competition' was being so successful. One identified reason was that Pacific Rim organizations appeared to have evolved internal capabilities in areas such as manufacturing and quality management that permitted them to offer the customer greater value than their Western nation counterparts. Various models have emerged concerning the internal capabilities or 'core competences' which firms must acquire to survive in today's global markets.

One model, based upon research in Europe and New Zealand, proposes that the key competences are strategy, finance, innovation, workforce skills, employee productivity, quality and information management. It is also proposed, however, that the managerial style of a specific organization will influence which competences will need to be given priority. The conservative-transactional firm, for example, will probably need to focus on employee productivity in order to optimize operating costs. This can be contrasted with an entrepreneurial-transactional firm which should probably place emphasis on acquiring a high level of competence in the development and launch of new products.

Fewer and fewer firms can now expect to exhibit all of the competences required to survive in today's highly complex and rapidly changing world. In response, many organizations are entering into alliances, joint ventures and/or network relationships with others within their market system as a path through which to overcome identified internal weaknesses.

The Emergence of Mass Marketing

Richard Tedlow (1990), a business historian at Harvard Business School, has analysed the life history of a number of well-known US companies in the automobile, electrical goods, retailing and soft drinks sectors. From his research on company behaviour both before and after the Second World War, he has formulated some generic guidelines concerning effective strategies for establishing successful mass market brands. These include:

1 Exploiting the economies of scale associated with mass production to generate high absolute profits by selling large volumes of low-margin goods.
2 Re-investing generated profits in high levels of promotional activity as a mechanism through which to shape and mould market demand.
3 Creation of a vertical system in which raw materials are sourced, production operations managed and products delivered to the final consumer. This vertical system usually involves integration within the firm of key steps within the production process (e.g. Ford motor company owning both car assembly and component manufacturing plants) accompanied by contractual relationships for other elements within the distribution system (e.g. the move by Coca Cola to reduce costs by supplying concentrate syrups to bottling companies who manage production and distribution in a specified market area).
4 Having achieved market dominance through being the first company to exploit a strategy of high volume/low unit prices, to then create economies of scale barriers to ward off attacks from competition.

Tedlow has proposed that during the twentieth century, long-term survival of the leading mass market companies necessitated a move from a profit-through-volume strategy towards a new operating philosophy based on segmenting the market and offering a variety of goods to the now more sophisticated and experienced customer. The higher costs associated with expanding the product variety were not a problem because (a) many market segments are quite large (thereby permitting some degree of ongoing economies of scale) and (b) even more importantly, the supplier now had the freedom to 'price in accord with the special value that a particular market segment places on the product, independent of the costs of production' (Tedlow 1990: 43).

In retailing, Tedlow presents the example of A&P after the First World War, who achieved market dominance through emphasizing vertical integration, offering private label goods and creating effective systems to manage multiple store locations. After the Second World War, however, the company failed to recognize the implications of emerging trends of customers, namely (a) moving from the city to new houses in the suburbs, (b) seeking greater in-store product choice and (c) wishing to purchase branded goods being advertised on television. By not responding to an increasingly segmented world, the company subsequently lost ground to competitors such as Safeway and Kroger.

The Onset of the Marketer's Dilemma

By the 1960s, the demonstrable success of the f.m.c.g. (fast-moving consumer goods) companies such as General Foods, Procter & Gamble and Colgate–Palmolive caused some marketers to begin to believe that their management discipline was the fundamental cause of corporate success and that their activities should be seen as the centre of a universe around which the rest of a company's operations should revolve.

By the late 1970s, the influences of the OPEC oil crisis and the application of Keynesian economics to achieve full employment through increased public sector expenditure combined to create a world in which sustaining profit growth within Western nation firms became increasingly difficult. For many marketers, the task of building customer loyalty was replaced with the more urgent priority of fulfilling the financial community's demands for continued growth in corporate earnings in an increasingly economically unstable world. Return on Investment (ROI) began to be seen as much more important than delivering customer satisfaction. To support higher dividend flows and share values, marketers concerned with job security rapidly understood that their boards would only endorse strategies which either reduced costs by cheapening the product and/or restricted implementation of new product development projects to those which involved minimal investment in new capital assets.

This scenario did not go unnoticed by the new tiger nations of the Pacific Rim who clearly understood that to become global firms, they needed to enter both American and European consumer markets. Recognizing that the 'old world competition' had moved from customer to shareholder satisfaction, they directed their energies towards developing better products and, by exploiting their labour cost advantage, making goods available at significantly lower prices. Within a very short period of time, Western nation firms in durable goods market sectors such as automobiles, cameras, motorcycles, photocopiers, televisions and typewriters found that the competitor was no longer another domestic plc, but instead firms based in Japan and Taiwan.

As this text was being written, the dramatic fall in the Hong Kong stock market, the wave of bankruptcies in Japan and the need for the International Monetary Fund (IMF) to make massive loans to shore up the Korean economy does raise the question of whether the Pacific Rim 'economic miracle' can be sustained into the twenty-first century. The author's perspective is that the current problems being faced by these countries, although demonstrating the risks of funding economic development through governments condoning low rates of interest as in Japan, or approving loans well in excess of capability to repay from probable revenue flows as in Korea, can be overcome because their firms will still be able to exploit the benefits associated with retaining technological leadership over Western nation competitors in key consumer markets such as electronics and automobiles. Furthermore, even if some of the tiger economies do not ever totally recover from their current traumas, it must be remembered that mainland China is clearly laying the foundation stones for seeking to become a leading economic player in the new millennium.

Rebuilding a Competitive Edge

The recognition that the Pacific Rim was the location of the new industrial revolution prompted massive efforts by both academics and management practitioners in the 1980s to understand the reasons behind the decline of

Table 2.1 *Summary of findings concerning research on the characteristics exhibited by growth firms*

Coopers & Lybrand (1994) study of UK 'super growth' firms
- Perceive their markets as intensely competitive.
- Are flexible decision-makers.
- Seek leadership through offering superior quality in a niche market.
- Deliver superior pre/post sales service.
- Use technology-driven solutions to achieve a superiority position.
- Emphasize fast, frequent launch of new/improved products and draw upon external sources of knowledge to assist these activities.
- Emphasize application of technology and techniques such as cross-functional teams, process re-engineering to optimize productivity.
- Recognize the need to invest in continual development of their employees.
- Rely mainly on internal profits to fund future investments.

Cranfield pan-European study (Burns 1994)
- Seek niches and exploit superior performance to differentiate themselves from competition.
- Operate in markets where there is only an average-to-low intensity of competition.
- Utilize clearly defined strategies and business plans to guide future activities.
- Rely mainly on internally generated funds to finance future investment.

Comparative study of German and UK food-processing firms (Brickau 1994)
- German firms emphasize acquisition of detailed knowledge of external factors capable of influencing performance.
- German firms can clearly specify their competitive advantages.
- German firms seek niches exploited through a superiority positioning.
- German firms use strategies and plans to guide future performance.
- German firms concurrently seek to improve products through innovation and enhance productivity through adoption of new process technologies.
- German firms fund investment mainly from internal fund generation.

Study of New Zealand exporting firms (Lindsay 1990)
- Emphasis on R&D to achieve continuous innovation and gain control of unique technologies.
- Orientation towards achieving 'world-class' superiority in specialist niches.
- Use structured plans based upon extensive information search to guide future performance.
- Exhibit a very entrepreneurial management style and encourage employee-based decision-making.
- Strong commitment to using superior quality coupled with high productivity as a path to achieving competitive advantage.

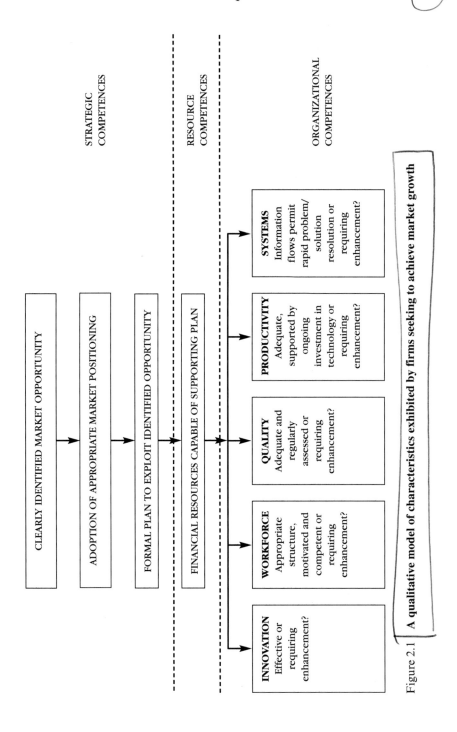

STRATEGIC
COMPETENCES

RESOURCE
COMPETENCES

ORGANIZATIONAL
COMPETENCES

CLEARLY IDENTIFIED MARKET OPPORTUNITY

ADOPTION OF APPROPRIATE MARKET POSITIONING

FORMAL PLAN TO EXPLOIT IDENTIFIED OPPORTUNITY

FINANCIAL RESOURCES CAPABLE OF SUPPORTING PLAN

INNOVATION
Effective or
requiring
enhancement?

WORKFORCE
Appropriate
structure,
motivated and
competent or
requiring
enhancement?

QUALITY
Adequate and
regularly
assessed or
requiring
enhancement?

PRODUCTIVITY
Adequate,
supported by
ongoing
investment in
technology or
requiring
enhancement?

SYSTEMS
Information
flows permit
rapid problem/
solution
resolution or
requiring
enhancement?

Figure 2.1   **A qualitative model of characteristics exhibited by firms seeking to achieve market growth**

Western nation companies and the factors influencing the success of the tiger nation corporations. One of the ground-breaking texts in this area was the book entitled *In Search of Excellence*. Written by Peters and Waterman (1982), it presented the results of research undertaken by the McKinsey Consulting Firm to define the attributes exhibited by America's best-managed companies.

Although reinforcing the fundamental principle that customer satisfaction rather than the short-term needs of the financial community should drive corporate philosophy, the text also proposed that achievement of excellence is founded on a complex interaction within the organization of the seven factors of strategy, structure, systems, style, staff, skills and shared values.

The added insights demonstrated by McKinsey's approach of studying the interaction of intra-organizational variables when seeking to understand factors influencing performance have subsequently resulted in the technique being adopted by other researchers. The results of four such studies are shown in Table 2.1.

By drawing upon the data in Table 2.1, it is possible to evolve a generic model (Figure 2.1) of internal strategic, resource and operational competences which can have a critical influence on the goal of achieving market-driven growth. Given the functional interactions proposed in Figure 2.1, it is posited that the marketer cannot restrict analysis of capability to just the marketing department, but will have to extend assessment of competence across other key areas of activity within the organization.

Strategic Competence

Complacency is dangerous in a world where competitors sit like vultures waiting to exploit any mistakes that might be made by others operating in the same market sector. Under these circumstances, the long-term survival of all organizations is critically dependent upon the ability both to identify new market trends and to determine how the internal capabilities of the organization can be used to exploit emerging opportunities.

In some cases this opportunity-exploitation responsibility may be vested in the entrepreneurial skills of one individual (e.g. Richard Branson's influence within his diversified Virgin empire, or Anita Roddick's, as the founder of Body Shop). In other situations, although there is an identified leader to whom success is often attributed, this individual typically seeks to build a strong senior management team to sustain performance well beyond the point at which he or she may retire from corporate life (e.g. Jack Welch, the President at G.E. Corporation, or Lord King during his tenure as Chairman of British Airways).

Tom Cannon (1996) has proposed that an organization's strategic competence can be evaluated by testing articulated competitive position against the five criteria of being distinctive, sustainable, appropriable, usable and measurable. Achievement of a positive rating against all of these criteria is probably unlikely unless the organization has created effective systems for carefully monitoring the external environment and ensuring the ongoing development of appropriate internal competences.

Financial Resource Competence

Most marketers are attracted by any proposition that offers revenue growth. Too few, however, take into consideration the impact of a growth strategy on a firm's profitability and/or fund flow position. If then at a later date a new, potentially very exciting, proposition requiring further investment comes along, they may find their cavalier attitude towards overall financial viability can result in the firm being unable to borrow from shareholders, and/or the financial community, the money required to implement the new marketing initiative.

The capability to resource a new project is illustrated by the example in Table 2.2 of two firms in the clothing industry, both of whom operate manufacturing operations and have their own retail outlets. Ten years ago, the two companies embarked on market expansion programmes – Company A by acquiring a competitor and Company B through carefully controlled, internal growth.

Table 2.2 *Comparative financial performance (£ millions)*

	Company A		Company B	
	1987	1997	1987	1997
Profit and loss account				
Sales	100	200	100	150
Gross profit	57	80	57	90
Other expenses	44	76	44	67.5
Net profit	13	8	13	22.5
Profit as % sales	13.0	4.0	13.0	15.0
Balance sheet				
Current assets	50	120	50	75
Current liabilities	20	90	20	30
Net current assets	30	30	30	45
Fixed assets	30	60	30	45
Long-term loans	20	45	30	45
Capital employed	30	45	30	45

Industry sector research indicated that although overall sales for up-market fashion goods clothing are beginning to flatten, major growth is forecast for the sports/leisurewear clothing market. Furthermore, an opportunity exists to acquire a successful, international well-known, vertically integrated company in this latter sector. The probable cost of the acquisition is £25 million.

Company A's marketers soon discover that access to new funds through further borrowing and/or issuance of additional equity is impossible because recent performance has already caused the financial community to label the firm as a poor credit risk. This is in contrast to Company **B** who encountered no problems raising new capital through a mixture of shares and long-term debt. Consequently they were able to execute an acquisition which offers the opportunity of doubling the size of their business over the next 10 years.

This lack of financial orientation among many marketers is probably caused by the fact that many start their careers working in large national or multi-national firms. Many of these organizations tend to have adequate cash reserves and/or a financial track record which allows them to borrow from external sources such as banks or the stock market. In addition, the tendency in these organizations is for the balance sheet and fund flow management to be seen as the 'sole preserve' of the accounting department. Consequently few marketers are able to gain appropriate experience in developing marketing plans which are compatible with optimization of an organization's working capital, asset balances and/or external fund-raising position.

Innovation

To prosper and grow all organizations need to engage continually in finding new ways of improving their products and process technologies. In the case of conservative-transactional or conservative-relationship firms, primary innovation management competence will probably be biased towards optimizing the efficiency of their procurement, production and logistics operations.

An example of this philosophy is provided by Finland's most successful forest products company, United Paper Mills (UPM). Despite an overall world decline in demand for paper in the late 1980s, UPM continued to make investments in new paper-processing equipment. Profits have increased and, in addition, the company has acquired new competences which permitted entry into the lucrative markets of manufacturing high-value-added products such as magazine paper and newsprint (Hornell 1992).

In contrast, within the mobile telephone market, although manufacturing process capability is important, long-term survival is currently more dependent upon skills in new product development. The Nordic firm Ericsson has been able to build a dominant position in world markets by exploiting research expertise in the fields of digital radio and digital signal processing to support the rapid development of new models offering improved performance in areas such as weight, size and operating life.

Successful innovation may also offer the added benefit of restoring the financial fortunes of a firm. At the end of March 1997, for example, the US chip manufacturer Advanced Micro Devices unveiled K6, a microprocessor for PCs which, it claimed, can handle calculations faster than the Intel Pentium Pro chip and will sell at 25 cents less than the market leader's product. This announcement caused analysts on Wall Street, who previously had been forecasting a loss of up to three cents per share, immediately to upgrade the company credit rating. Not surprisingly, this event was rapidly followed by a major upswing in the traded value of AMD shares (Parkes 1997).

Workforce

In most markets, because all firms understand the nature of customer need and internal operations utilize very similar production technologies, it is often extremely difficult to achieve a long-term sustainable advantage over competition. Consequently, as demonstrated by the impact of significantly upgrading the quality of in-flight services on airlines such as British Airways and Scandinavian Airlines in the late 1980s, in some cases the only way to reverse a declining market share is to invest heavily in the creation of a motivated and appropriately structured workforce.

Clearly, therefore, no marketer can ignore the Human Resource Management (HRM) practices within their organization when considering future marketing strategies. Unfortunately over recent years, however, the field of 'people management' seems to have attracted numerous gurus who claim, sometimes with an almost religious fervour, that their solution is the only way to proceed. Examples of these 'new faiths' include concepts such as Management By Objectives (MBO), employee empowerment and the creation of organic organizations.

There is no question that employers who create appropriate working environments can expect higher levels of performance from their workforce. It is vital to understand, however, that employee motivation and job satisfaction are influenced by complex interactions between socio-demographic, economic and cultural factors. Hence the marketer would be well advised to ignore some of the 'mine is the only way' advice offered by the management consultancy fraternity. Instead they should seek to understand what causes certain employees to consistently achieve high performance standards within the organization, and then determine how effective management of these factors can contribute to building a market lead over competition.

Quality

In the late 1970s, Western nation firms began to realize that Pacific Rim competitors were using superior quality to establish new beachheads in global markets. Possibly the real irony in this situation was the fact that it had been American experts such as A. Deeming and P. Crosby who, ignored in their own country, had taught the tiger nations how to use quality as a very effective weapon through which to build customer satisfaction.

Perhaps not unsurprisingly, the 1980s were a period when quality became a strategic priority for firms such as IBM, Xerox, Ford and Rolls Royce. Schonberger (1990) has described the development of effective quality management practices as a journey through the phases of correction, prevention, cost-based quality and ultimately a desire to serve the customer. Correction-based quality was founded on what is now considered to be an outmoded concept – namely, waiting until something goes wrong and then initiating remedial work to correct the fault. By moving to prevention quality, the organization develops processes which minimize the occurrence of the mistakes which cause the defects. A widely adopted approach in the prevention procedure is to seek registration under process certification schemes such as BS 5750 and ISO 9000.

Studies by researchers such as Schoeffler et al. (1974) have clearly demonstrated that companies whose products are perceived to be of a higher quality will enjoy higher profits and a larger market share. Recognition of this fact has permitted quality to move from an operational, process management issue concerned with cost minimization to a board-level topic of fundamental relevance in the planning of future corporate strategies. Having gained acceptance for the idea that quality should underpin strategy, it has been a relatively small conceptual step for organizations to understand how quality could provide the basis for sustaining long-term customer loyalty. Within only a very short space of time, Western nation case examples have emerged of how good practice provided the foundation stone for market success (e.g. Milliken Corporation in the US textile industry and Avis Corporation in the international car rental market).

Productivity

Productivity is usually measured in terms of level of value-added activities per employee and/or per number of hours worked. By increasing productivity in terms of value-added/employee or per hour of labour input, the firm can expect to enjoy an increase in profitability. This effect can occur in a number of ways. First, if productivity rises, the company can more efficiently utilize available capacity to manufacture more goods or services. Second, if productivity is increased by employees being furnished with better equipment, or when human labour is replaced by a machine, costs per unit of output may fall. Third, if improved productivity is reflected in higher quality, this may permit the firm's output to command higher prices in the market. Fourth, the firm may direct attention at seeking ways to improve productivity within supplier firms which in turn is reflected by a fall in the cost of input goods (Hornell 1992).

In addition, the Western world has lost market share to Pacific Rim firms who, as with quality, recognized the importance of productivity as a strategic weapon to increase sales. Studies of Japanese industry have revealed that adoption of concepts such as lean production, concurrent engineering and JIT manufacturing have all contributed to this country's manufacturing firms being able to generate very healthy levels of profit through the very simple idea of offering their customers higher quality goods at lower prices.

The fundamental importance of productivity as a profit driver is illustrated by the massive decline in the competitiveness of American and European car manufacturers in world markets during the 1980s. As in the case of quality, firms such as General Motors, Volkswagen and Rover Group (now owned by BMW) recognized the strategic implications of the widening productivity gap between themselves and their counterparts in countries such as Japan and Korea, these firms have implemented major initiatives to regain their lost status as world class manufacturing companies.

Given the major influence of productivity on organizational performance, it is very clear that this is an area of internal competence which will have significant influence on marketing planning. Thus, for example, a conservative-transactional producer of UPVC window frames for the replacement window market, who has failed to place sufficient emphasis on improving productivity through investment in automated extrusion equipment, will undoubtedly find that plans for continued market growth are frustrated by more efficient competitors using price as a mechanism for eroding their customer base.

Hence all marketers would be well advised to ensure that their organizations have in place a benchmarking scheme for carefully monitoring competitor productivity, and that data from this activity are used in ongoing re-assessments of how to enhance employee productivity through actions such as revising process procedures, increased employee training and investment in new technologies. Without such actions, the marketer should not be surprised to discover that selected strategic positions have been eroded because competitors are more effective at optimizing employee productivity.

Information Systems

With a philosophy of seeking to respond to identified customer needs, not unsurprisingly most marketers are critically aware of the importance of creating information systems for monitoring the external environment. For many years, marketers have used published sources, panel data (e.g. Nielsen store panels) and a variety of research techniques (usage and attitude studies, focus groups, customer satisfaction survey) to track and respond to changing customer behaviour. A common failing of many of these approaches is that limited marketing budgets often mean that studies are only infrequently undertaken (e.g. many major firms execute usage and attitude surveys on an annual or bi-annual basis) and/or some data sources are not linked to other information being acquired by the firm (an accounting department's standard costing system, for instance, which is not compatible with the manufacturing operation's computer and therefore is not used to optimize costs during the development of production schedules).

The advent of low-cost, extremely powerful computers clearly offers a mechanism through which to develop integrated Management Information Systems (MIS). Furthermore, the move to computerized on-line order entry systems now permits the creation of data bases through which to monitor customer behaviour on a daily or even hourly basis.

One only has to observe the example provided by the impact on market performance provided to American Airlines through their development of the SABRE seat reservation system to realize that computer technology can deliver significant strategic advantage to an organization. Unfortunately, even today in many firms, information management is seen as the preserve of a centralized Computer Services Department whose managers are more interested in ensuring that they retain control of all decisions related to use of computers and/or approved software systems, than in providing effective decision support systems to line managers across the organization. Here again, therefore, the marketer will need to assess carefully an organization's data-management capabilities to ensure these are able to support delivery of defined levels of customer service and additionally permit rapid diagnosis of problems likely to impact the firm's reputation in the market place.

Competence Prioritisation

Although high standards of competence across all areas of activity is the goal of the world class firm, it is extremely unlikely that the organization has either the time or resources to achieve this aim. Under these circumstances, firms will need to assess carefully both the standards achieved by competitors and also decide which competences should receive priority for further enhancement in terms of supporting the organization's marketing strategies.

Thus the conservative-transactional firm producing standard products and seeking to deliver a strategy of offering the best possible price/quality combination would probably be well advised to give priority to optimizing employee productivity. This competence will also be of importance to conservative-relationship orientated firms, but, additionally, attention to HRM and information system competences will be needed in order to deliver a strategy based on working in close partnership with the customer.

Entrepreneurial-transactional firms should probably give the highest competence priority to managing innovation in order to fulfil the strategy of always offering superior products. Given that customers in this sector of the market are more concerned with product performance than low price, this type of firm might be too concerned about concurrently achieving high ratings for employee productivity. Similarly, entrepreneurial-relationship orientated firms will need to pay attention to innovation competence. In this latter case, however, the philosophy of working in close partnership with customers will also demand high levels of competence in the areas of HRM and MIS.

The interaction and relative importance of internal competences has been examined in a study of manufacturing firms in the UK. Discriminant function equations generated in this research were subsequently used to develop a computer software tool which can evaluate alternative competence enhancement strategies in small manufacturing firms (Chaston and Mangles 1997). The plots in Figure 2.2 are of a firm for which the owners rated all areas of competence as neither adequate/nor inadequate, thereby resulting in a prediction by the software tool of zero future revenue growth. As shown in Figure 2.2, by increasing innovation competences from neither adequate/nor inadequate to adequate, the tool predicts the firm can expect revenue growth. Similar competency improvements in the areas of HRM, quality and information systems have minimal impact on future revenue. In contrast, by increasing employee productivity competency to adequate, the predicted revenue growth is of a scale even higher than that achieved through enhancement of innovation management capability.

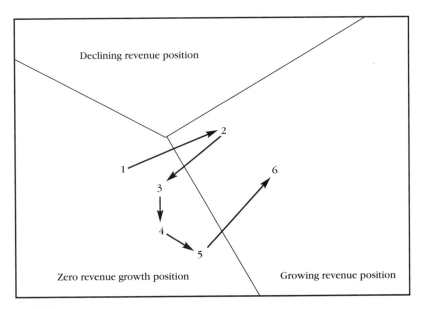

KEY

1 All competences at neither adequate/inadequate level
2 Move to average competence in innovation
3 Move to average competence in HRM
4 Move to average competence in quality management
5 Move to average competence in information system management
6 Move to average competence in management employee productivity

Figure 2.2 **Territorial discriminant function map plotting impact of changing competences**

Subsequent repetition of this research for hi-tech manufacturing firms and service sector firms has generated very different discriminant function equations. This suggests that, compared to the situation found in small manufacturing firms, revenue growth is influenced by very different combinations of internal competence in these latter two industrial sectors.

External Sources of Competence

Studies initiated by the Nordic business schools on the performance of Swedish firms in international markets revealed that many companies, when confronted with a competence inadequacy (e.g. not owning appropriate technology or not having the marketing skills to enter a new market sector) these organizations tended to seek solutions to this problem by entering into network relationships with other firms (Hakansson 1989). Hakansson further concluded that one of the commonest forms of business networking was forming alliances to achieve faster rates of product and/or process innovation.

Conway (1997) has constructed a morphological template in an attempt to define all of the potential participants (or 'actors') which a firm might seek to bring together in the formation of a network to overcome an identified innovation competency problem. These include:

1 Upstream innovators found from among the firm's suppliers.
2 Downstream actors found within the firm's customer base.
3 Horizontal actors found from firms within the same level of the market system.
4 Knowledge actors such as universities and research institutes.
5 Regulatory actors (e.g. governments or statutory bodies).
6 Wider environmental actors (e.g. environmental pressure groups).

The implications of the Conway template are that the firm who decides that internal innovation competences are insufficient to adequately support future marketing plans is now able to consider the formation of external alliances to overcome this problem. Implementation of this alternative solution will not be easy, however, because the firm will need to assess carefully (a) the exact nature of the competence enhancement to be acquired through the formation of the network and (b) how other participants which it will seek to recruit can gain mutual benefit from the proposed relationship. Hippel's (1988) research study would tend to suggest that the relative importance and potential contribution these various types of actor can contribute will vary depending upon whether the innovation is of a major versus a minor nature and upon the accepted 'norms' of relationship formation which already exist within a specific industrial sector.

References

Brickau, R. (1994) 'Responding to the Single Market: a comparative study of UK and German food firms' unpublished PhD dissertation, University of Plymouth.

Burns, P. (1994) Keynote address, Proceedings 17th ISBA Sheffield Conference, ISBA, Leeds.

Cannon, T. (1996) *Welcome to the Revolution: Managing Paradox in the 21st Century*, London: Pitman.

Chaston, I. and Mangles, T. (1997) 'Core capabilities as predictors of growth potential in small manufacturing firms', *Journal of Small Business Management*, 35(1): 47–57.

Conway, S. (1997) 'Focal innovation action-sets: a methodological approach for mapping innovation networks', Research Institute Working Paper RP9702, Aston University, Birmingham.

Coopers & Lybrand, (1994) *Made in the UK: The Middle Market Survey*, London: Coopers & Lybrand.

Hakansson, H. (1989) *Corporate Technological Behaviour: Co-operation and Networks*, London: Routledge.

Hippel, Eric von (1988) *The Sources of Innovation*, London: Oxford University Press.

√Hornell, E. (1992) *Improving Productivity for Competitive Advantage: Lessons from the Best in the World*, London: Pitman.

Lindsay, V. (1990) *Export Manufacturing – Framework For Success*, Wellington: New Zealand Trade Development Board.

Parkes, C. (1997) 'AMD posts surprise profit', *Financial Times*, 9 April: 40.

Peters, T.J. and Waterman, R.H. (1982) *In Search of Excellence: Lessons from America's Best Run Companies*, New York: HarperCollins.

Schoeffler, S., Buzzell, R.D. and Heany, D.F. (1974) 'Impact of strategic planning on profit performance', *Harvard Business Review*, March–April: 137–45.

Schonberger, R.J. (1990) *Building a Chain of Customers: Linking Business Functions to Create the World Class Company*, London: Hutchinson.

Tedlow, R.S. (1990) *New and Improved: The Story of Mass Marketing in America*, Oxford: Heinemann.

3 The External Environment

Understanding the nature of the external variables which may influence organizational performance can be achieved by creating a map of the marketing system of which the organization is a part. The role of the marketer is then to focus on those variables which are most likely to impact future performance.

Within the core market system, the typical variables which need to be monitored are end users, intermediaries, competition and suppliers. Surrounding this core system is the macroenvironment which contains variables of a more generic nature such as prevailing economic conditions and changes in political climate.

The traditional view of market systems is that of participants exhibiting a transactional orientation in many cases accompanied by the maintenance of adversarial relationships. More recently, however, this perception is beginning to change. In both tangible goods and service markets, members of the system actively seek ways of mutually enhancing performance through adopting a more co-operative attitude. An example is the increasingly popular practice of manufacturers and retailers in many consumer goods markets forming customer–supplier chains.

In the small-business sector, formal co-operation between firms often leads to the creation of 'business networks'. These have the attraction of permitting organizations to pool resources, thereby enhancing aspects of the marketing process and/or permitting the development of expanded product portfolios.

The Market System

A typical visual representation (Figure 3.1) of a market system will contain a 'core market' surrounded by a macroenvironment. Contained within the core are the components specific to the production and supply of products or services within an industrial sector. Sectoral components usually include the suppliers, producers, intermediaries and end user market. In many industrial markets and some consumer markets, intermediaries may be absent because the producer may elect to deal direct with the end user (e.g. a chemical firm supplying fertilizers direct to farmers or an outdoor clothing manufacturer

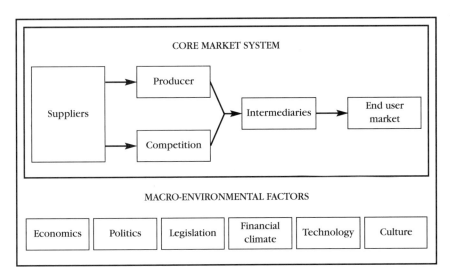

Figure 3.1 **A market system model**

marketing goods to consumers through the medium of a mail-order catalogue).

The macroenvironment contains generic variables which have an impact on virtually all market systems. Typical macroenvironmental variables include prevailing economic conditions (e.g. a downturn in the economy affecting house construction); political manifestos (e.g. the move by Western governments to privatize public sector monopolies such as telecommunications); changes in legislation (e.g. revised food handling laws following an outbreak of food poisoning); emerging new technologies (e.g. the impact of the Internet in providing an alternative approach to making international telephone calls); financial conditions (e.g. impact on consumer spending of an increase in credit card interest rates) and culture (e.g. impact of growing awareness of 'green issues' on customer purchase behaviour).

For an organization to establish and sustain an effective marketing strategy, the marketer must have a very detailed understanding of all of the variables which exist within their core market and the surrounding macroenvironment. This knowledge will provide the basis for identifying both opportunities and threats that may impact future performance. Without this understanding, the future of the organization is at risk because it may fail to identify a new threat or move with sufficient rapidity to exploit a newly emerging opportunity ahead of competition.

For example in America over recent years, consumers have begun to seek greater variety in their purchase of 'take-away' foods. In 1997, McDonald's Corporation, the founder of the 'hamburger revolution', reported a downturn in US sales which in part was attributed to a change in customer eating patterns. The company's response to this market trend was to launch 'Campaign 55', a series of price cuts across their product line to recover market share. Behind the scenes the firm concurrently initiated changes to enhance product quality, speed up service and improve order accuracy (*Financial Times* 1997). In contrast, other fast food operations such as Taco Bell and Pizza Hut, who had already begun to extend the variety of items offered in their outlets, appear to have been less affected by this new trend in customer purchase patterns.

Another example of fortunes being affected by market circumstance is the impact of the computer on the publishing industry. As their end user market has begun to respond to the benefits offered by using technology such as the CD-ROM to acquire information, some publishers who continue to produce only books have lost sales to those competitors who more rapidly embraced IT as an alternative medium through which to fulfil changing demands within the market place.

In attempting to manage demand, many firms face the problem that their market system is linked to other systems further downstream in their industry. A producer of engine blades would probably define their end user market system as the manufacturers of aero-engines. This latter group of firms are suppliers within the aircraft manufacturing market system, who in turn are suppliers to the airlines, who in turn are providers of services to the world travel market. Thus engine blade manufacturers, whose revenue is influenced by the number of aircraft being purchased by the airlines, would need to undertake downstream market research if they wish to comprehend how trends in the airline passenger market will impact order patterns for their blades from aero-engine firms such as Rolls Royce, GE or Pratt & Whitney.

The End User Market

In seeking to understand future purchase decision trends, the marketer will usually have to perceive the end user market as consisting of a series of 'nested shells' (Rangan et al. 1995) of the type shown in Figure 3.2. The outer shell, or generic market, contains all the individuals and organizations who may at some time decide to enter the core end user market to purchase products or services. Thus, for example, all manufacturers of industrial components in a country might be perceived as potential customers in a core market for a certain type of Computer Numerically Controlled (CNC) machine tool. Only those companies who use automated manufacturing processes would, however, represent a customer base for this CNC equipment. Nevertheless, the size of the core market will be influenced by trends in the generic market such as (a) the degree to which component manufacturing firms are moving towards total automation of production processes and (b) whether the total number of this type of manufacturing firm in the country begins to decline as the Original Equipment Manufacturers (OEMs), to whom they supply goods, decide to purchase more components from overseas producers.

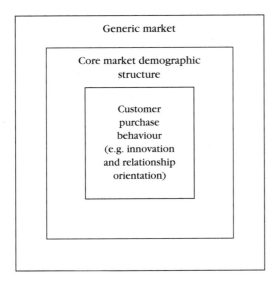

Figure 3.2   **A multi-shell end user market**

Within the core market, the demographics of the customer population have a significant impact on total demand. In both consumer and public sector markets, the usual demographics which should be monitored by the marketer are age, sex, marital status, income, education and occupation. Thus, for example, a government seeking to manage the provision of public sector medical services for the elderly would be well advised to examine changes in the age profile of the population and also the capability of the economy to generate sufficient taxes to support the provision of healthcare within a welfare state system.

In industrial markets, relevant demographic data will usually include variables such as the size of specific industrial sectors, number of companies within each sector, purchase patterns in relation to company size and location of customers. Thus a company marketing networked, computer-based, order-entry systems may define their core market as all firms within the financial services industry. They would then have to monitor trends within sub-sectors such as banking, insurance and stockbroking. In the UK this firm would currently no doubt be very carefully tracking moves by the High Street banks to provide 24-hour, telephone-based, banking services and, most recently, noting that massive investments are being made to create new customer service centres around the Glasgow area in Scotland.

Alternatively, this firm might conclude that supplying order-entry systems in the UK financial services sector market is becoming too competitive and that an appropriate response is to expand into the travel industry. Given the trend by travel service providers such as the major world airlines to locate their passenger reservation systems offshore in lower labour cost countries (e.g. Eire or India), this revised marketing strategy will probably have implications in terms of the need to create a new, internationally orientated marketing operation.

A characteristic of most markets is that customers exhibit variation in buying behaviour. This phenomenon is illustrated by the inclusion of the inner purchase behaviour shell in Figure 3.2. There are various ways of defining purchase decisions, but possibly the most relevant approach is to divide the shell into the following four sub-shells:

1   Conservative-transactional orientated customers seeking:
    ● the best available price/quality/value product combination;
    ● standardized products;
    ● wide availability in outlets, thereby minimizing the purchase location search;
    ● access to information systems designed to resolve problems rapidly during pre-purchase, purchase and/or the consumption phase.
2   Conservative-relationship orientated customers seeking:
    ● product/service combination which delivers complete customer-specific solution;
    ● customized product/service solutions based on the standard specification used by the majority of the customers within the market sector;
    ● being supplied with product/service(s) which offer ever more effective solutions to identified customer usage problems;
    ● information systems which very rapidly assist in resolving any errors in solution provision;
    ● supplier employees committed to creating close relationships with the customer.
3   Entrepreneurial-transactional orientated customers seeking:
    ● product/service(s) which uses latest innovations to deliver outstanding performance, in many cases exceeding the performance requirement articulated by the market;
    ● promise of being offered even more innovation in the future which will further extend the benefit offering of existing leading edge product/services(s);
    ● providers deeply committed to being entrepreneurial in all areas associated with serving customer needs;
    ● culture of employees always challenging current market performance 'norms'.
4   Entrepreneurial-relationship orientated customers seeking:
    ● suppliers offering product/service(s) which clearly contributes to ensuring that the customer's output is also of a superior nature;
    ● providers orientated towards helping customers achieve even more innovation by further extending the performance boundaries of their output;
    ● providers clearly committed to working in partnership with customers to mutually satisfy each other's desire for continuous innovation;
    ● culture of both parties jointly seeking to challenge current market performance 'norms'.

Company revenue in any of these sectors can be calculated using the formula:

Sales = (number of customers in the generic market) × (proportion of generic market customers entering the core market) × (proportion of customers in specific purchase behaviour sub-shell) × (annual value of purchases by an average sub-shell customer) × (1 – proportion of sales achieved by competition)

In terms of achieving higher revenue in the future, the above equation suggests that the organization has a number of options. These include seeking to expand the generic market, attracting more customers into the core or sub-shell market, increasing customer annual purchase volume and/or persuading customers to switch from competitors' products. If the resultant forecast indicates that the combined impact of all of these actions still does not fulfil the organization's long-term revenue goals, then the next option might be that of seeking new opportunities by expanding into other product or market sectors (e.g. a diesel engine manufacturer in the truck industry deciding to enter the marine engine market supplying products to shipyards building luxury motor yachts; or a chain of hotels who have traditionally focused on the tourism market seeking to diversify their product portfolio by upgrading their facilities to attract more guests from the business traveller market).

Intermediaries

The primary role of intermediaries is to accept the responsibility for executing all the tasks necessary to link the producer to the end user market in those cases where the latter is unable or unwilling to manage the delivery process. An example of this scenario is that of the f.m.c.g. companies such as Kellogg, Heinz and Unilever who utilize the services of the large supermarket chains to distribute their products to households in developed nation economies.

In selecting an appropriate intermediary, the producer must take into account factors such as the purchase behaviour within the end user market (e.g. consumers may be prepared to travel up to 100 miles to find a specific brand of furniture, but would be unwilling to exhibit the same behaviour when purchasing a box of detergent), the willingness of the intermediary to carry their goods (e.g. the problems currently being created for the f.m.c.gs by supermarket chains wishing to expand sales of their own-label products and therefore reducing the number of equivalent branded items in their stores) and the capability of the intermediary to provide appropriate support services to the market (e.g. discount retailers who are not prepared to offer installation or repair services on electrical goods which they sell).

It is critical for the producer to identify emerging trends either in customer buying patterns and/or in the intermediary's willingness to service the end user market. Possible forces of change which producers will need to monitor are summarized in Figure 3.3. An example of an end user behaviour shift is that which has occurred in the business sector of the Personal Computer (PC) market where many large customer organizations are now requiring distributors to go beyond just 'selling boxes' and to provide advice on selection, installation and post-purchase operation of sophisticated computer systems. To exploit this trend a number of distributors, known as Value Added Resellers (or VARs), now specialize in supplying certain types of system and/or serving specific market sectors. In the late 1980s, IBM's orientation towards emphasizing the importance of industrial customers dealing direct with their sales force possibly resulted in this organization being rather slow in building strong relationships with the leading VARs. It is felt by some industry observers that the outcome of this decision was that sales were adversely affected in those sectors of the market which preferred to purchase their systems through VARs instead of dealing direct with computer manufacturers.

An example of the impact of new technology on intermediary behaviour is provided by Electronic Data Interchange (EDI). These systems permit firms to automate their order entry, logistics and stock control systems by linking their computers directly with that of their suppliers. Thus a small producer of specialist electronics components who lacks the capability to offer an EDI facility may find that major distributors in overseas markets such as Germany are unwilling to carry their products because this would involve returning to a manual product procurement operation.

Power shifts in the intermediary system are an opportunity or a threat depending upon whether the producer recognizes signs of change and is able to sustain relationships with an intermediary who is in the process of gaining dominance over competitors. The same risk also exists for a producer who fails to realize that new intermediaries are seeking to enter their market system. For example, up until the mid-1980s in the UK, the bulk of low-cost petrol was sold through garages not owned or linked by contractual agreements to the major oil companies such as Texaco, Esso and BP. The primary suppliers to

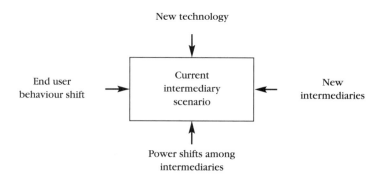

Figure 3.3   **Forces of change within an intermediary system**

the independent garages are the smaller oil companies who produce low-cost fuels by purchasing their crude oil from whatever happens to be the cheapest source available from around the world. During the late 1980s, however, UK supermarket chains began to add garage forecourt operations to their larger out-of-town hypermarkets and within only a few years have become dominant players in the petrol market. Thus those small independent oil companies who failed to recognize the important new role of supermarket chains in the petrol retailing market eventually found their sales were declining because many of their traditional customers were being forced out of business in the mid-1990s by a petrol price war which broke out between the supermarkets and the major oil companies.

Competition

A vital responsibility assigned to the marketer is that of recognizing the nature of competition, the potential threat competitors may represent, and the development of appropriate response strategies. Possibly the most widely known source of theories on the effective management of competitors is Michael Porter, the Harvard Business School Professor, whose first major text (Porter 1980) has subsequently been followed by a whole series of writings on this critically important issue.

He has proposed that competitive threats can be classified into five major types:

1   The threat of other producer firms already operating within the market sector seeking to increase market share (e.g. the ongoing battle between brands such as Heineken versus Fosters lager around the world).
2   The threat of customers moving upstream to also become producers and/or using their purchasing power to dominate terms and conditions of purchase (e.g. a telephone company starting to manufacture its own telephones; or car manufacturers who might use their purchasing power to demand price reductions from their component manufacturers during periods when world car sales are falling).
3   The threat of a supplier moving downstream to become a producer or using their control over critical resources to dominate terms and conditions of sale (e.g. lumber companies entering the furniture manufacturing business; or a natural gas producer seeking to increase prices to electricity generators using gas-fired power stations during a period when very cold weather has created an increase in world energy prices).
4   The threat of a substitute entering the market (e.g. a new cancer drug which vitiates the need for a piece of specialist medical equipment used by clinicians who traditionally have treated the cancer by carrying out major surgery on their patients).

5   The threat of a new entrant who was not previously a major player in the market (e.g. the recent entry of the Korean firm Daewoo into the US and European car markets).

Suppliers

Traditionally marketers have focused their attention on monitoring the downstream components within their market system. The risk of this somewhat myopic approach was clearly demonstrated by the oil crisis in the 1970s when the OPEC countries sought to gain greater control over the pricing and consumption of crude oil. Many Western world products such as plastics, automobiles and electrical goods made affordable by using low-cost hydrocarbon feedstocks as inputs to high-volume/low-unit manufacturing operations (e.g. nylon shirts) or during consumption, required the customer having access to low-cost energy sources (e.g. V6-engined cars).

The impact of the OPEC restriction of supplies and their concurrent demand for higher crude oil prices was to trigger a global recession which caused marketers, possibly for the first time, to assess carefully the impact of scarce resources on the future positioning of products in their respective markets (e.g. the need for US automobile manufacturers to begin to offer their customers smaller cars; or the requirement of construction firms to improve insulation levels in new houses in order to reduce occupants' energy bills).

More recently, some firms have begun to realize that suppliers, as well as possibly being able to constrain input resources, can also be a major source of new opportunities. For example, most of the recent advances in the modern computer's data-processing capability have not come from the laboratories of the computer manufacturer, but instead from the entrepreneurial behaviour of their suppliers (e.g. Intel Corporation's ongoing efforts to produce a new computer chip even more powerful than their world-beating Pentium product; or the diverse range of Windows products developed by Microsoft Corporation).

Over the last few years, the growing recognition of the importance of working closely with key suppliers has caused many OEMs to move from the traditional, conflict-based negotiation style of using purchasing power to drive down input prices, towards scenarios based on achieving mutual benefits from their supplier–customer relationships (Peters 1987). This change in management practice is often described as 'building stronger supplier–customer chains'. It usually involves firms mutually determining how to optimize responsibilities for the various stages of the value-added processes associated with the production and delivery of goods to end user markets (Storey 1994).

In Britain the Japanese car manufacturer Nissan, for example, has introduced the Cogent programme to help suppliers develop self-sufficiency in both design and right-first-time delivery of components. The ultimate aim of this scheme is to further enhance employee productivity within the Nissan car assembly operation and cut time from design to market launch of new models from 40 months to 30 (Lorenz 1997).

Market System Co-operation

The traditional approach to the management of market systems as espoused by transactional orientated marketers is to consider other elements within the system as elements with whom to trade on an 'arm's length basis' or to treat as sources of potential or real competitive threat. Research on supplier–customer behaviour by the Nordic business schools and subsequent follow-up studies by members of the European Industrial Marketing and Procurement (IMP) group revealed the apparent contradiction that in many markets the various actors within the system often exhibit preference for building relationship based on co-operation, not confrontation.

Other researchers have subsequently found examples of this collaborative approach to market system management in other parts of the world. One extremely well documented example of the concept are the *keiretsus* in Japan. These conglomerate-type industrial groups consist of a complex web of interacting independent companies which co-operate with each other as systems through which to share skills and resources to achieve sustainable competitive advantage in world markets (Collins and Doorley 1991). A similar example from another part of the world is that of Benetton, the global leisure-wear company. Their core organization is based in Italy and acts as a hub organization orchestrating the activities of independent retailers who stock the brand and of the numerous small garment operations who manufacture the company's products.

A number of reasons have been proposed to explain the trend of firms seeking to build strategic partnerships with other organizations which in past were often seen as the enemy within a market system (e.g. Lockheed and General Dynamics in the aerospace industry). A theme common to many of these partnerships is that collaboration is the only viable option for firms seeking to survive in an increasingly turbulent and competitive world (Cravens et al. 1993; Hamel et al. 1989; Webster 1992).

The cost of being competent in every area of technology, which has always been accepted as an operational constraint confronting the smaller firm, is now also seen as a massive obstacle for even the largest of corporations. Hence firms are increasingly coming together to bid for a specific contract (e.g. a proposed alliance between Vickers and British Aerospace to market armoured vehicles in the Middle East) or to form longer-term strategic partnerships (e.g. the various aerospace firms who constitute the European Airbus consortium which was formed to challenge Boeing Aircraft Corporation's dominance of the world civilian passenger jet market).

Lacking the resources and/or expertise to operate successfully in every major market around the world is often another stated reason for the formation of co-operative relationships between large multi-national corporations. This concept has been extremely popular with Western nation firms seeking to enter European Eastern Bloc markets such as Hungary, Poland and Russia following *perestroika* and the subsequent collapse of communism in these countries.

Not all these ventures have, however, proved as successful as originally hoped. One such example is the Radisson-Slavyanskay hotel project involving a partnership between Paul Tatum, an American entrepreneur, the US Radisson hotel chain and the City of Moscow. Unfortunately the relationship between the partners became extremely strained and reached the point where, at one stage, Tatum was physically barred from the hotel. He reacted fiercely to regain control of the venture, including invoking a court action to prove the original contractual agreements were being ignored. Tragically the final outcome in this affair was that Tatum was assassinated in an attack which has subsequently been attributed to the Moscow Mafia (Pratley 1997).

The not infrequent failure of many strategic alliances over the years has caused Day (1990) to propose that successful partnerships are difficult to achieve because of:

1   Changing strategic priorities within the partner organizations.
2   Lack of appropriate systems to ensure rapid, effective joint decision-making on issues vital to the operation of the alliance.
3   Conflicts arising because of cultural and management style differences.
4   After a period when specified performance goals are not being achieved, one or more of the partners becomes disillusioned and reduces their commitment to seeking ways for overcoming identified operational problems.

In some cases the need to cover all key markets around the world is determined by an organization's desire to provide a 'seamless service' to the customer. This objective is a reason why, over recent years, many of the world's airlines have formed partnerships with others in their industry to enable them to better assist their passengers travelling both between and within countries (e.g. the transglobal partnership involving Air Canada, ALM, Antillean Airlines, Aloha Airlines, Ansett, British Midland, Gulfstream International, Lufthansa, National Airlines of Chile, SAS, Thai Airways and United Airlines).

Small Business Networks

Miles and Snow (1986) proposed that the 1990s will be characterized by a de-integration of large firms as these organizations begin to establish 'dynamic networks' based on new forms of contractual relationships with other independent firms. At the core of the Miles and Snow network paradigm is a lead organization fulfilling the role of a 'broker' orchestrating the inter-firm collaboration process. Jarillo (1986), although reaching a similar conclusion about the potential for business networks in a changing industrial world, believes the overwhelming pressure to further reduce operating costs would be the primary factor underlying the creation of these new entities. Subsequently, Johnson and Lawrence (1988) developed their Value Added Partnerships (VAPs) theory of networking in which independent companies collaborate in the management of transaction costs associated with the flow of goods and services along the entire value-added chain. An example of this approach was provided by Lorenzoni and Ornati (1988) in their study of Northern Italy regional clothing networks.

During the 1980s in Denmark, the government working with the Danish Technological Institute sought to encourage growth in the Small and Medium-Size Enterprise (SME) sector through the creation of business networks. In those industrial sectors or geographic regions where there are no large firms to fulfil the role of hub facilitator, there was a need for independent network brokers to manage the processes of identifying potential opportunities for small-firm networking, seeking potential network members from within the local business community and acting as a mentor/facilitator in the creation of a new, commercially viable, trading entity.

Studies of economic development initiatives which utilize business networks to stimulate SME sector growth have revealed that sharing of resources to achieve greater scale in the execution of marketing processes is one of the commonest reasons for smaller firms to enter into a partnership with other organizations. The following are examples of some of the networks which have been created:

1   Ten Danish landscape gardening firms interested in the opportunities available in the construction of golf courses who realized that, by acting individually, none of them would be considered of a size sufficient to be awarded major contracts in overseas markets such as the USA.
2   A group of Danish organizations including fishermen, processing companies and a hospital who came together to develop new health products which use the sea as the primary source of basic ingredients.
3   A group of small appliance and telecommunication retailers sharing marketing, planning and promotional costs. As a network they were able to obtain a contract to market the best-selling modular telephone in Denmark; whereas, acting individually, none of them would have been considered of a size sufficient to be granted the agency.
4   Eleven Danish textile manufacturers who produce different products have formed a network called 'CD-line'. While continuing to operate independently in their traditional markets, the consortium has been able to enter West Germany, marketing a complete range of image clothing for employees in large corporations such as banks and car makers.

5   Four Danish furniture companies collaborated in the design of a new range of furniture for the Netherlands market and jointly resourced the opening of an export sales office to market the range in that country.
6   Three Norwegian furniture firms who formed a network to supply all of the equipment needs for the Winter Olympics in Lillehammer.
7   Four Norwegian producers of kitchen equipment who formed a network to offer total system catering solutions for oil platforms in the North Sea.
8   Four Norwegian fish farming equipment manufacturers who have developed a complete range of products in order to begin offering total farm management systems in overseas markets.

On the basis of these and other examples, it appears there are two dimensions associated with the formation and operation of small-firm marketing networks. One is the sharing of expertise/resources to more effectively manage marketing processes directed at increasing sales to current customers, gaining access to larger customers in existing markets or entering completely new markets. The other dimension is in the area of revising the product offering either through the combination of existing products to offer an enhanced proposition or through the development of an entirely new range of products.

By combining these two dimensions, as demonstrated in Figure 3.4, one can generate the following nine different collaborative pathways from which firms can then select the best option for enhancing their marketing operations:

Cell 1 where sales of existing products to existing customers are increased by a pooling of resources (e.g. a group of small furniture manufacturers who create a single sales force to represent all of their products in the market place).
Cell 2 where pooling of resources permits access to new customers for existing products (e.g. a group of cheese producers already distributing their products through local retailers, who can now gain access to national supermarket chains because together they can offer a full range of cheeses from a single source).
Cell 3 where sales of existing products can be increased by pooling of resources to permit entry into a new market (e.g. a group of component manufacturers in the leisure craft industry who pool promotional resources to develop new export markets).
Cell 4 where the pooling of resources permits offering of an enhanced product to current customers (e.g. a group of accountants drawing upon their various areas of specialist expertise to offer a complete financial management services portfolio to their clients).
Cell 5 where pooling of resources leads to the creation of an enhanced product proposition which can assist in gaining access to new customers (e.g. a group of specialist management trainers who create a 'complete training solution' package which means they will now be considered as viable potential suppliers to large, multi-national corporations).

Cell 6 where pooling of resources to enhance an existing product permits entry into a new market (e.g. a group of specialist computer software designers who normally work as sub-contractors for system provider firms, combining their skills to move into the systems provision market).

Cell 7 where the pooling of resources permits the creation of a new product marketed to existing customers (e.g. a group of hotels creating their own package holiday operation).

Cell 8 where pooling of resources creates a new product for sale to new customers in an existing market (e.g. a group of fresh-juice processors who distribute their product through small retailers, developing a new longer-shelf-life product which means they can now market their output to national retail chains).

Cell 9 where pooling of resources leads to the development of a new product to create access to new markets (e.g. a group of civil engineering firms each specializing in specific aspects of construction who create a total project design and management system which permits them to enter overseas markets offering a complete infrastructure management capability).

Market Product	Existing market(s)		New market(s)
	Existing customers	**New customers**	**New customers**
Existing product	1 Sharing of market management resources to increase existing customer sales	2 Sharing resources to achieve scale effect to gain access to new customers	3 Sharing market management resources to execute new market entry strategy
Merged product line to enhance product position	4 Increased sales to existing customers by offering an enhanced product proposition	5 Access to new customers through offering an enhanced product proposition	6 Gaining access to new markets through offering an enhanced product proposition
New product	7 New sales to existing customers through launching new product	8 Gaining access to new customers by launching new product	9 Gaining access to new markets through offering new product

Figure 3.4   **Alternative business networking marketing relationship strategies**

References

Collins, T.M. and Doorley, T.L. (1991) *Teaming up for the 1990s*, Homewood, IL: Irwin.

Cravens, D.W., Hipp, S.H. and Cravens, K. (1993) 'Analysis of co-operative relationships, strategic alliance formation and strategic alliance effectiveness', *Journal of Strategic Marketing*, March: 32- 41.

Day, G.S. (1990) *Market Driven Strategy*, New York: The Free Press.

Financial Times (1997) 'McDonalds cuts breakfast prices to increase sales', 3 April.

Hamel, G., Doz, Y.L. and Prahalad, C.K. (1989) 'Collaborate with your competitors – and win', *Harvard Business Review*, Jan.–Feb.: 135–6.

Jarillo, J.C. (1986) 'Entrepreneurship and growth: the strategic use of external resources', unpublished doctoral dissertation, Harvard Business School.

Johnson, R. and Lawrence, P.R. (1988) 'Beyond vertical integration – the rise of value adding partnership', *Harvard Business Review*, July–August: 54–68.

Lorenz, A. (1997) 'Nissan drives to new heights', *Sunday Times*, 6 August, Business Section: 7.

Lorenzoni, G. and Ornati, O.A. (1988) 'Constellation of firms and new ventures', *Journal of Business Venturing*, 3: 23–36.

Miles, R.E. and Snow, C.C. (1986) 'Network organization: new concepts for new forms', *The McKinsey Quarterly*, Autumn.

Peters, T. (1987) *Thriving on Chaos*, New York: Alfred Knopf.

Porter, M.E. (1980) *Competitive Strategy: Techniques for Analysing Industries and Competition*, New York: The Free Press.

Pratley, N. (1997) 'Russian gold rush slows to a hard slog', *Daily Telegraph*, 5 April: B2.

Rangan, V.K., Shapiro, B.P. and Moriarty, R.T. (1995) *Business Marketing Strategy: Concepts and Applications*, Chicago: R. Irwin.

Storey, J. (ed.) (1994) *New Wave Manufacturing Strategies: Organizational and Human Resource Management Dimensions*, London: Paul Chapman Publishing.

Webster, F.E. (1992) 'The changing role of marketing in the organization', *Journal of Marketing*, 56 October: 1–17.

4 Strategy and Positioning

(For many years advocates of mass marketing held the view that seeking market leadership was the only route through which to maximize ROI. More recently it has been recognized that small, specialist firms can achieve similarly high ROIs by focusing on meeting the needs of a specific market niche. The concept of exploiting variation in customer need is now also understood by large firms who segment markets by offering a diverse range of products or services.

(For a firm effectively to execute a marketing strategy usually requires the adoption of a 'market position' which communicates to the customer how the organization can fulfil their product needs.)Classic Porterian theory suggests there are four generic positions available to firms. However, by adding to the two standard variables of low cost and superior performance the concepts of multi-performance and 'mass customization', the number of alternative positions can be greatly expanded.

Products and services typically exhibit a sales pattern indicating the existence of a product life cycle. The position of a product on the life cycle curve can influence the nature of the marketing mix which should be utilized to affect customer purchase behaviour. One approach to defining appropriate marketing mix strategies is to recognize that early in the life cycle customer uncertainty is high. Uncertainty declines with experience and thus by the maturity phase of the life cycle, variables such as price and sales promotion will have an increasingly stronger influence over purchase decisions. The concept of changing levels of certainty can also be used to define the nature of the product portfolio most capable of contributing to long organizational success.

Mass Versus Niche Marketing

It has long been accepted that mass production offers the opportunity for major cost reductions by exploiting economies of scale. Subsequently it has also become apparent that further cost savings are offered by a phenomenon known as the 'experience curve'. First observed during the Second World War in the Californian B29 bomber assembly plants and the Kaiser shipyards building pre-fabricated Liberty Ships, this curve reflects the fact that as workers gain experience there is a steady ongoing decline in unit production costs.

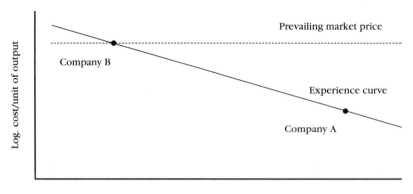

Figure 4.1   **An experience curve**

As shown in Figure 4.1, the experience curve is usually presented as a plot of the logarithmic cost per unit of output against the logarithmic value for cumulative output. (The only reason for plotting experience curves in a logarithmic form is that this permits negatively exponential data to be presented in the more understandable form of a straight line.) In Figure 4.1 Company A, through the production of large quantities of output, has reached the extremely advantageous position of being able to control the destiny of Company B. For in the event that Company B becomes an irritant, Company A can respond by (a) reducing the prevailing price to a level which is below Company B's current costs; (b) increasing promotional spending to the point where the market is no longer aware of B's existence; and/or (c) re-investing profits in the development of new, even more superior, products.

In view of this situation, it is clearly the case that becoming a mass market leader is an extremely attractive proposition for virtually any organization. This is why, even today, large firms around the world continually strive to steal sales from competition as a fundamental element in the process of achieving market domination. The other factor influencing the popularity of market leadership is, of course, the appeal it has to marketers. They have long understood the value to their own careers of involvement in the management of a nationally or internationally recognized, brand leadership success story.

As most organizations are not just interested in high sales, but also seek to generate an adequate ROI, marketers were gratified by research in the 1970s which demonstrated a strong relationship between the degree to which firms dominate markets and the impact this has on ROI. The Profit Impact of Management Strategies (or PIMS) study concluded that businesses which have a market share of greater than 40 per cent can usually also expect to enjoy an ROI of greater than 30 per cent (Buzzell et al. 1975). This conclusion was of course music to the ears of marketers, who felt totally exonerated from any criticism about continuing to request, even during periods of economic downturn, larger marketing budgets to support their latest plan to increase market share further.

There is no question that in a large market in which customers exhibit homogeneous demand for a product, striving to achieve a dominant position through implementation of a mass marketing strategy is an extremely viable concept. Unfortunately, what some proponents of the 'big is always best' management philosophy appear to ignore is that in many markets customers often exhibit heterogeneous purchase behaviour. This situation thus permits consideration of an alternative strategy – namely, instead of seeking to dominate the market by offering a standardized product, to make available specialist product(s) specifically directed at meeting the needs of a smaller, more select group of customers (Roach 1981). For, as demonstrated by Figure 4.2, although it may not generate the same level of absolute profits as mass marketing, the concept of specialization (or 'niche marketing') can offer the organization an extremely acceptable ROI.

Managers who are totally convinced that growth is beneficial, whatever the circumstances confronting the organization, would be well advised to consider carefully the ROI implications described in Figure 4.2. For as can be seen from the diagram, should Company B decide to seek to join Company A by moving from a niche to a mass market position, then it must expect a period, before enjoying the rewards of higher market share, during which ROI will be dramatically reduced.

An added risk in this scenario is that during periods of economic recession, curves of the type shown in Figure 4.2 may shift downwards, and in the trough between the two peaks ROI might approach zero. Thus if a firm which funded growth by raising new long-term debt at 10 per cent interest during an economic boom is then confronted by the onset of a recession, it is very possible that an inability to service interest charges from profits will emerge, with bankruptcy being a likely outcome.

This scenario is exactly that which, during the late 1980s, faced many UK

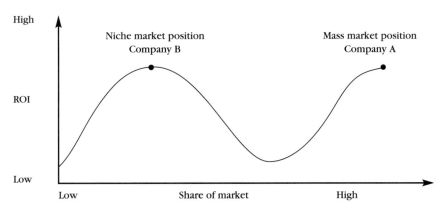

Figure 4.2 **Comparison of mass versus niche marketing strategies**

firms which had implemented major market growth programmes. One of the few firms which appears to have managed a return from the brink of disaster by recognizing the risk of sustaining a growth strategy in a recession by implementing a trading contraction response, was the UK upmarket fashion and interior design firm, Laura Ashley. The only outstanding question is the scale of contraction and management change that will be required within the firm before a complete recovery becomes a certain outcome.

A well publicised example of a niche player who was not swayed by the advice that growth is always good for a business was the UK specialist sports car manufacturer, Morgan. The company was featured in a television documentary starring the ex-ICI chairman, John Harvey-Jones. He visited the factory, noted the three-year waiting list for a Morgan car and recommended a major increase in capacity to exploit market demand. The company chairman, Peter Morgan, who clearly intuitively understood the benefits of a niche positioning, questioned the validity of this recommendation and, in this author's opinion, was wise enough to refuse to make any significant changes in the firm's marketing strategy.

Recognition of the benefits of high ROI from a niche position has caused some theorists to suggest that mass marketing is an outmoded concept in Western nation firms because companies occupying a niche are in a very secure position, safe from competitive threats from larger, mass market orientated firms. In the past when mass marketing was based on large plants manufacturing average quality, standardized goods, this theory probably had some validity. More recently, however, Pacific Rim mass market firms by adopting lean manufacturing philosophies have begun to produce a very diverse range of extremely high-quality goods. This new capability, as demonstrated by the impact of the Toyota Lexus on the sales of luxury car manufacturers such as Mercedes Benz, now permits the mass marketing orientated company effectively to threaten even firms which have sought to protect themselves from competition by becoming niche marketers.

Market Segmentation

Although offering specialist products to a limited number of customers used to be perceived as the role of the smaller firm, even large multi-nationals now accept that serving the varying needs of specific groups of customers may be more advantageous than merely offering a single, standardized product to all areas of the market. More usually known as 'market segmentation', the process involves identifying variations in buyer needs and determining how these can be fulfilled with specifically tailored products or service offerings.

Initially firms tended to use very simple taxonomies for segmenting markets, such as customer location or socio-demographics. For example, a construction company segmenting the market on the basis of customer income, might build dwellings across the complete market spectrum from two-bedroom terrace houses for young couples seeking their first starter home, through to large, detached houses for high-income business executives.

In many cases, however, a single socio-demographic variable has been found to be a somewhat crude tool upon which to define customer segments. As a result, many organizations now use multi-attribute segmentation which can involve combining together two or more socio-demographic factors. Thus, for example, many banks use the variables of age, income and social class as the basis for developing specific product portfolios aimed at meeting the different needs of customer groups in the consumer financial services market.

life strategy chapter 4.

Another approach is to divide customers into groups on the basis of their knowledge, benefits sought, attitudes and/or use of product. Haley (1963) provided one of the earliest reported examples of behavioural segmentation which was based upon the benefit customers sought from different brands of toothpaste. He was able to identify four different benefit segments, namely price, medical treatment, personal appearance and flavour. The marketer can also consider segmentation based on product usage rates. Many beer companies have found that their heavy usage customers exhibit common behavioural traits (e.g. a brand of beer may be heavily consumed by 18–25 year old males who are strong football supporters). This knowledge can then be exploited in terms of how the product is positioned in the market and also in the selection of the media vehicles used to promote the beer's benefit claim.

In consumer goods markets, as time has gone on and organizations have gained experience of market segmentation, more sophisticated techniques such as basing segments on the psychographic variables of life-style or personality has become increasingly popular. To a large degree this change has become necessary because research using traditional measures such as socio-demographics has often revealed that these taxonomies are not sufficiently sensitive to permit effective classification of actual customer behaviour. One recent example of life-style segmentation is that provided by Pepsi-Max who selected young snowboarders as a primary user group and feature the sport in their television commercials.

(Texts on business-to-business marketing appear to indicate that industrial marketers, although somewhat slower in their adoption of market segmentation, are now very reliant upon the technique to optimize the selective targeting of marketing effort.)Bonoma and Shapiro (1983) have proposed that the possible variables that can be used in industrial markets include demographics, operating variables, purchasing behaviour, situational factors and the personal characteristics of the individual(s) making the purchase decision. Another approach is to segment industrial markets on the basis of benefit sought. Robertson and Barich (1992) have suggested a taxonomy based on the stage reached in the purchase decision process by dividing customers into the three groups of first-time prospects who have not yet purchased, novices and sophisticates.

To a certain degree, advances in segment classification have been made possible by the rapidly increasing availability of computerized relationship data bases containing detailed records of customer purchase patterns (e.g. those generated by electronic shop tills using Universal Product Codes, or 'bar codes', to track purchase patterns of individual consumers shopping in their local supermarket). A further contribution to process has been the continued improvement in the data-processing capacity of desktop PCs which now permits even the smallest of firms to rapidly execute the segment identification task using statistical analysis techniques such as factor or discriminant function analysis.

In recent years, various academics and practitioners have strongly supported the concept of 'mass customization'. This philosophy proposes that every customer can be considered as a market segment with products or services being customized to suit individual, specific needs (Vandermerwe 1996). Two of the factors used to justify the appeal of the approach are (i) the power of relationship data bases to isolate and track individual customer purchase patterns from sources such as credit card transactions, and (ii) the advent of flexible, lean manufacturing technologies which permit an almost 'batch production' philosophy to be utilized to vary instantly the specification of products on the assembly line.

In reality product customization is not a new idea in that, for many years, it has been a standard operating practice within those industries in which each customer exhibits heterogeneous need and makes a high unit value purchase (e.g. merchant banks assisting firms seeking investment advice; construction firms involved in projects such as building new hotels or hospitals). The only real change that has occurred in recent years is that advances in information management and product/service production technologies now permit the concept to be affordable in markets constituted of customers each purchasing lower unit value products (e.g. the Dell Corporation which uses direct marketing techniques to supply customers with machines which are constructed to suit the buyer's specific data-processing requirements).

Thus, in considering the validity of adopting a mass customization philosophy, the marketer would be well advised to continue to use the long accepted rules of segmentation – namely, that to be successful, the identified segment must be of an adequate size, the higher costs of servicing customer needs can be recovered through charging higher prices, the segment is accessible to the supplier and, if at all possible, the selected marketing position is resistant to the subsequent entry of competitors.

Generic Positioning

By combining the concepts of niche versus mass marketing and the product proposition to be offered to customers, Michael Porter (1985) evolved the theory that there are four possible generic strategic options available to organizations, namely *cost leadership, differentiation, focused cost leadership* and *focused differentiation.*

BASIS OF PRODUCT PERFORMANCE PROPOSITION

	Cost	Superior performance
Mass market	Cost of leadership	Differentiation
Niche market	Focused cost of leadership	Focused differentiation

MARKET COVERAGE

Figure 4.3 **A competitive advantage alternative positioning matrix**

Cost leadership is based upon exploiting some aspect of the output generation process which can be executed at a cost significantly lower than that of
the competition. There are various sources of this cost advantage such as
lower input costs (e.g. the price paid by New Zealand timber mills for logs
produced by the country's highly efficient forestry industry), in-plant production costs (e.g. lower labour costs enjoyed by Japanese firms locating
their video assembly operation in Thailand or US mail order companies
locating the order-fulfilment activities in Mexico) or delivery costs reduced
by the near proximity of key markets (e.g. the practice of some major beer
producers who locate micro-breweries in, or near to, major metropolitan
areas). *Focused cost leadership* exploits the same proposition, but the company occupies a specific niche or niches servicing only part of the total
market (e.g. a horticulture enterprise which operates an on-site farm shop
offering low-priced, fresh vegetables to the inhabitants of towns within the
immediate area).

Porter has proposed that focused and cost leadership represent a 'low
scale advantage' because it is frequently the case that eventually a company's capabilities will be eroded by rising costs (e.g. as an economy moves
from developing to developed nation status, unions are able to persuade
employers to pay higher wages and to improve terms and conditions of
employment) or their market position is usurped by an even lower cost
source of goods (e.g. Russia's post-*perestroika* entry in the world arms markets offering extremely competitive prices on the latest military hardware).

The generic strategy of *differentiation* is based upon offering superior performance and Porter argues that this is a 'higher scale advantage' because (a)
the producer can usually command a premium price for output and (b) competitors are less of a threat, for to be successful they must be able to offer a
even higher performance specification product. *Focused differentiation*, which
is typically the preserve of smaller, more specialist firms, is also based on a
platform of superior performance. The only difference is that the firm specializes in serving the needs of a specific market sector or sectors (e.g. the
Cray Corporation which supplies 'super computers' to the aerospace and
defence industries).

The other attraction of differentiation is that there is a multitude of
dimensions which can be exploited in seeking to establish a product or service

which is superior to competitor offerings. Garvin (1987), for example, has proposed that in relation to superior quality there are seven different dimensions which might be considered: features, actual performance, conformance to quality expectations specified by customers, durability, reliability, style and design. In addition to dimensions associated with the physical product, organizations can also exploit other aspects of the purchase and product utilization process by offering outstanding service across the areas of ease of ordering, delivery, installation, customer training, maintenance, repair and post-purchase product upgrades.

The core attributes of many products and services are often very similar (e.g. liquid detergents, life insurance) and the customer would be hard pressed to distinguish any real technical difference between the performance offered by the various suppliers in a market sector. Under these circumstances, one way to differentiate the firm from the competition is to use promotion as a means of creating a 'perceived difference' in the minds of the consumer (e.g. Fairy Liquid in the UK being positioned as an effective washing-up detergent which, because of a very mild formulation, can exploit the emotive phrase 'hands that do dishes can be as soft as your face', or Commercial Union's commitment to rapidly settling customers' loss claims – communicated by an advertising campaign using the message that they will 'not make a drama out of a crisis').

Although a very useful conceptual tool, the Porterian strategic option model may involve the major risk that if users exhibit blind allegiance to theory, they may incorrectly decide that the four alternative positionings are mutually exclusive. Available case materials would suggest that in the past, for example, many Western nations assumed that one should strive to be either a low-cost leader or the producer of superior, differentiated goods. Thus, for example in the 1980s, in response to the high labour costs associated with delivering the country's Social Charter, German firms concentrated on premium priced, superior goods market sectors. In Spain, on the other hand, lower labour costs stimulated the establishment of factories orientated towards serving downmarket, price-sensitive sectors.

This situation can be contrasted with Pacific Rim firms whose Confucian approach to decision-making appears frequently to result in the generation of superior, holistic solutions. In the case of strategic options, advances in flexible manufacturing permitted them to develop products which concurrently offer high standards of performance and low price. Their ability to achieve this goal in areas such as video cameras, cars and televisions was a key factor in contributing to the achievement of major market share gains during the 1980s.

As Western nation firms began to recognize this new threat, their response was to fundamentally re-assess all aspects of their internal operational processes. This involved application of a bundle of techniques which subsequently came to be known as 'business process re-engineering' (Hammer and Champy 1993). Although initially the orientation of such projects tended to focus on lowering operating costs, over time many corporations found that by

PERFORMANCE

	SINGLE BENEFITS		COMBINED BENEFITS
Mass market	Cost leadership*	Differentiation*	Value and performance differentiation
Mass customization	Customized cost leadership	Customized differentiation	Customized value and differentiation
Focused	Focused cost leadership*	Focused differentiation*	Focused value and differentiation

(*The original four Porterian Strategic Options)

Figure 4.4   **An expanded strategic options matrix**

revisiting fundamental assumptions about business processes (e.g. materials handling, or processing customer enquiries), new work methods began to emerge that not only enhanced productivity but also revealed new ways of employee working that increased organizational flexibility. These in turn permitted a move away from offering standard goods or services towards 'mass customization' of company offerings.

A case example quoted by Hammer and Champy (1993: 241) is the impact of re-engineering on the American fast food chain Taco Bell. Their CEO, John Martin, having described what he calls their 'journey', makes the point that 'because of our efforts to re-engineer our operations and to think of growth not in terms of a four-walled restaurant but in terms of points of distribution, we expect numbers to skyrocket. Vending machines, supermarkets, schools, street corners – you name it, we'll be there.'

Thus on the basis of the above materials it seems reasonable to suggest that marketers can significantly increase the number of strategic options available to them by adding the options of multi-performance and mass customization to the traditional Porterian strategic options matrix. As shown by Figure 4.4, this action increases the number of options from four to nine.

Product Life Cycle

When a product is first introduced, sales are low and costs usually exceed revenue. Over time, sales will rise because the number of customers trying the product increases and some of these customers adopt the product as a regular item within their purchase portfolio. Eventually all users have entered the market and sales will plateau. Then, at some time in the future, customers are offered a better product (e.g. the advent of the railway which meant fewer firms needed to use canals to distribute bulky cargoes) and sales decline.

This predictable variation in sales pattern over time is often described in the context of a Product Life Cycle (PLC) curve which, as shown in Figure 4.5, is typically presented in the form of a four-phase process – Introduction, Growth, Maturity and Decline. Although some academics have questioned the existence of the PLC in the real world, it is nevertheless a useful conceptual tool for determining appropriate strategies according to the current position of a product on the curve.

One way of using the PLC concept is to consider that the curve is a reflection of the level of uncertainty among both customers and suppliers. As shown in Figure 4.6, at the Introduction stage both parties in the transaction face a high level of uncertainty. The customer is uncertain about issues such as the nature of product benefit, likely price, purchase process and possible problems which might emerge during usage. Equally, the supplier often lacks information on issues such as the real size of the market, structuring of the distribution system, selection of the most appropriate production technology and the speed with which customers will adopt the product. As the product enters the Growth phase, both parties acquire understanding of various aspects of managing the transaction process. Typically this knowledge acquisition process is faster for the supplier than the customer and consequently uncertainty remains higher among this latter group.

Eventually through personal usage and/or contact with other users, customers gain greater understanding, and by the Maturity phase their level of certainty approaches that of the supplier. At the onset of Decline, the customers usually remain certain about the product but uncertainty increases among suppliers over issues such as how long the product will survive, the implications of needing to restructure the distribution system and the degree

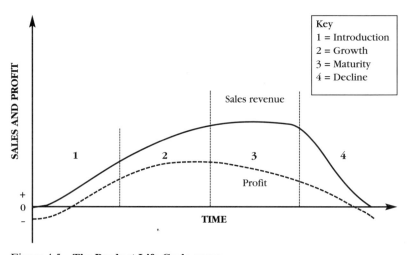

Figure 4.5   **The Product Life Cycle curve**

SUPPLIER UNCERTAINTY

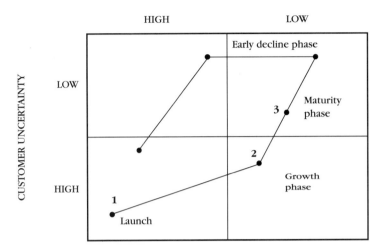

Figure 4.6   **A customer/supplier uncertainty matrix**

to which repair and renewal of capital assets will be required to sustain the production process as sector sales trend downwards. Towards the end of the Decline phase even customers, faced with problems over matters such as locating a supplier, obtaining spare parts and/or individuals willing to repair the product, may also begin to become uncertain about whether to remain a loyal user or whether to switch to a more up-to-date product offering.

As shown in Table 4.1, the concept of customer uncertainty is very useful in determining appropriate actions in the selection of the marketing mix to be used depending upon the current position of a product or service on the PLC curve.

Uncertainty and Marketing Style

In selecting the strategy of building market share through the launch of a new product, the organization has a choice of options in relation both to the customer target to whom the new product will be directed, and the degree to which the new product is different from existing items. Combining these two dimensions generates an alternative new product strategy matrix of the type illustrated in Figure 4.7 which can be used to determine the degree of risk associated with the various innovation options being considered by an organization.

The lowest risk option is the Product Upgrade proposition which involves offering an improved product to existing customers. Higher risk is associated with offering the existing customers a completely new, Replacement Product.

Table 4.1   *Marketing mix selection*

PLC Phase	Introduction	Growth	Maturity	Decline
Customer uncertainty	Very high	High	Average	Low
Product	Single product offering understandable core benefit	Expansion of product line to exploit emerging alternative benefit needs	Continued line expansion to offer increased variety and/or increased value to customers	Reduced variety to meet needs of remaining core
Price	High but within value boundaries of initial adopters	Remaining high but falling to reflect production economies and to broaden market appeal	Continuing to decline to reflect value boundaries of average customers	Continuing to fall to justify continued use by remaining loyal customers
Above-line promotion	Education on primary benefit offered by product	Continued education plus assisting repeat purchase/ increased usage	Sustain loyalty of existing customers and stimulate switching from competition	Minimal reminder level activity
Below-line promotion	Added value to stimulate trial	Added value to stimulate repeat usage	Added value to sustain loyalty/stimulate brand	Added value to reward loyalty/extend product life
Distribution	Selective via outlets capable of aiding customer education	Expanded to increase purchase convenience	Further expansion to maximize purchase convenience	Reduction to minimal level acceptable to remaining customers

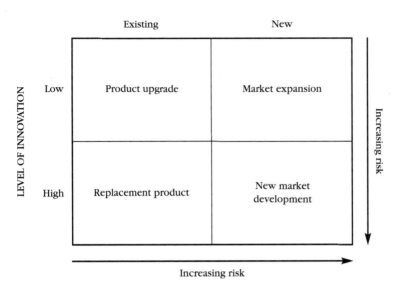

Figure 4.7 **Alternative new product strategy matrix**

This is because initially the organization cannot be certain that customers will wish to switch to the new, improved product and/or that no operational problems will emerge as the firm scales up the new production technology to service growing market demand. In the case of a Market Expansion proposition, although the firm will have few worries about managing the production technology, there are significant risks associated with the fact that the firm has minimal experience of servicing customer need in the new market sector. Clearly, however, the highest level of risk is associated with the New Market Development proposition which involves uncertainties in relation to both customer and technology management.

Although once an organization comprehends the factors contributing to risk and actions can be taken to minimize the chance of failure, different management styles confer certain advantages in relation to the type of innovation strategy to be implemented. In an existing market, relationship orientated firms can reduce risk by entering into innovation partnerships with their customers. In terms of the scale of innovation, product improvements usually create added value and, therefore, firms which have a customer base built upon offering the highest level of value standardized goods are most likely to succeed when adopting this form of innovation. In contrast, the entrepreneurial firm, which specializes in introducing new standards of performance, is more likely to succeed by focusing on the development of completely new product forms.

By overlaying the new product strategy matrix with the combined implications of the benefits of forming relationships in existing markets and the issue of conservative versus entrepreneurial product development, the following conclusions can be reached concerning the influence of marketing style on relative probability of success:

1 Conservative-relationship firms are most likely to have an advantage over other marketing styles by concentrating on Replacement Product strategies involving the development in partnership with customers, propositions designed to offer higher value (e.g. a bank which has developed a strong relationship with small firms by providing an effective portfolio of traditional banking services introduces an Electronic Fund Transfer System specifically aimed at being compatible with the level of IT systems being used in the SME sector clients).

2 Conservative-transactional firms are most likely to have an advantage over other marketing styles by concentrating on exploiting capabilities developed in one sector to enter another area of the market (e.g. a private sector bus firm established as a result of public transport privatization in the UK, drawing upon acquired skills in creating efficient passenger service delivery operations to enter the newly privatized rail transportation market).

3 Entrepreneurial-relationship firms are most likely to have an advantage over other marketing styles by working with their existing customers to develop radically new ways of satisfying market need (e.g. a firm specializing in water chemistry analysis working in partnership with water companies to develop new remote sensing, water chemistry monitoring systems).

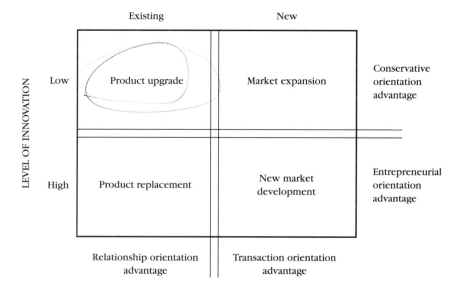

Figure 4.8 **Alternative market styles and new product strategies**

4   Entrepreneurial-transactional firms are most likely to have an advantage over other marketing styles by focusing on using innovation to develop completely new markets (e.g. a firm with R&D expertise in bioluminesce using this technology to develop new ways of tagging chemicals for use by paediatricians wishing to diagnose prior-to-birth genetic defects that can cause food metabolism problems in the human foetus).

Uncertainty and Product Portfolio Management

In seeking to evolve a tool for helping their clients manage their portfolio of products more effectively, the Boston Consulting Group evolved a decision matrix based on the two dimensions of market share and rate of market growth (Heldey 1977). The theories underlying the 'BCG matrix' are that (a) high market share products generate large profits and (b) the earlier a product achieves market domination, the more likely is the case that this share will be retained as the market moves into the Maturity phase on the Product Life Cycle.

Although the original model has proved extremely popular with marketers, it has faced a number of criticisms. Doyle (1998), for example, points out that:

- Market growth may be an inadequate description of overall industry attractiveness.
- Market share is an inadequate proxy for relative competitive strength.
- The analysis is very much influenced by which definition of market is used.
- The model assumes strategic business units are independent, whereas products may share resources such as machine tools, warehousing systems, etc.

One way of dealing with some of the criticism about using market share to describe industry attractiveness is to accept the view recently expressed by Slywotzky (1996), that what managers should assess is sales revenue of a product relative to proportionate share of total corporate value contained within a market sector. For publicly quoted companies, corporate value can be calculated by summing the variables of quoted market value (i.e. total shares issued multiplied by current market value/share) and long-term debt.

If a company has a calculated corporate value of £100 million, total sales of £50 million, and a specific product achieves sales of £10 million, then share of corporate value equals percentage share of total sales times corporate value; that is, (£10m × 100/£50m) × £100m = £20 million. By calculating corporate value for competitors' products it is then possible to use share of total market corporate value for the product category in place of the market share dimension in the BCG matrix using the formula:

UNIVERSITY OF HERTFORDSHIRE LRC

% share of market value = (product's specific corporate
value/total corporate value
for all products in the market segment) × 100

By concurrently replacing market growth on the BCG matrix with the new dimension of product uncertainty in Figure 4.9, it is then possible to determine appropriate marketing strategies for a product portfolio which are more reflective of the objectives of value maximization and management of risk. As described earlier, during the Introduction and Growth phases of the PLC, uncertainty is high because suppliers need to convince customers that adopting their specific product is the correct decision. By the time a market moves into the Maturity phase, most customers have become loyal to a specific product and their level of confidence is high.

If a supplier's product has achieved a dominant share of total corporate market value by the time the market has reached Maturity then, because customers are extremely confident about their purchase choice, the supplier will only have to expend limited funds as a percentage of sales on promotional activity to sustain market position. Hence this product, the 'Value Cow', will contribute a significant proportion of the company's total corporate value which in turn will be reflected by a high traded market price for the company's share.

In contrast the 'Value Dog' product is in the unenviable position that (a) low value generation by the product will depress the company's share price and (b) the sales growth needed to increase the company's traded share price

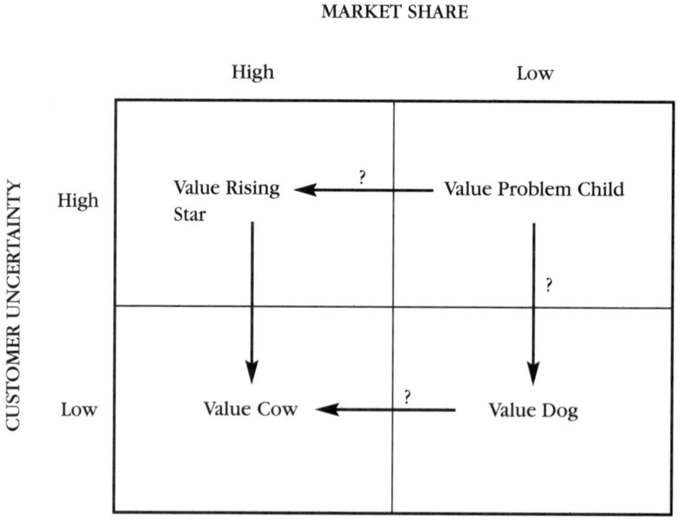

MARKET SHARE

Figure 4.9   **Modified BCG matrix**

can only come from stealing sales from a market leader. Because this latter firm's customers are now highly certain about the correctness of their product choice, then the company with a Value Dog product will have to spend a huge amount of funds and/or dramatically reduce price in order to stimulate switching by eroding customer loyalty. In most cases this strategy is not financially viable, which is why Value Dog products are rarely able to overthrow Value Cows in most markets.

An exception to this rule can occur where the leader company(ies) has become complacent to the point of clearly not being interested in meeting the changing needs of the customer. Under these circumstances disenchanted customers are only too willing to switch loyalty. This has frequently been exploited by Pacific Rim firms acting to steal sales from their Western nation counterparts in mature markets (e.g. the success of the Japanese car companies in both Europe and the USA during the 1980s). The other alternative for the Value Dog is to implement actions that create 'attitude disruption'. This will cause uncertainty in the minds of customers as they re-assess their previously strongly entrenched product usage habits and values. Examples of the latter approach are Volvo's emphasis on car safety and reliability instead of style/speed in the car market, Haagen-Daz's advertising their brand of ice-cream as an exotic, adult eating experience and the Midland Bank's launch of Direct Line 24-hour telephone banking as a challenge to conventional high street consumer banking.

If a firm has a low market value share product during a high market uncertainty phase, (i.e. a 'Value Problem Child'), then the most appropriate time to act is when customers are still at the stage of finalizing their decision about which supplier offers the best proposition. Consequently, firms with a low share of total market value are well advised to act while customer uncertainty is still high by upgrading the performance proposition offered by their Value Problem Children and attacking 'Rising Value Stars' (e.g. IBM's successful recovery strategy against Apple Corporation in the PC market). Conversely, owners of Rising Value Stars need to recognize the potential vulnerability of their current position and to re-invest funds from Value Cows into maximizing customer certainty over product choice with the aim, if possible, of driving their product into the Maturity phase on the PLC curve.

References

Bonoma, T.V. and Shapiro, B.P. (1983) *Segmenting the Industrial Market*, Lexington, MA.: Lexington Books.

Buzzell, R.D., Gale, B.T. and Sultan, R.G. (1975) 'Market share – a key to profitability', *Harvard Business Review*, Jan.–Feb.: 34–42.

Doyle, P. (1998) *Marketing Management and Strategy*, London: Prentice-Hall.

Garvin, D.A. (1987) 'Competing on the eight dimensions of quality', *Harvard Business Review*, Nov.–Dec: 101–9.

Haley, R.J. (1963) 'Benefit segmentation: a decision orientated research tool', *Journal of Marketing*, July: 30–5.

Hammer, M. and Champy, J. (1993) *Re-engineering the Corporation: A Manifesto for Business Revolution*, New York: HarperCollins.

Heldey, B. (1977) 'Strategy and the business portfolio', *Long Range Planning*, February: 1–14.

Porter, M. (1985) *Competitive Advantage: Creating and Sustaining Superior Performance*, San Francisco: Free Press.

Roach, D.C. (1981) 'From strategic planning to strategic performance: closing the achievement gaps', *Outlook*, Spring: 3–9. New York: Booz, Allen, Hamilton.

Robertson, T.S. and Barich, H. (1992) 'A successful approach to segmenting industrial markets', *Journal of Marketing,* December: 5–11.

Slywotzky, A.J. (1996) *Value Migration: How to Think Several Moves Ahead of the Competition,* Boston, MA.: Harvard Business School Press.

Vandermerwe, S. (1996) *The Eleventh Commandment: Transforming to Own Your Customers*, Chichester: J. Wiley.

5 Selecting Strategies and Constructing Plans

Whichever management philosophy is practised within an organization, the planning process will usually cover the three issues of 'where are we now?', 'where do we wish to go?' and 'how do we wish to get there?' One tool which can be useful in this analysis is the Directional Policy Matrix which simultaneously addresses the issues of internal capabilities and market attractiveness.

In some cases the situation analysis reveals that a firm lacks the capability to exploit available opportunities. An increasingly popular solution is the formation of a business network (e.g. the vertical network created by Benetton to design, manufacture and retail designer clothing). The Directional Policy Matrix can also be used in determining appropriate strategies for business networks.

There is now widespread acceptance of the idea that during the planning process, the organization must identify which core competences are critical to establishing and maintaining a strong market position. One approach for competence identification is the application of Porter's Value Chain model.

Most marketing plans contain the standard elements of Situation Review, SWOT (strengths, weaknesses, opportunities, threats), Issues, Objectives, Strategy, Strategic Mix, Action Plan, Financial and Control Systems. During the implementation of the plan, however, the organization will need to give careful consideration to the marketing tactics required (a) to attack competitors and (b) to defend existing business from others within the market system.

Implications of Alternative Philosophies

The alternative philosophies of management discussed in Chapter 1 might, at first sight, be expected to create problems in attempting to define a standardized approach for evolving strategies and marketing plans. As illustrated in Figure 5.1, however, although the alternative philosophies have differing start points for initiating process, in reality the final outcome of seeking to identify appropriate actions for the future is very similar.

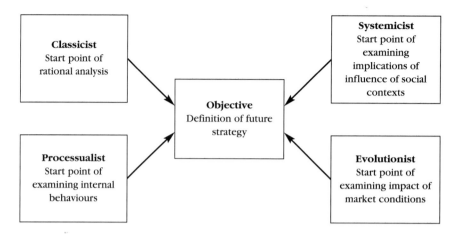

Figure 5.1 **Alternative philosophies to determine strategy**

During the evolution of strategy, managers adopting any of the four philosophies, will, either formally or informally, undertake the activity of analysing prevailing internal and external conditions confronting the organization as the basis for defining necessary action plans. Possibly the only real difference is that Processualists and Systemicists will begin with an analysis of internal organizational issues, whereas Evolutionists will first examine market conditions and Classicists will attempt a concurrent analysis of both internal and external circumstances.

A more likely area of difference between organizations engaged in planning activities will be that associated with the influence of uncertainty. For, as shown in Figure 5.2, this variable will probably result in one of four planning outcomes depending upon prevailing circumstance. In a market where over the medium term, both external and internal circumstances are reasonably certain, then this will probably result in a strategy and plan which is merely an extension of current practice. This situation is most frequently encountered in mature markets where customer needs and the technology which provides the basis for delivering benefit, are both clearly understood (e.g. the consumer goods market for branded petfoods).

In a market where customer need is understood, but alternative approaches to structuring the organization to meet customer need are thought to exist, then the strategy and plan will be of an organizationally adaptive nature (e.g. life insurance companies experimenting with alternative models ranging from localized one-to-one services delivered by an insurance sales person through to the provision of services using telephone-based, direct marketing techniques). In contrast, where appropriate organizational form is understood, but customers are exhibiting variation in obtaining need fulfilment, then competing firms may be forced to use very different marketing strategies (e.g. the current situation in the North American and UK Cola markets where some consumers continue to exhibit a preference for multi-national brand

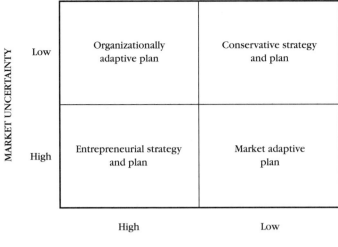

Figure 5.2   **Influence of uncertainty on planning philosophies**

names and therefore respond to classic branded goods mass-marketing techniques; whereas more price-orientated consumers are switching to other brands such as Virgin Coke or the generic products offered by the major supermarket chains).

The last scenario described in Figure 5.2 is that of high uncertainty for benefits sought by customers and the most appropriate organizational structure for servicing this need. In this situation, one can expect firms to exhibit very entrepreneurial behaviour, experimenting with both product offerings and organizational structure throughout the period when uncertain conditions prevail and nobody really comprehends what optimal form of either the product/service portfolio or organizational entity will ultimately emerge. A current example of this scenario is provided by the recent introduction of income tax self-assessment in the UK which has generated a variety of entrepreneurial reactions ranging from restructuring within traditional accountancy practices through to the launch of self-learning, PC-based, computer systems.

Strategy Development in an Uncertain World

Hamel and Prahalad (1994: 13) have suggested that 'Competition for the future is competition to create and dominate emerging opportunities . . . to stake out new competitive space.' They further recommend that '. . . a firm must unlearn much about its past . . . recognize that it is not enough to optimally position a company within existing markets . . . develop foresight into the whereabouts of tomorrow's markets'.

In offering guidance on how to achieve this aim, Hamel and Prahalad rely very heavily on the concept of understanding the probable nature of future market conditions and ensuring the organization has acquired competences appropriate for achieving ongoing success. Their definition of a successful firm is one which is able to predict the future accurately, acquire core competences ahead of competition and thereby become the dominant player within an industrial sector.

Clearly this is a conceptual philosophy which in practical terms only a minority of firms can ever aspire to achieve. Nevertheless, the logic of the process associated with examining market circumstance and at the same time having the internal capability to determine future strategies is a technique which virtually all organizations should find acceptable. Furthermore it does seem that this technique, which was originally developed by Classicist marketers, is applicable no matter which managerial philosophy is being used by the organization.

Matching Competence to Market

One of the simplest, yet most powerful tools, for concurrently examining both competence and market attractiveness is the Directional Policy Matrix pioneered by Shell in Europe. In North America the equivalent tool is more usually known as the GE-McKinsey Matrix (Robinson et al. 1978). The start point in building the matrix is to first determine which factors influence (a) whether or not markets being served are attractive propositions and (b) what competences are required in order to perform effectively in markets being served.

Factors influencing market attractiveness will vary by both industrial sector and nature of marketing style adopted by the organization. Examples of relatively standard factors which might be considered in virtually any situation include:

- Size of market (with larger markets usually being seen as more attractive than smaller markets).
- Market growth rate (with rapidly growing markets usually being seen as more attractive than zero growth, mature markets or markets in decline).
- Intensity of competition (with markets where competitive intensity is low usually being seen as more attractive than those where intensity of competition is high).
- Stability of technology (with markets where process technology is well defined usually being seen as more attractive than markets where major uncertainty still exists about which technology is the most appropriate).
- Customer price sensitivity (with markets where customers are product-performance-orientated usually being perceived as more attractive than those where price is the overwhelmingly dominant influence in the customer purchase decision).

Relationship orientated firms would probably consider that willingness of customers and/or suppliers to enter into close collaborative partnerships would also be a critical factor influencing market attractiveness. Conversely, highly entrepreneurial firms might specify willingness of customers continually to seek new and improved products or services as the dominant factor influencing any classification of market attractiveness.

Relevant internal competences known to critically influence performance will also vary by industrial sector and marketing style orientation of the organization. Examples of standard competences which are applicable in virtually any situation include:

- effectiveness and efficiency of process technology in relation to impact on costs of production;
- quality of products and/or services;
- modernity of fixed assets relative to average asset life within the sector;
- financial resources (generated from operation and/or acquirable through additional external borrowings);
- skill levels of the workforce.

Within transactionally orientated firms, given their need to optimize their output of high-value, standard goods, significant emphasis would also be given to internal capability issues such as effectiveness of procurement, production capacity in relation to future demand and effectiveness of information systems to diagnose rapidly causes of variance in operational costs. Conversely, highly entrepreneurial firms might consider issues such as creativity of staff, time to develop new products from concept through to launch, and ability to create new products to support entry into new market sectors as critical areas of internal competence.

The key factors having been defined, the next stage in the process is to rate these factors on some form of scale. Possibly the commonest approach is a scoring system ranging from a low of 1 through to a high of 10. The average total score is found by dividing summated total scores by the number of factors used in the analysis. This generates an overall score for market attractiveness and internal competence. Data are then usually interpreted by entering scores on a directional policy matrix of the type shown in Figure 5.3.

As can be seen from the DPM diagram in Figure 5.3, resultant positions in the matrix guide the organization towards adoption of the following generic strategies:

Cell 1 where the low market attractiveness and company competence means there is minimal opportunity. Hence the company (assuming they also have operations in other more successful sectors) should withdraw from the market immediately.

Cell 2 where low internal competence implies poor future prospects, but withdrawal should be a phased process because this will avoid major financial write-downs for redundant capital assets.

MARKET ATTRACTIVENESS

		Low	Average	High
COMPANY COMPETENCE	Low	1 Immediate market withdrawal strategy	2 Phased market withdrawal strategy	3 'One-off' significant capability upgrade strategy
	Average	4 Phased market withdrawal strategy	5 Sustain current strategy	6 Capability enhancement strategy
	High	7 Resource withdrawal strategy	8 Market expansion strategy	9 Leadership retention strategy

In obtaining C
but ≠ in retaining C's

Figure 5.3   **A directional policy matrix**

Cell 3 which offers a highly attractive market that a company cannot afford to ignore. Hence the strategy is to make a significant investment in upgrading competence in one last attempt to become successful. If, however, the investment does not deliver the required competence upgrade, then a departure strategy would be the next action.

Cell 4 where, as for Cell 2, low market attractiveness implies poor future prospects, and again withdrawal should be a phased process because this will avoid major financial write-downs for redundant capital assets.

Cell 5 where both competence and market attractiveness are rated average. For many organizations, this type of classification applies to a core business area generating a major proportion of total revenues. Hence the existing operation should be managed to sustain current market share (e.g. if the market begins to grow, increased revenue should be used to support higher promotional expenditure; conversely, if market size declines, promotional spending is reduced in direct relation to any decrease in total revenue inflows).

Cell 6 where competence is lower than market attractiveness and, therefore, the organization should invest in upgrading internal capabilities to the point where they are compatible with market opportunity.

Cell 7 where, because competence is higher than market attractiveness, the organization is probably over-resourcing the marketing operation. Hence resources can probably be withdrawn and because this will have minimal impact on revenue, profitability will rise.

Cell 8 where the firm can exploit an above-average competence as the basis for moving into new market sectors.

Cell 9 is a highly attractive market in which the organization, because of above-average competence, has achieved a leadership position. This will demand ongoing investment in order to protect the operation from any competitive threats.

Application of the DPM Tool

Brymor Ltd manufactures the component materials used by UK companies who fabricate and install new and replacement windows. The industry originally used aluminium as the standard material for window frames. The first significant technological advance was the introduction of 'double glazed' frames containing two pieces of glass which, by creating a thermal barrier, offer superior heat conservation properties.

Approximately 50 per cent of industry unit volume comes from sales in the domestic housing market, with the balance of sales split between industrial products (windows, shop fronts, office buildings, etc.) and the public sector (Local Government and Housing Association dwellings, etc.).

Important trends in the domestic market were the introduction of low-cost, plastic (or UPVC) frames and, for performance orientated end users, the introduction of 'composite frames' made by coating aluminium with polyvinyl compounds. The industrial market mainly still considers that aluminium is the best material for meeting their specifications for durability and variability of shape.

Brymor supplies (i) bar lengths of all four product types (i.e. aluminium, thermal break aluminium, UPVC and composites) to customers who wish to fabricate windows, and (ii) window-frame kits to customers who wish to install frames without any involvement in fabrication. Although limited industry data prevents an accurate assessment of market share, Brymor is believed to be a market leader in the supply of premium quality, advanced design, bar lengths and kit form products. In an attempt to avoid becoming involved in price-based competition, the firm has developed downstream relationships with window fabricators and installers who make their purchase decisions on the basis of factors such as product quality, just-in-time deliveries and provision of technical support to help resolve any very significant technical problems which may be encountered during either the pre- or post-purchase phase.

Factors such as market size, intensity of competition, orientation towards co-operation by customers, manufacturing costs, modernity of production assets and workforce skills were used to develop the DPM matrix shown in Figure 5.4. As can be seen from this example, the firm has some products which fall in the phased withdrawal and resource withdrawal categories, a core thermal break business, an area for competence enhancement, a market expansion opportunity and the need for new product investment to retain leadership in the composite materials market.

MARKET ATTRACTIVENESS

		Low	Average	High
		Immediate withdrawal No relevant product	**Phased withdrawal** No relevant product	**One-off upgrade** No relevant product
	Low			
	Average	**Phased withdrawal** Aluminium products supplied to price sensitive customers in industrial markets	**Sustain position** Thermal break products in both industrial and domestic markets	**Capability enhancement** Improve product and service quality of UPVC products in both markets
COMPANY COMPETENCE	High	**Resource withdrawal** Aluminium products supplied to small fabricators/ installers in domestic market	**Market expansion** Enter market for fabrication of large customized specification conservatories for domestic and industrial markets	**Leadership retention** Invest in new product development for composite products

Figure 5.4   **The Brymor DPM analysis**

DPM in Business Network Formation

A preliminary analysis of prevailing market conditions may prove that the organization working in isolation will never be able to achieve a specified vision. Possibly one of the most dramatic examples of this scenario was that facing Luciano Benetton who wanted to establish a global fashion goods business. He recognized that in Italy the industry suffered from an 'artisan perspective'. Hence the solution was the formation of a business network that could retain the flexibility to respond rapidly to new fashion trends while at the same time creating an 'industrial orientation' based on the use of vertical integration to achieve economies of scale (Jarillo and Martinez 1988).

The outcome has been the creation of a world-wide network with Benetton acting as a global hub orchestrating all aspects of managing a vertically integrated design, manufacturing, logistical and retailing operation. Styling is done outside the company by drawing upon a number of international freelance designers. More than 80 per cent of manufacturing is undertaken by other firms within the network but the critical phase of dyeing assembled garments is retained as an in-house responsibility. Logistics are undertaken mainly by other firms. The retail operation consists of 6,000 independent shops assisted by a team of approximately 100 agents who work under the direction of Benetton area managers.

For an organization which concludes that formation of a business network is a possible strategic solution, the first step is to undertake research with other organizations to determine the opportunities for collaboration. As shown in Figure 5.5, there are four possible outcomes. Outcome 1 is that no perceived opportunity exists. Outcome 2 suggests that market collaboration may be advantageous (e.g. a group of office furniture firms combining their products, thereby placing themselves in the position of entering new overseas markets with a much broader product portfolio). Outcome 3 suggests there may be a cost advantage from collaboration (e.g. a group of independent building supplies distributors forming a procurement network to achieve scale in negotiating larger discounts from suppliers). The fourth possible outcome offers the dual benefits of achieving both marketing and cost advantage (e.g. a group of tile manufacturers each agreeing to specialize in the production of floor tiles instead of all producing small runs of the same items, and using this more efficient manufacturing capability to launch a new range of high-value flooring products).

Having identified a possible idea, the group of firms can then determine which factors affect market attractiveness and the competences required to serve markets. This knowledge will provide the basis for constructing a Directional Network Policy Matrix of the type shown in Figure 5.6.

MARKET ADVANTAGE FROM COLLABORATION

	Low	High
Low	1 No perceived opportunity for a business network	2 Perceived opportunity for a marketing network
High	3 Perceived opportunity for cost-advantage network	4 Perceived opportunity for a dual-benefit network

COST ADVANTAGE FROM COLLABORATION

Low   High

Figure 5.5 **A network opportunity matrix**

ASSESSMENT OF MARKET CONDITIONS

		Low	Average	High
ASSESSMENT OF INTERNAL ORGANIZATIONAL CAPABILITY	Low	Immediately terminate network formation process	Only progress formulation of an informal market management co-operation network	Postpone network formation until location of new firms capable of upgrading internal capability
	Average	Only progress formation of an informal internal productivity network	Progress formation of formal network but seek additional network members with market management or internal capability skills	Progress formation of formal network but actively seek new network members with capability to lead internal productivity enhancement
	High	Progress formal network formation while concurrently progressing additional market opportunity search	Progress network formation but seek new market sector opportunities to fully exploit capabilities of network members	High priority progression of formal network formation due to strong evidence of potential

Figure 5.6   **A directional network policy matrix**
(*Source:* Chaston 1996)

Selecting Core Competences

Having matched markets to capability using an analysis tool such as the DPM, the next issue confronting the firm is to select which core competence(s) will be the driving force upon which to build future market success. A frequently quoted example of an organization which illustrates this approach is the Japanese computer giant, NEC (Kobayashi 1986).

Originally a supplier of telecommunications equipment, the firm realized that the communications and computer industries were on a convergent path because both exist to serve the needs of customers wishing to manage information electronically. The identified opportunity was that of becoming global provider of systems which simultaneously handle voice, data and image traffic. To be successful, the firm recognized that excellence would be required in three areas – namely distributed data processing using networked computer systems; evolving electronic components from simple integrated circuits to ultra large-scale integrated circuits; and the move from mechanical to digital switching. By internal development of resources and the formation of both technology and market access alliances, the company has been able to develop core competences that have supported revenue growth from $3.8 billion in 1980 to over $30 billion in the early 1990s.

Possibly one of the most useful tools for the selection of core competence is Porter's (1985) Value Chain concept. This model, as shown in Figure 5.7, proposes that opportunity for adding value comes from (a) the five core processes of inbound logistics, process operations, outbound logistics, marketing and customer service, and (b) the four support competencies of management capability, HRM practices, exploitation of technology and procurement.

For firms operating in transactional markets, assessment of the value chain is primarily restricted to analysing internal added-value activities to determine potential sources of competitive advantage. In relationship orientated markets, firms are more able to examine how horizontal partnerships with other firms at the same level in the market system and vertical partnerships with suppliers and/or customers can be used to identify how their specific value-added activities when linked with others can best determine competitive advantage.

Jarillo (1993) has posited that analysis of the precise value chain role an organization will undertake within a market system is a crucial step in the determination of future strategy. A fundamental objective in this process is to ensure that the organization is able to maximize its contribution to value-added activities within the system. He further points out that the exact nature of opportunity may change over time. An example he uses to illustrate this point is the computer industry where in the past the producers of hardware were able to enjoy most of the profits generated by value-added activities. More recently, however, as the knowledge of the technology associated with the assembly of 'boxes' has become more widely available, then greater profits have begun to accrue to those who have retained a 'lock on key technologies' (e.g. Intel in the manufacture of microchips; Microsoft in the area of operating systems and software applications).

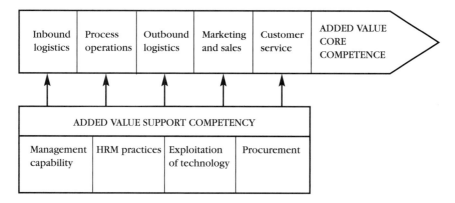

Figure 5.7 **A value chain model**

A Value Chain Example

Brymor's analysis of their market system indicated that as the majority of end user markets are seeking standard products, there is little point in seeking to act as a highly entrepreneurial organization. Within the standard product, transactional market sectors, price-based competition involves a value chain in which the size of company provides economies of scale in procurement, size of operation and investment in highly automated bar extrusion equipment. This sector is seen as the preserve of the very large, vertically integrated window companies. Hence Brymor has decided to concentrate its value chain analysis around serving the sectors in which customers exhibit a collaborative orientation in their purchase of high-quality, standard products.

Discussions with fabricator/installers and installers in this sector revealed a need for quality, order-entry convenience, JIT delivery, access to technical support to resolve complex installation problems and assistance in marketing. These data caused Brymor to focus on (i) their outbound logistics operation, (ii) marketing competence in the role of assisting their customers' own local marketing efforts and (iii) provision of technical services as the primary areas of their internal value chain capable of sustaining a competitive advantage within the replacement window market. Furthermore the firm recognized the importance of both product quality and rapid information interchange between the customer interface and manufacturing does mean that capability enhancement to at least to a 'best in industry' standard is required in areas such as process worker skills, total quality management and operation of the their computer-based MIS.

Developing the Marketing Plan

The format and contents of marketing plans depend upon the size of the organization (most small firms, for example, produce very short plans whereas in multi-national branded goods companies, the plan can approach the size of a small book), the attitude of the organization to the degree of formalization required within the annual planning cycle process and accepted sector conventions (e.g. consumer goods companies typically produce much more detailed plans in comparison to their counterparts in many industrial markets).

Whatever the selected format, the areas which should be covered in a typical marketing plan are summarized below:

- situation review
- strengths/weaknesses/opportunities/threats (SWOT) analysis
- summary of key issues
- future objectives
- strategy to achieve objectives

- marketing mix for delivering strategy
- action plan
- financial forecasts
- control systems
- contingency plans

Within the situation review, there should be coverage of the strategic situation facing the organization. This will be based on a description of market size, market growth trends, customer benefit requirements, utilization of mix to satisfy customer needs, activity of key competitors and the potential influence of changes in any of the variables which constitute the core and macro-environmental elements of the market system.

The internal capabilities of the organization are reviewed within the context of whether they represent strengths or weaknesses which might influence future performance. Market circumstances are assessed in relation to whether these represent opportunities or threats. This SWOT analysis, when linked to the situation review, provides the basis for defining which key issues will need to be managed in order to develop an effective plan for the future.

The degree to which marketing objectives will be defined can vary tremendously. Some organizations will merely restrict aims to that of specifying overall forecasted sales and desired market share. Other organizations may extend this statement by breaking the market into specific target segments and providing detailed aims for sales, expenditure profits for each product and/or market sector.

The marketing strategy will define how, by positioning the company in a specific way, stated marketing objectives will be achieved. The marketing mix section will cover how each element within the mix (product, price, promotion and distribution) will be utilized to support the specified strategy.

The action plan section will provide detailed descriptions of all actions to be taken to manage the marketing mix, including timings and definition of which specific individual(s)/department(s) are responsible for implementing the plan. The financial forecasts will provide a detailed breakdown of revenue, cost of goods, all expenditures and resultant profits. Many organizations will also include forecasts of fund flows and, via a balance sheet, the expected asset/liability situation.

Control systems should permit management, upon plan implementation, to identify rapidly variance of actual performance versus forecast and furthermore to offer diagnostic guidance on the cause of this variance. To achieve this aim, the control system will focus on measurement of key variables within the plan such as targeted market share, customer attitudes, awareness objectives for promotion, distribution targets by product and expected versus actual behaviour of competitors.

Contingency plans exist to handle the fact that actual events rarely happen as predicted by the plan. If the organization has already given thought to alternative scenarios prior to the beginning of the trading year, then if actual events are at variance with the plan, management is more able to implement immediately actions to overcome encountered obstacles. The usual approach for achieving this goal is that during the planning cycle the marketer examines the implications of alternative outcomes (e.g. the impact of actual sales revenue being 25 per cent higher or 25 per cent lower than forecast). Having reached conclusions from this analysis, the marketer then includes alternative plans as a component of the overall actions for which senior management approval is being sought.

Marketing Tactics

The key to the effective implementation of a marketing plan is the selection of tactics to be used in concurrently attacking competitors and defending the company against competition. As the concept of a strategic approach to the marketing process gained in popularity, it prompted some writers to suggest that there were close similarities between the principles of military warfare and the management of the marketing process (James 1985; Reis and Trout 1986).

Figure 5.8 illustrates the five alternative tactics through which to attack the competition. Military theory has established that, as was tragically demonstrated on the Western Front during the First World War, if a frontal attack is to be successful, the aggressor must be in possession of much greater resources than the defender. In the case of marketing battles, this superiority can be achieved by using various combinations of product performance, creation of a distinctive market position, promotional spending and/or lower prices.

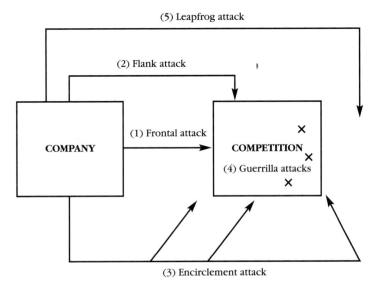

Figure 5.8   **Attack tactics**

An example of this type of approach is provided by the 1997 re-launch of Elida Fabrige's Organics range of haircare products aimed at taking market share from the market leader Pantene. The Organics product was put through a design revamp and a £15m TV campaign focused on the root-nourishing nutrients and shine-enhancing qualities of the reformulated product. These activities were accompanied by a national price promotion and sampling push directed to 10 million households (Anon. 1997).

It is necessary to register, however, that in all too many cases the optimism of the marketing strategist about the predicted outcome of a frontal assault is often not borne out by subsequent events. The need to identify a scapegoat in failure scenarios is probably the primary reason one regularly sees an announcement in the trade press along the lines of 'Following a strategy review by senior management, company X is sorry to announce the departure of their Marketing Director.'

A flank attack, which is targeted at an area poorly defended by the competition, is usually much less demanding of resources than a frontal attack. If the initial assault establishes a beach head, this territory gain can provide the basis from which to expand into the defender's market hinterland. This approach has often been used by Pacific Rim companies when mounting their initial attack on markets in North America (e.g. Matsushita's market entry, initially producing video recorders sold under the brand names of large American electrical goods manufacturers and acting as a supplier of private label goods for retailers such as Sears Roebuck).

Encirclement follows the strategy of simultaneously attacking on a number of fronts. As a strategy it requires that the attacker has the resources (a) to mount a very large-scale, initial assault and (b) once success becomes evident, can follow up to consolidate early share gains which have been achieved. The massive scale of the strategy means that very few examples can be found in the literature. One of the most well documented was that of Seiko during the period when the microchip was beginning to replace mechanical movements in the world watch industry. Seiko exploited the benefits of microchip technology to create a portfolio of branded watches to cover all price/quality combinations. They then overwhelmed competitors on a global basis by building distribution in all sectors of retailing from up-market jewellers through to discount catalogue houses.

Guerrilla warfare, in both military and commercial scenarios, is usually a strategy adopted by small operations attacking a much larger enemy. The key philosophy behind guerrilla warfare is to avoid a pitched battle with the enemy by immediately leaving an area of territory if the enemy mounts a large-scale, retaliative response. Consequently, in the world of marketing, the strategy is usually employed by smaller firms who select areas of territory poorly served by larger, national firms (e.g. small courier and parcel delivery services; small software firms customizing standard software platforms to suit the needs of companies who cannot afford the costs of having bespoke software developed to meet their specific data-processing requirements).

If, in a review of the market, the potential attacker decides competition is too well entrenched, then an alternative strategy is to mount a leapfrog attack. This involves the firm initiating an action which essentially by-passes the competition. An example is provided by Toshiba who decided they could never build an effective brand franchise in the UK television market by competing in a head-to-head confrontation with well-entrenched, European manufacturers. Their solution was to use superior technology to completely revise picture quality standards in the industry and then launch a new range of televisions which operated using flat square tube technology (FST).

Although marketers tend to find that planning new attacks on the enemy is much more exciting than defending a current business position, clearly all firms must have a strategy for responding to competitive threats. Five primary types of defence strategy are illustrated in Figure 5.9.

As demonstrated by the importance of castles during the Middle Ages, the classic form of retaining existing territory is to mount a position defence by constructing strong ramparts to keep out any enemy. In the world of marketing, the position defence is typically based upon building extremely high levels of customer loyalty. The potential problem of position defence for commercial organizations is, however, that the defender often becomes complacent behind the castle walls and does not recognize that the enemy is making inroads into the organization's customer base. One of the saddest examples of this scenario is IBM who built a global business in the computer industry based on unmatched customer loyalty in the business-to-business and business-to-public sector markets. Then, having ignored threats such as those posed by the advent of the networked PC and more powerful operating systems, the company awoke at the beginning of the 1990s to find customer loyalty had been completely eroded away by competitors more strongly committed to fulfilling the changing needs of customers in these two sectors.

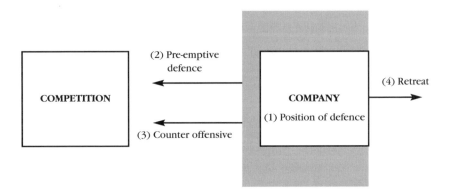

Figure 5.9 **Defence tactics**

Given the old military adage that 'attack is the best form of defence', clearly firms would be advised wherever possible to consider pre-emptive defence strategies in which, having identified a possible threat, they take action ahead of the competition. An excellent example of this philosophy is Microsoft who repeatedly observe advances being made by competitors in the software industry and then move to introduce another upgrade to retain their market leadership position.

Waiting until one is attacked and then mounting a counter-offensive does have the advantage of not having to respond before one comprehends the real nature of the competitive threat. Nevertheless it is probably a response to be avoided because there is always the risk that by waiting until 'you see the whites of the enemy's eyes', you are then forced to allocate a massive increase in marketing resources to recover the inroads the competitor has already started to make in the market place. An example is the Xerox Corporation which over the last few years has been forced to make large-scale investments in R&D, manufacturing technologies and organizational structure in order to regain lost ground in the photocopier market to competitors such as Canon.

Finally, if a careful review of circumstances reveals that the competitor has the potential to overwhelm the company completely, then there is little point is staying to defend a position which eventually will be overrun by the enemy. In these circumstances, the defender is well advised to withdraw to a more protected area of the market while determining how development of new, superior product/service propositions might permit recovery of lost market position at a later date. An example of this scenario is that of Lotus who in the 1980s lost their dominant position in the computer-based spreadsheet market to new software products such as Microsoft's Excel package. Having been acquired by IBM, Lotus are now using their world-beating Lotus Notes product as a platform from which to reposition themselves as the leading providers of Intranet-based intra- and inter-office 'groupware' communications systems.

References

Anon. (1997) Relaunching Organics', *Marketing*, 17 April: 4.

Chaston, I. (1996) 'Critical events and process gaps in the D.T.I. SME structured networking model', *International Small Business Journal*, 14(3): 71–84.

Hamel, G. and Prahalad C.K. (1994) *Competing for the Future: Breakthrough Strategies for Seizing Control of Your Industry and Creating the Markets of Tomorrow*, Boston, MA: Harvard Business School Press.

James, B. (1985) *Business Wargames*, London: Penguin.

Jarillo, J.C. (1993) *Strategic Networks: Creating the Borderless Organization*, Oxford: Butterworth-Heinemann.

Jarillo, J.C. and Martinez, J.I. (1988) *Benetton, S.p.A., Harvard Business School Case*, Boston, Mass.: Harvard Business School Press.

Kobayashi, K. (1986) *Computers and Communication: A Vision of C&C*, Cambridge, MA.: MIT Press.

Porter, M. (1985) *Competitive Advantage: Creating and Sustaining Superior Performance*, San Francisco: Free Press.

Reis, A. and Trout, J. (1986) *Marketing Warfare*, New York: McGraw-Hill.

Robinson, S.J.Q., Hitchens, R.E. and Wade, D.P. (1978) 'The directional policy matrix – tools for strategic planning', *Long Range Planning*, 11: 42–51.

6 Buyer Behaviour

Early writings on buyer behaviour, by drawing mainly upon observations of American tangible f.m.c.g. markets, assumed that purchase processes are transactional and that the customer passively accepts what is offered by the supplier. More recent studies of industrial and service markets have raised doubts about the validity of these early models because researchers found evidence of co-operation and proactive interactions between customers and suppliers during the execution of the purchase decision process. These observations strongly influenced the emergence of early theories concerning relationship marketing as a route through which to build long-term customer loyalty.

Understanding of buyer behaviour is essential to the management of the marketing process (e.g. determining when and how promotional information should be made available to customers). Increasingly it is also recognized that by undertaking detailed studies of buyer behaviour, the resultant knowledge can often provide the basis of identifying new sources of competitive advantage. Examples of this approach include the computer direct marketing organization, Dell Corporation and Procter & Gamble working in partnership with Wal Mart to evolve more effective logistics systems.

A critical element in the new approach to managing supplier–customer interactions is the creation of trust and commitment. This usually evolves from both parties exhibiting reliability and integrity. Once trust and commitment has been established, it is extremely difficult for a competitor to then gain a foothold in the market sector.

Effective launch of new products also requires a detailed understanding of variations in customer behaviour. This theory is usually presented in the context of the Diffusion of Innovation curve. When applying the curve to manage process, the organization will need to take into account the influence of transactional versus relationship marketing styles among customer groups.

Introduction

Buyer behaviour as a marketing discipline has tended to parallel evolving theories about strategic marketing with interaction between these two schools of thought being a somewhat rare event. The danger of this situation is that marketers may fail to appreciate the importance of understanding the buyer during the crafting of appropriate strategies and developing of effective marketing plans. This conclusion is reinforced by the views expressed by Engel et al. (1986: 7) who, in commenting on consumer marketing, propose that 'marketing starts with the analysis of consumer behaviours which are those acts of individuals directly involved in obtaining, using, and disposing of economic goods and services, including the decision processes that precede and determine these acts'. To further reinforce their views, these authors also state that 'understanding consumer motivation and behaviour is not an option – it is an absolute necessity for competitive survival' (Engel et al. 1986: 8).

The dominant influence in the early literature of marketing processes in American consumer goods markets has resulted in the creation of buyer behaviour models in which the buyers are passive and only react to seller stimuli by purchasing or not purchasing. The seller is seen as the active manager of process and, furthermore, the relationship is posited as one in which the seller interacts with a general market, rather than with individual customers (Ford 1990).

In the 1970s and 1980s, it became increasingly obvious that effective management of business-to-business markets cannot be achieved by merely assuming industrial scenarios can be treated as an extension of traditional, transactional, consumer goods marketing philosophies. Instead both academics and practitioners began to realize that industrial marketing theory is grounded in the critically important issue of adequately managing interactions within the buyer–seller relationship. Some of the most important contributions to theory in this area were made by the various European researchers working on a cross-border programme known as the Industrial Marketing and Purchasing (or IPM) project.

An added impetus to recognizing the important role of buyer behaviour has been the paradigm shift associated with the acceptance of relationship marketing as a fundamental principle in the management of many consumer and industrial market sectors. In an attempt to demonstrate the importance of the interaction between buyer behaviour and marketing theory, Gummesson (1994) has proposed that successful management of process demands that the seller emphasizes the use of customer behaviour data for bonding the seller to the customer as the basis for sustaining purchase loyalty. He, along with other academics, argues that traditional, transactional marketing theory ignores the important influence of buyer behaviour because it places too much emphasis on stealing customers from the competition.

Building Buyer Behaviour Models

Over the years academics and market researchers have developed a vast array of techniques for studying customer behaviour. These range from simple attitude and usage studies through to the development of complex multivariate equations that define the relationship between sales and all of the variables within the marketing mix.

One tool available to the researcher is observation of all phases of the purchase process from need identification through to post-purchase evaluation as the basis for constructing flow models of the buyer behaviour process. The advantages offered by such models are that they can provide:

- an explanation of all of the underlying variables which might influence the customer's product usage patterns;
- a frame of reference upon which to build a more effective marketing plan;
- knowledge of the information which should be used by the organization to track customer purchase patterns and assess the effectiveness of the organization's marketing activities.

One can use the activities associated with the purchase of toothpaste as the basis for illustrating the basic components that will typically be found in a basic buyer behaviour model. The customer first recognizes the need to purchase more toothpaste by observing that the current tube in the bathroom is almost empty and, therefore, adds the item to the weekly shopping list. Once at the supermarket, the individual reviews product availability by noting which brands are on the shelf. Having identified the presence of the family's favourite brand and observed there are no significant in-store offers on other brands, the individual purchases the product and, on arriving home, places the new tube of toothpaste in the bathroom for use by the family.

The activities described above can be translated into a formalized five-phase model of the type shown in Figure 6.1. External information is that data supplied by sources such as the promotional activities of the supplier and by any intermediaries who might be involved in the product distribution process. In this case, the information sources might include the competing claims made in the advertising campaigns of toothpaste manufacturers and the supermarket's in-store merchandizing activities.

Internal information comes from those sources not under control of supply chain members, and, as suggested in Figure 6.1, these might include the product usage experience of both the purchaser and the purchaser's family.

The type of model shown in Figure 6.1 assumes that the customer is acting rationally and making systematic use of available information. It is necessary to register that some academics have expressed concerns about the validity of using buyer behaviour models to assist the marketing process. East (1990), for example, holds the view that the models are of little use because the relationships between variables are often poorly specified and, therefore, cannot be tested. He also argues that 'the actual sequence of decision-making in the real world may be different and that problem solving is probably better explained as a series of associations of thought and feeling, rather than as a logical inference.'

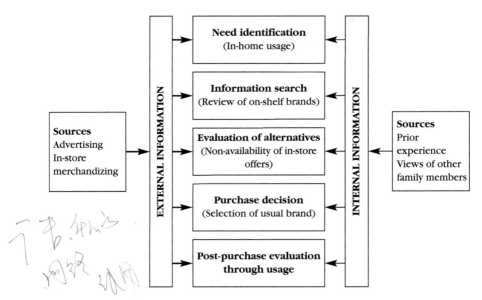

Figure 6.1   **A five-phase buyer behaviour model**

Clearly all such criticisms contain some validity and certainly in the case of purchase decisions involving a series of feelings, the 'buyer modelling' school of thought would totally accept that other research techniques would be needed to gain insights over those factors which are key influencers of behaviour (e.g. the application of psychoanalytic techniques pioneered in the early 1950s by Ernest Dichter (1960)). Possibly what is more important for model builders, however, is to identify in their specific studies how the factors of involvement, differentiation and time pressures may influence customer behaviour.

Munch and Hunt (1984: 114) have proposed that involvement is the 'level of perceived personal importance and/or interest evoked by a stimulus (or stimuli) within a specific situation'. From this definition it can be concluded that in cases of low involvement (e.g. the decision to purchase coffee from a vending machine) the customer will rapidly progress through the problem-solving model in Figure 6.1. Over time, however, the repeated use of the vending machine will evoke memory patterns that create feelings which ultimately may influence future purchase patterns. This scenario, however, does not invalidate logical problem-solving models; it merely suggests that in examining possible future marketing programmes, the marketer should use intuitive common sense and not always bother with attempting to construct a customer purchase behaviour model.

In relation to the issue of differentiation, when the customer perceives that available choice alternatives offer a vast array of different benefits, then he or she is more likely to undertake an extensive period of information search and evaluation of alternatives prior to reaching a purchase decision. Where there are no genuine differences between offerings, however, the customer is most likely to use a single factor such as convenience in determining which product to purchase (e.g. the car driver who needs petrol observes two garages offering competing brands of fuel at similar prices and drives on to the forecourt of the garage on the same side of the road, thereby avoiding having to wait for a gap in the oncoming flow of traffic).

Similarly, when the customer is under extreme time pressure, it is unlikely that he or she will embark on an actively reasoned decision process. The business executive running late for a meeting will probably, for example, ask the secretary to 'grab me whatever is available from the canteen', and not embark on a detailed discussion of available takeaway establishments in the surrounding area and/or the different offerings which might appear on their respective menus. Therefore, although there is validity in the views expressed by the anti-modelling fraternity, in those cases where the customer is considering a high involvement product category, can differentiate between alternative offerings and is not facing extreme time pressures, then it does seem reasonable to suggest that insights can be gained from examining the nature of the rational problem-solving process being utilized.

Probably some of the strongest benefits for a modelling approach are provided by applications in industrial markets. For here the marketer faces the major complication that more than one individual from the buyer organization may become involved in the purchase decision process. To illustrate this situation, we can remain with our toothpaste example, but now turn to the situation of the manufacturer seeking to repackage the product in a new, more customer friendly, container. As can be seen from Figure 6.2, need recognition involves consumers, the advertising agency and the marketing department. Once the firm determines there is an opportunity to progress the idea, other parties within the organization become involved as the project progresses through to completion. It is apparent from Figure 6.2 that for a packaging supplier to be successful in obtaining the contract for the new item, they will need to ensure they are not just having conversations with the procurement department, but also initiate dialogues with numerous other individuals both within and outside their customer's organization.

Webster (1973) made one of the earliest attempts at using stage process models to describe the purchase process in industrial markets. Robinson et al. (1967) have also used a similar approach, but suggested an extended form of the basic five-phase model based upon an eight-step decision process called BUYPHASE. This consists of the following phases:

1 Anticipating/recognizing need and probable solution.
2 Determining the characteristics of the required product/service.
3 Defining the quantity to be procured.
4 Searching and qualifying potential sources.
5 Requesting proposals from potential providers.
6 Evaluating submitted proposal and selection of appropriate source(s).
7 Implementing the formal purchase process.

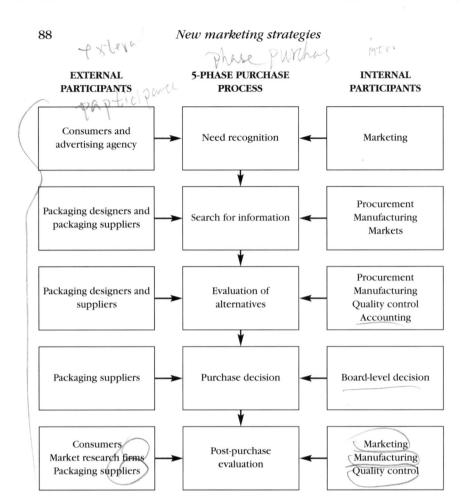

Figure 6.2 **Participants in an industrial purchase scenario**

8   Using post-purchase usage experience to provide feedback for utilization
    when seeking to place possible future, repeat purchase, orders.

Subsequently Webster and Wind (1972) introduced the concept of risk
management within industrial markets. They proposed that the purchaser
would act to reduce perceived risk by using mechanisms which might include
(a) acquisition of additional information both from suppliers (e.g. by
requesting the submission of detailed bid documents) and from other industry sources such as the sector's trade association, (b) extending the breadth
and duration of the information evaluation phase (e.g. defence contract
negotiations between government aerospace suppliers might take two to
three years before a final specification is agreed by all parties) and (c) 'source
loyalty' (i.e. favouring suppliers with whom the buyer has an existing
relationship).

Empirical research has shown that source loyalty is a key factor across most industrial markets. This fact clearly demonstrates how important it is for a prospective vendor to emphasize the proven superior, competitive advantages of their products when seeking to induce buyers to switch from existing sources of supply. In some cases, however, outsiders may never obtain the chance to put their case to the buyer because the latter organization operates an 'approved supplier list' and will only contract with firms on this list. The use of approved suppliers is especially widespread among public sector purchasing organizations. Hence, one of the recent actions of the European Community to increase public sector competitiveness has been the introduction of legislation requiring national governments and government-funded organizations such as hospitals, to expand their approval lists to include suppliers from outside their own borders.

Source of Competitive Advantage

By the mid-1980s, many firms finally began to realize that because they and their competitors in a market sector use very similar management techniques across all areas of their operation (e.g. all purchase Nielsen store panel data; employ television advertising to communicate benefit claims; operate the same machinery in their manufacturing processes; buy raw materials from the same sources) identifying opportunities for differentiating their offering in the market place had become extremely difficult. At this juncture, some of the more far-sighted firms began to realize that the buyer behaviour process model might provide new sources of competitive advantage.

Dell Corporation, for example, recognized that consumers seeking good advice and rapid response to problems were often not receiving this type of information from many of their local retail, home computer, outlets. This caused the company's founder to recognize that by building a direct marketing operation capable of communicating directly with end users, it would be possible to enhance the role of the supplier in the provision of external information. As one of the first firms into interactive telephone selling, the company achieved a massive lead over other computer manufacturers and this enabled the firm to emerge as a new, dominant force in the world PC market (Rapp and Collins 1994).

Another example of exploiting process is provided by the marketing giant Procter & Gamble. This firm's dominant position in f.m.c.g. markets around the world had apparently caused them to adopt the view that their size permitted them to dictate terms to their intermediaries on the grounds that retailers cannot survive without P&G products on their shelves. For some years a number of industry observers had been expressing the view that the growing strength of competition should be a warning bell to P&G that their somewhat dictatorial attitude was beginning to impact market share.

Following discussions between Lou Pritchett, P&G's US vice-president of sales, and Sam Walton, the founder of the Wal-Mart Corporation, Procter clearly recognized that there was a need to build closer relationships with intermediaries. Subsequent meetings between executives at all levels across the organization soon revealed that the existing Wal-Mart purchasing system was creating undesirably high inventory levels. P&G used a computerized inventory replenishment system to model an optimal order pattern for Wal-Mart. Initially applied to the Pampers diaper product, P&G then extended their research to examine the entire Wal-Mart's warehouse system. This eventually led to P&G creating an automated replenishment system in which Wal-Mart no longer needed to be involved in day-to-day stock management activities. The outcome of this project was that Wal-Mart reduced their excess and out-of-stock problems, P&G's on-time delivery reached 99.6 per cent and both parties made significant cost savings in their inventory management operations (Wiersema 1997).

Dell and P&G are both examples of essentially transactional orientated firms (the former an entrepreneurial-transactionalist and the latter a conservative-transactionalist) creating competitive advantage through gaining understanding of the buyer behaviour process. Similar benefits are available to relationship orientated firms, but to be successful it is probable they will have to become even more deeply involved with their customers.

To illustrate this fact, one can use an example of what has traditionally been a transactional-orientated market, namely baby foods. In France, Nestlé Foods faced the problem that they were a poor number two to the dominant Bledina brand owned by BSN. Research on customer behaviour caused Nestlé to realize that by exploiting their knowledge of the problems confronting young mothers, they could begin to build brand share by developing a much closer relationship with their customers. To initiate this relationship, Nestlé created rest stops alongside motorways which they staffed with hostesses to help parents feed and change their babies. They also created a toll-free number which mothers could call to obtain baby-nutrition counselling advice and established a database of 220,000 new mothers that permitted the firm regularly to mail free packages of product samples six times during the first two years of the baby's life. In just four years, these various actions have combined to move Nestlé from nowhere to a 30 per cent share of the French baby food market (Rapp and Collins 1994).

Commitment and Trust

In seeking to exploit knowledge of buyer behaviour to achieve competitive advantage, it is critical that the relationship marketer recognizes the importance which trust and commitment play in building customer loyalty. Traditional transactional marketing tends to focus on managing the purchase process as a series of discrete, separate activities (e.g. the use of in-store money-off coupons to reward current customers and concurrently tempt other customers away from purchasing their usual brand). Relationship marketing is based upon the concept of the buyer and seller working in partnership to achieve mutually satisfactory goals. In supply chain situations, for example, this may be reflected by the purchaser being willing to contract for a three-year period with the supplier. In return, this latter organization will implement investment activities such as the creation of a distribution centre next to their customer's premises from which product can be drawn down on a daily basis.

Service industries are also finding that a partnership orientation between supplier and customer is critical to sustaining purchase loyalty. The emergence in recent years of a banking culture which is credit-risk aversion driven linked to an increasing centralization of lending decisions has been found to be a major impediment to building trust and commitment between banks and their customers. Wood et al. (1995), for example, concluded banks will continue to lose customers unless their managers at a local level were orientated towards establishing close relationships with customers and permitted to make decisions without continually referring the matter to a central lending authority which had little understanding of the specific issues the local manager had taken into account in recommending a positive response to a borrowing request.

Exhibiting traits of reliability and integrity leads to firms beginning to trust each other to make decisions which have positive outcomes and to avoid creating situations which might have an adverse impact on the seller–buyer relationship. In discussing the factors influencing the formation of effective relationships, Morgan and Hunt (1994) have posited that there are five precursor variables influencing commitment and trust – namely, relationship termination costs, relationship benefits, shared values, effective communication and avoidance of opportunistic behaviour.

The assumption over termination costs is that, where these are high, all parties will try to overcome differences of opinion because all wish to avoid the economic impact of severing the relationship. Thus, for example, in the case of Korean power stations which have designed their system to burn a specific blend of Australian coal and the mining company in Australia which has invested in a mixing plant to produce this coal, both parties would suffer if it became necessary to terminate the contract. The power station, if unable to find an alternative supplier, would have to reconfigure its burners and the mining company would have an idle mixing plant.

The coal example can also be used to illustrate the requirement of mutual benefit. The mining company has a long-term contract for a significant proportion of total output and the power station is assured of supplies at a stable price. Creating and sustaining this relationship is critically dependent upon both parties sharing common values. The mining company must be more interested in achieving stable sales and therefore be prepared to forgo opportunistic situations of re-entering commodity markets during periods of rapidly rising prices. Conversely, the power company must be orientated towards the goal of meeting long-term customer needs and be willing to ignore any higher short-term, profit opportunities that might be available by

(a) procuring bargain priced coal during periods of supply glut and (b) not passing on these temporary cost savings to the customer in the form of lower electricity bills. This example of pricing behaviour within the relationship also shows that by putting priority on supply stability, both parties have accepted that price-driven opportunistic behaviour is clearly unacceptable if they seek to develop a relationship based upon mutual trust and commitment.

The role of communication in the relationship is to ensure that both parties keep each other informed of events that might disrupt the flow of goods or services through the supply chain, for, as suggested by Mohr and Nevin (1990: 37), 'communication can be described as the glue that holds together a channel of distribution'. Thus if the coal-mining firm in the above example encounters an extraction problem which might affect deliveries, it should immediately communicate this fact to the Korean power station. Conversely, if the generator is expecting a downturn in demand that might impact future purchases, this information should rapidly be communicated to their supplier in order that the latter organization can review future production schedules.

Network Behaviour

The critical importance of trust and commitment within buyer–seller relationships can be further demonstrated by an examination of their importance within business networks. The American Hospital Supply network was created as a strategic response to environmental developments. Beginning in 1977, a growing number of US hospitals were encountering cost pressures and, to contain this situation, decided to centralize their procurement operation to obtain larger volume discounts. A distributor of healthcare products, American Hospital Supply, wanting to capitalize on this situation, signed a blanket agreement with several buying groups. Though no prices were listed, the company agreed as a matter of trust that its prices would always be competitive. It also agreed to hold prices below specified, maximum percentage increases and to pay volume rebates based upon the hospitals' annual purchases. To apply some degree of peer pressure within the network, it was agreed that no hospital would qualify for a volume rebate unless all other hospitals in the group reached a required minimum purchase volume (Pillsbury 1982). American Hospital Supply also secured the right to 'match it or walk away' under which the hospitals agreed to provide the supplier with any information on bid prices submitted by competitors.

Business networks may often consist of firms who traditionally have been in fierce competition with each other. Under these circumstances, a critical first phase in the network formation process is to find a way of replacing old behaviours with relationships based on mutual trust. In some cases this is achieved by the network members agreeing to continue to compete with each other in their traditional markets, but to 'bury the hatchet' and work together to enter successfully a new market sector. One such example is provided by New Zealand farm equipment suppliers who have formed an export network to expand overseas, but still operate independently of each other within the domestic agricultural supplies market. An observation about this network communicated to the author by the broker who was employed to create this new trading entity is that, over time, as the joint overseas trading experience created stronger trust and commitment between the participant firms, this has gradually been followed by a reduction of the intensity of rivalry between these organizations in their domestic market as each has realized that even here co-operation is probably a more productive way of building market share.

Product Adoption Behaviour

A common practice among many f.m.c.g. firms is to adopt a mass market approach of immediately seeking to gain widespread distribution for a new product and to underpin the launch with heavy promotional spending. This approach has a fundamental flaw in that it assumes all customers are willing to change their product usage patterns immediately and switch to the new offering. Yet as Rogers (1983) has suggested, there exists an 'innovation diffusion process' which he proposes can be characterized as a normal curve containing the following five adopter groups:

1 *Innovators* are venturesome individuals, who are sufficiently willing to try new ideas so that they are often prepared to accept that the product is so new that performance may be less than perfect.
2 *Early adopters* are opinion leaders within their industrial and/or personal social groups, who are willing to try new ideas ahead of others but who make careful assessment of potential risk before placing an order.
3 *Early majority* are people who try new ideas ahead of the majority, but typically delay initial purchase until information from early adopters indicates the new product is meeting claims made by the supplier.
4 *Late majority* are those who tend to be sceptical about new ideas and avoid purchase until there is clear evidence that the new product is successful.
5 *Laggards* are traditionalists who are suspicious of change and will delay purchase until the new product has been in the market for a significant period of time.

The speed with which a new product gains market acceptance and is adopted by the five different customer types on the diffusion curve, is influenced by a whole range of factors which the marketer will need to understand in designing a successful market launch. These include relative product advantage,

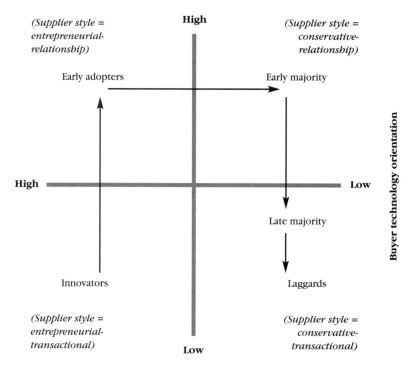

Figure 6.3 **A high-tech customer adoption model**

compatibility, product complexity, product divisibility (i.e. the degree to which the product can be tried on a limited basis) and communicability (i.e. the degree to which the benefit claims can be easily described to potential users) (Gatignon and Robertson 1985).

The influence of these factors is relatively small in the case of an easily understood consumer product. Consequently, in only a very short period of time, a new product of this type will usually gain widespread acceptance within the market (e.g. the snowboard which only arrived on the scene in the late 1980s, and on the *pistes* in some areas of the world snowboarders now outnumber the skiing population).

As shown in Figure 6.3, however, producers of technically complex products usually face a much harder time gaining acceptance of their product. For in many cases the major differences in buyer behaviour between the various customer groups on the innovation diffusion curve will demand completely different marketing strategies.

Figure 6.3 was constructed by undertaking interviews with the owner-managers of small, high-tech firms in the UK involved in the manufacture of components and test equipment for the electronics industry. Style of marketing of selected firms was identified by asking respondents to classify their operations using the Covin/Slevin (1988) entrepreneurship scale and the relationship/transactional scale described in Chapter 1. Respondents were then asked to describe their own marketing philosophy and the purchase behaviour exhibited by their major customers.

Entrepreneurial-transactional firms tend to draw upon the latest technological breakthroughs in their sector as the basis for developing new-to-the-world propositions. The majority of their customers are researchers working in scientific institutions, R&D laboratories or quality control departments within manufacturing firms, who are also deeply fascinated by the exploitation of the latest technology, and for whom moving forward the frontiers of knowledge is often more important than purchase of a reliable product which has a proven application. In many cases the owner-managers within the supplier firm, having provided a solution to a customer problem, are more interested in moving on to a new project than seeking to gain a high volume of sales for their previous new product idea. Management of the marketing process is often undertaken by the firm's researchers who operate in a world where customers find out about their new product expertise through word-of-mouth recommendations within the same sector of industry or academia.

New ideas based upon the latest technology often require the involvement of the customer to help the supplier firm in the development of a truly new effective product. This fact is clearly recognized by entrepreneurial-relationship firms who proactively seek to form innovation partnerships with like-minded customers in order to develop together a new product offering genuinely superior performance (e.g. some of the R&D firms originally involved in exploiting the laser, who worked in partnership with industrial welding equipment and medical equipment firms to pioneer the application of this technology in their respective industrial sectors). An alternative approach to innovation is for the entrepreneurial-relationship firm to open discussions about the current problems confronting its customers as the basis for determining how they might work together in the formulation of a solution.

The marketing process of the entrepreneurial-relationship orientated firm is one which relies heavily upon word-of-mouth recommendations, but additionally requires that the firm has a clear idea about which firms among their customer group are early adopters willing to take risks in the process of identifying new, often radical solutions to existing problems. An example of this is the software firm Lotus which persuaded the accounting and consultancy giant Price Waterhouse to enter the era of the 'electronic office' by purchasing 10,000 copies of their then unproven Lotus Notes product.

Once the market begins to recognize the widespread take-up of a new product by early adopters, the early majority will begin to become interested in the benefits of this latest innovation. Unlike innovators or early adopters, the early majority take a much more pragmatic attitude to new products. Proven, superior benefits to the user are significantly more important than the nature of the technology which has permitted the development of the product (Moore 1991).

At this stage in the life of the product, the supplier will need to begin to use the more traditional marketing tools to convince the market that the new product is clearly capable of outperforming existing products. The market expansion task is made significantly easier if the supplier has an in-depth knowledge of the customer. Extensive customer knowledge is why at this point on the Product Life Cycle Curve, unless the entrepreneurial-relationship firms are willing to change their marketing orientation, their role in the life of the product often passes into the hands of conservative-relationship firms. These organizations are often larger firms who have typically monitored the progress of any new innovation, and when they feel the majority of the market is willing to adopt the new product, they will enter the sector offering a specific solution targeted at customers known to be dissatisfied with the performance of existing products.

An example of this dissatisfaction scenario is provided by Oracle, who carefully monitored the growing concerns that their customers were exhibiting over the fact that many new database software products were designed to operate on specific hardware platforms. This meant that it was often impossible effectively to integrate different information systems within their organizations. Oracle's solution was to launch a database system which was compatible with most hardware systems, thereby enabling their customers to begin to create fully integrated Management Information Systems.

The late majority is usually completely uninterested in technological advances. Instead they are influenced by the fact that the product has proven capabilities, is widely used within their market sector and is realistically priced relative to existing products. Servicing this type of customer is best undertaken by larger firms who can exploit scale in their manufacturing operation, have a marketing operation capable of implementing large-scale promotional campaigns and a distribution operation able to service a diversity of market channels. Typically these are the skills found within conservative-transactional marketing operations and a current example is provided by Canon's increasingly global domination of the laser printer market.

Laggards are only really motivated by proven solutions available at low prices. The strong price orientation across this group of customers means that their needs are best served by very large, conservative-transactional firms who specialize in producing and distributing a large volume of goods at highly competitive prices (e.g. the Korean electronics firms who now dominate the consumer video-recording machine market).

References

Covin, J.G. and Slevin, D.P. (1988) 'The influence of organisational structure on the utility of an entrepreneurial top management style', *Journal of Management Studies*, 25: 217–37.

Dichter, E. (1960) *The Strategy of Desire*, New York: Doubleday.

East, R. (1990) *Changing Consumer Behaviour*, London: Cassell.

Engel, J.F., Blackwell, R.D. and Miniard, P.W. (1986) *Consumer Behaviour*, 5th edn, Chicago: Dryden Press.

Ford. D. (1990) *Understanding Business Markets: Interaction, Relationships and Networks*, London: Academic Press.

Gatignon, H. and Robertson, T.S. (1985) 'A proposition inventory for new diffusion research', *Journal of Consumer Research*, March: 849–67.

Gummesson, E. (1994) 'Making relationship marketing operational', *The International Journal of Service Industry Management*, 5(5): 5–20.

Mohr, J. and Nevin, J.R. (1990) 'Communication strategies in marketing channels: a theoretical perspective', *Journal of Marketing*, 54, October: 36–51.

Moore, G.A. (1991) *Crossing the Chasm*, New York: HarperBusiness.

Morgan, R.M. and Hunt, S.D. (1994) 'The commitment–trust theory of relationship marketing', *Journal of Marketing*, 58, July: 20–38.

Munch, A. and Hunt, S.D.(1984) 'Consumer involvement: definition issues and research directions', in T. Kinnear (ed.), *Advances in Consumer Research*, Provo, Utah: Association for Consumer Research. 11: 113–27.

Pillsbury, A.B. (1982) 'The hard-selling supplier to the sick', *Fortune*, 26 July: 51–61.

Rapp, S. and Collins, T.L. (1994) *Beyond MaxiMarketing: The New Power of Caring and Sharing*, New York: McGraw-Hill.

Robinson, P.J., Faris, C.W. and Wind, Y. (1967) *Industrial Buying and Creative Marketing*, Boston: Allyn and Bacon.

Rogers, M. (1983) *Diffusion of Innovation*, New York: Free Press.

Webster, F.E. (1973) 'Modeling the industrial buying process', *Journal of Marketing Research*, 2(3): 251–60.

Webster, F.E. and Wind, Y. (1972) *Organizational Buying Behaviour*, Englewood Cliffs, NJ: Prentice-Hall.

Wiersema, F. (1997) *Customer Intimacy*, London: HarperCollins.

Wood, D., Collett, N., Ertuk, I. and Schell, C. (1995) 'Customers call the banks to account', *Financial Director*, November: 20–5.

7 Business-to-Business and Institutional Marketing

Studies in both Europe and the USA have validated the view that business-to-business markets exhibit certain unique characteristics.(These include factors such as nature of demand, complexity of the buying process, buyer power and the nature of the buyer–seller relationship.)

To manage business-to-business markets effectively, suppliers and their customers usually need to focus on how mutual advantages can be identified in downstream markets. One approach is to examine marketing planning in the context of the two dimensions of reducing uncertainty and determining the potential for forging long-term functional relationships from which all parties can benefit.

Over the last two decades, management of the business-to-business marketing process has been strongly influenced by JIT and TQM because both processes are dependent upon the formation of closer customer–supplier relationships. The IMP group has further extended relationship theory by evolving a model concerned with the actors, resources and activities which exist within a market system.

In the case of institutional markets, growing problems over the funding of the welfare state has resulted in governments acting to revise management practices within public sector institutions such as hospitals and schools. Initially errors were made because it was assumed that concepts from the commercial world such as responding to competition and acting to totally satisfy customer need could be introduced without any form of modification to reflect the actual circumstances facing public sector organizations. Recently more realistic management paradigms have been evolved which more adequately reflect the real circumstance that demand exceeds supply and sufficient resources will never be made available to fulfil totally customer expectations.

Business-to-Business Marketing

The early authors of business-to-business marketing texts often adopted an approach which was clearly rooted in a consumer goods, transactional marketing framework. The only difference was that these authors, when discussing issues such as strategic planning and the selection of an appropriate marketing mix, attempted to present examples of practice in terms of industrial market scenarios.

Researchers seeking to validate the theories presented in such texts soon found, however, that actual marketing practices in industrial sectors were often very different from those espoused by many business school academics. Some individuals explained that their inability to find examples of convergence between theory and practice was a reflection of the fact that most industrial firms did not really understand basic marketing concepts. More perceptive members of the academic community posited the alternative view that lack of convergence between theory and practice might be due to business-to-business marketing processes being very different from f.m.c.g. marketing. They concluded that what was needed was first to observe actual managerial processes in use on a day-to-day basis and then, from these data, begin to formulate appropriate management paradigms.

Some of these researchers concentrated on determining whether differences in market structure influenced the marketing process (Powers 1991), while others concentrated on understanding buyer behaviour. By the early 1980s, academics, mainly in America, had been able to clarify differences which exist between consumer and industrial markets. Consequently, they were able to provide guidance on how such variations might influence the marketing process. Other American academics such as Sheth (1973), and Webster and Wind (1972) began to construct and validate realistic buyer behaviour models reflecting the real nature of events which occur in industrial markets.

Meanwhile in Europe, the Nordic business schools were applying a grounded theory approach to researching industrial markets. Their studies raised questions about the validity of assuming it was appropriate to apply theories based upon the utilization of the classic confrontational, transactional strategic planning models of the type espoused by academics such as Michael Porter. Wider recognition of the Nordic school of thought concerning the existence of alternative, collaborative buyer–seller relationships in industrial markets was achieved through the formation of the pan-European IMP research group.

Concurrently some academics in America such as Jackson (1985) also began to question the correctness of rigidly adhering to purist transactional management approaches when studying industrial markets. The outcome of such research led to the conclusion that in many cases successful firms were more likely to achieve market leadership through the exploitation of relationship orientated marketing principles.

By the end of the 1980s, most academics had accepted that certain fundamental aspects of the industrial marketing process were unique to the sector. Additional stimuli were provided through (a) the realization that many industrial marketers could be assisted by drawing upon theories and concepts being generated by research on service sector firms and (b) the advent of IT which was bringing about massive changes in processes associated with the marketing of industrial goods. The net outcome has been that by the 1990s, business-to-business is an area of marketing deserving its own unique paradigms. Furthermore, industrial marketing also provides an excellent source of managerial practices which marketers can transfer back into other sectors such as consumer goods, not-for-profit and service industry marketing.

Characteristics of Business-to-Business Markets

Business-to-business marketing has been described as 'the marketing of goods and services to commercial enterprises, governments and other non-profit institutions for use in the goods and services that they, in turn, produce for resale to other industrial customers' (Corey 1991: 4). This definition implies that the type of customer and nature of goods purchased are both very different from consumer markets where goods are bought for the purpose of final consumption. This means that business-to-business markets are likely to exhibit the following attributes (Powers 1991; Rangan et al. 1995):

Derived Demand

Because the supplier's product or service is to be incorporated into an output for which their customer will seek to generate sales revenue, one characteristic of business-to-business markets is that demand will be of a 'derived' nature. For example, the demand for house bricks in the domestic housing sector of the construction industry will be critically influenced by the number of consumers over a 12-month period who are willing to purchase new dwellings.

One key implication of derived demand is that because business-to-business customers purchase in response to what they perceive are the economic cycle trends in their downstream final consumption markets, industrial marketers often have to adopt a much longer-range planning orientation than their counterparts in consumer goods markets. Due to the fact that demand is often more volatile than in consumer goods markets, an added complication for the business-to-business marketer is that sales revenue can fluctuate quite dramatically. This is especially true in the market for new plant and equipment, because a given percentage of increase in consumer demand can eventually lead to a much larger percentage increase in the demand for the buildings and machinery required to produce additional output.

Thus, in the case of the brick industry, producers can initially probably handle an upswing in home starts by adding further shifts and/or having employees work overtime. If, however, the building boom continues, there could then be a 100 per cent surge in the demand for brick-processing equipment. This is then followed by a demand downturn because the 'one-off' expansion in brick-making capacity is sufficient and the brick producers will probably not need any additional new machinery for another two or three years.

Total demand in business-to-business markets also tends to be relatively inelastic (i.e. buyer behaviour, at least over the short term, is not strongly influenced by supplier price changes). This is because customers are usually unwilling and/or unable to make major changes in their plans merely to respond to a change in the prevailing price of a component which only constitutes a minor element in their overall costs. Thus, in the brick example, construction firms are unlikely to double the number of their new home starts just because the brick producers find they are able to reduce prices by 50 per cent.

Complexity of Buying Process

In consumer markets, the decision-maker is often a single individual who is buying a relatively simple product or service. In industrial markets, the sale of a single piece of capital equipment might involve the supplier in negotiations with the customer's purchasing, engineering, manufacturing, financial and legal departments before a purchase decision can be reached. Additionally, the new equipment may involve complex technologies, some of which have yet to be commercialized. Hence purchase negotiations between buyer and seller will probably involve complex discussions about product specifications, development lead times and customization of design to suit specific application scenarios (e.g. discussions between a shipbuilder and a shipping company seeking to purchase a new form of bulk carrier that has new advanced automated freight-handling facilities, in order to further improve shipboard operational productivity, thereby reducing the time spent in harbours loading and unloading cargo).

A side-effect of buying process complexity is that the time taken to reach a purchase decision and the life of the sales contract are both of a much longer duration than in many consumer goods markets. The reason is that the buy decision will often have a long-term impact on the customer's operation (e.g. Railtrack in the UK, having selected the firm to up-date their railway signalling system, will probably expect to be using the same equipment for 10–20 years). Thus, understandably, the purchaser will spend a considerable time making sure they have chosen the best available option. Furthermore, in these situations, having successfully negotiated a sale, the producer can often safely assume that expected sales revenue will continue to flow from the contract for several years. The implications for the business-to-business marketer, however, is that although they have fewer potential customers towards whom promotional efforts will need to be directed, failure to win only a small number of bids can create massive problems over sustaining future plant throughput, which in turn may lead to workforce redundancies and/or plant closures (e.g. British Aerospace being forced in the mid-1990s to curtail drastically the activities of their executive jet division).

Buyer Power and Location

In contrast with most consumer goods markets, business-to-business markets tend to have fewer customers who individually purchase a large proportion of their suppliers' total output. Producers of items such as generators for power stations, for example, can often literally count the number of customers on the fingers of two hands. Additionally, the specialist industrial sector infrastructure required by many manufacturing companies often results in their location in geographically concentrated areas (e.g. the large number of multi-national electronics firms in the area known as Silicon Glen in Scotland).

The advantage to the marketer is that this concentration of power and geographic clustering of customers means direct marketing and one-to-one selling are economically viable propositions. As a result marketers can avoid the need for the massive promotional budgets which are mandatory in branded consumer goods markets where firms are seeking to communicate with a highly dispersed customer base. On the other hand, the small number of business-to-business customers means that the marketer must continually be ready to respond to the possibility that the purchasing organizations may exploit their tremendous buying power to place pressure on their suppliers to offer significant price reductions or risk losing a major contract.

Buyer–Seller Relationships

The small number of customers in business-to-business markets and their potential to use their buying power to extract highly favourable terms from their suppliers does result in much closer buyer–seller relationships than those encountered in most consumer goods markets. Business-to-business marketers frequently find that the customer expects product offerings to be customized and that the supplier's marketing team must have the technical skills to handle customer concerns during both the pre- and post-purchase phases. It is quite usual, for example, in capital equipment markets such as the supply of automated metal tube production plants, for the customer to expect (a) to be permitted to spend extensive periods in their suppliers' factories during the design and manufacturing phases of the contract and (b) for their supplier's engineering team to live at the customer's site for many months while equipment is being installed and employees trained in the effective operation of the new machinery. Under these circumstances, a major role of the supplier marketer is to act as project co-ordinator in order to identify rapidly any problems which might arise and immediately to invoke appropriate actions for resolving customer concerns.

Buyer–Seller Interaction

The research by the IMP Group identified that the traditional model of the active seller and the passive buyer is just not borne out by observations of actual process in many industrial markets. These researchers concluded that the buyer–seller relationship is essentially one of active interaction between both parties in the relationship. Ford (1990) posits that the repeated occurrence of 'buying episodes' over time leads to the development of longer-term, mutually dependent relationships between the employees within the participant organizations. This perspective on the importance of employee interaction is supported by the earlier work of Hakansson and Ostberg (1975) who concluded that the social exchanges which occur between individuals from the buyer and seller organizations during repeated execution of the order-placement / order-delivery cycle lead to the development of clear expectations of each other's capabilities and responsibilities. Eventually these expectations become institutionalized to such an extent that they become incorporated into the operating procedures which form the basis of a long-term relationship.

As shown in Figure 7.1, within the core of a buyer–seller interaction model, certain variables such as technology, strategy and individual employee behaviour can all contribute towards influencing the relationship. Thus, for example, if both parties have a clear understanding of the technology upon which the seller's goods are based, this will simplify development of the market relationship (e.g. the UK manufacturer of turbine blades, Centrax Engineering, marketing their products to a manufacturer of jet engines such as Rolls Royce Ltd). Where there is a major technology knowledge gap (e.g. Mitsubishi's computer division marketing advanced, networked file servers to an insurance firm), then the supplier will have to demonstrate their desire to establish a relationship which is founded upon mutual trust and commitment. Typically this will only be achieved if the behaviour of the seller's employees is consistent with the long-term relationship formation objective (e.g. spending time explaining why a specific recommendation is being made and being very open about the strengths and weaknesses of product offered by other suppliers operating in the same market sector).

The macro-environment shown in Figure 7.1 contains variables of a wider context which can also influence the buyer–seller relationship. Examples include market structure (e.g. the degree of supplier choice available to the customer), market stability (e.g. minimal fluctuations in year-on-year sector sales trends which permit both parties to forecast reasonably accurately near future demand), industry internationalism (e.g. domestic suppliers and/or customers moving off-shore to further expand sector sales) and social system (e.g. the degree to which cultural trends cause customers to favour sourcing supplies from within their own nation).

Ford (1990) has grouped the marketing management implications of the interaction model under the two headings of 'limitations' and 'handling problems'. Within the area of limitations, for example, he suggests the

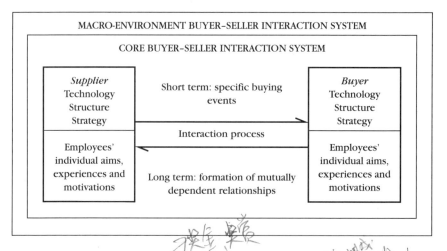

Figure 7.1 **An industrial buyer–seller interaction model**

supplier 'cannot be all things to all people'. Thus a firm specializing in the production of premium priced/premium quality components would face limitations if it also sought to meet the needs of customers seeking low price/low-quality goods. Handling problems are those activities associated with ensuring information and output fulfil the specific requirements of the customer. For example, most major OEMs now require that their overseas suppliers, in order to avoid production scheduling problems that might be created by component deliveries being disrupted by bad weather, maintain 'buffer stocks' at the customer's manufacturing plants.

Hakansson et al. (1976) have used the interaction model as the basis for defining how perceptions of both the buyer and the seller will influence the marketing process. They feel that possibly the most important variable is the degree of uncertainty which exists within the areas of customer need, market environment and management of the actual transaction. The usual response of the buyer to need uncertainty is to specify carefully contractual requirements in relation to issues such as product performance and delivery dates.

Market uncertainty may be seen by the buyer to exist in those cases where there is a diversity of choice because supplier offerings are highly heterogeneous in terms of product, quality and price. The buyer in this situation may need to consider carefully the implications of forming a long-term relationship with one supplier if it appears a better offer may become available from another source in the very near future.

Transaction uncertainty involves the issues of ensuring the product is delivered on time and meets the performance specifications agreed during the purchase negotiations phase. Where high levels of uncertainty exist (e.g. purchasing from an overseas supplier), the buyer may adopt the approach of requiring the signing of lengthy contracts which contain severe penalty clauses for any form of transaction error by the supplier.

As far as the supplier is concerned, it is also essential that the marketing management system contains elements designed to minimize the effects of uncertainty. First there is a need to ensure that the organization has the appropriate equipment, employee skills and production capacity for the delivered product to meet fully the buyer's specification. Where, for example, the contract involves a front-end period of extensive R&D to create a commercially viable product (e.g. the GEC Corporation's development of a new generation radar system for a contract to up-date air traffic control operations at a major airport), then clearly the supplier must ensure their organization can complete this first phase of the contract on time. Furthermore, in order to meet agreed delivery dates for the product, it is necessary that the final design does not subsequently create problems when the project enters the manufacturing phase.

Another dimension of uncertainty management for the supplier is to handle social interactions with the customer effectively in order that mutual trust and commitment can develop within the buyer–seller relationship. Typically, a critical element influencing this variable is the interchange of information (e.g. keeping the client up-dated on contract progress; confirming delivery dates; responding to enquiries from the customer's employees who are using the purchased items). If these are all handled efficiently, then customer uncertainty will be reduced. Conversely, poor information management can rapidly cause distrust to develop and this can easily result in the customer beginning to consider alternative sources of supply.

Given the critical influence of uncertainty in industrial market scenarios, Ford (1980) has proposed that effective management of the buyer–seller interaction demands that the supplier marketer must exhibit a high level of relationship management competence. He argues that to overcome any barriers which might exist between participant organizations, the supplier marketer will first need to analyse market conditions carefully to determine the exact nature of the relationship that each customer requires within a market sector. Having established which variables are critical (e.g. the 'closeness' of the relationship with suppliers required by the customer, or the degree of product customization which customers expect), then the marketer must decide how best to structure the organization's marketing operation to achieve delivery of buyer satisfaction. Furthermore, having created an initially effective buyer–seller relationship, the marketer will need to assess what ongoing activities will further enhance customer loyalty (e.g. inviting customer employees to become involved in joint project teams to examine issues such as optimizing quality and/or defining the operating performance parameters for components that would be suitable for incorporation into the customer's next generation of new products).

Solberg (1995) has proposed that development of effective industrial marketing strategies involves analysis both of opportunities to reduce uncertainty and of the potential to form long-term functional relationships. Possible factors influencing these two dimensions are shown in Table 7.1. Combining these two dimensions generates a Relationship Typology Matrix of the type shown in Figure 7.2, which suggests the existence of the following alternative relationship scenarios:

1   *Episodic Transactional Relationships*, in which it is not possible to reduce uncertainty or form long-term relationships with customers. In this case the supplier marketing strategy would need to be capable of handling market scenarios in which customer loyalty is low and purchase decisions are probably based on relative competitiveness of offering (e.g. a major insurance company which operates an annual contract rebidding scheme to decide who will supply consumable office materials such as pens, paper, staples, etc.).

2   *Contractual Project Specific Relationships*, in which the customer is willing to form long-term relationships with suppliers, but because their down-stream market is one in which their customers seek new bids for each new contract, it is impossible to guarantee ongoing purchases beyond the life of each contract (e.g. a major building company operating in the office block construction market, which, although wishing to continually employ the same suppliers of air-conditioning and plumbing systems, can only contract with these organizations for delivery of products and ser-vices for a specific project).

3   *Periodically Renegotiated Customer–Supplier Chain Relationships*, which exist in markets where the customer perceives real benefits from forming strong customer–supplier relationships, but where the possibility of changing market conditions does require a regular review of the ongoing nature of such relationships (e.g. supermarket chains contracting for the supply of own-label products from food processing companies).

4   *Long Term Customer–Supplier Chain Relationships*, in which factors such as the nature of technology, the investment required to produce next-generation output and indications of market stability combine to suggest that customers would be advised to develop long-term partnerships with a small group of suppliers (e.g. the relationships which often exist between OEMs and component suppliers in the computer industry).

Supply Chains and Networks

In the late 1970s Western companies were forced to recognize that their Pacific Rim competitors had dramatically raised the performance stakes in relation to the effective management of quality. Even as Western firms were responding to the strategic implications of TQM, they also rapidly had to learn about moving towards adopting a JIT orientation. Initially the focus of JIT was in optimizing the production of existing goods and services. Within only a few years, however, JIT principles were found to have important impli-cations in relation to reducing time-to-market for the development and launch of new products.

Table 7.1   *Influencing factors in industrial markets*

A   Possible actions for reducing uncertainty

Marketing plans based on careful analysis of markets and customers.
Selection of appropriate distribution channels to service customer need.
Commitment to extensive social interaction with customer employees.
Communication flows are carefully managed.
Contractual obligations are always fulfilled.
Building customer loyalty more important than generating new orders.
Ensuring organizational values are compatible with customer values.

B   Probable attributes indicating the potential for long-term relationships

Customers seeking complex products.
Customers seeking customized products.
Customers wishing to negotiate high-volume/long-term contracts.
Customers purchase on a frequent and regular basis.
Customers would face high switching costs in changing suppliers.
Customers require extensive ongoing product usage advisory support.
Customers seek ongoing post-purchase maintenance/service support.
Customers seek solutions demanding high level of supplier R&D.

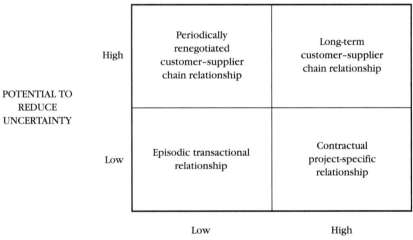

Figure 7.2   **An industrial market relationship typology matrix**

As firms sought to become immersed in TQM and JIT, they soon realized that these concepts could not succeed if organizations sustained their traditional adversarial relationships with other organizations within their market system. Achieving quality goals and evolving a rapid, more flexible approach to the management of manufacturing processes demands the forging of new, closer links between all members of the market system. An eloquent proponent of this new orientation was Schonberger (1990) who tabled the idea of forming 'customer chains'. Subsequently this philosophy has gained wide-spread acceptance and is now usually referred to as 'supply chain management'. Originally initiated as a change in managerial practice within industrial markets, the concept has subsequently gained equal popularity in many consumer goods market systems.

For the industrial marketer in many market sectors, an ability to both understand and manage relationships within the supply chain is fundamental to sustaining competitive advantage. The Nordic school, complemented by subsequent research by the IMP Group, has contributed the three-component network model of market system management which can greatly help the industrial marketer to determine the interaction of forces which will influence the effective management of supply chains (Hakansson 1987). The three elements of this triadic model presented in Figure 7.3 are:

1 *Actors* – the individuals and groups of individuals within the organizations who are members of a specific market supply chain.
2 *Resources* contained within participant organizations which are utilized in the production of products and services for both internal and external consumption.
3 *Activities* which constitute the processes associated with the production and delivery of products and services within the market supply chain.

Lee and Billington (1992) have proposed that market system managers also need to be totally aware of the multitude of pitfalls which can cause failure of a supply network to deliver end user satisfaction. By building upon

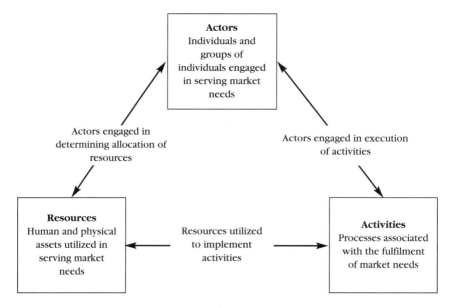

Figure 7.3 **Triadic network variables influencing supply chain operations**

their identified areas of potential risk and exemplifying the process by application to the photocopier supply chain illustrated in Figure 7.4, it is possible to suggest that the following issues should be of concern to business-to-business marketers at all levels within a supply chain system:

1 *Final customer-driven performance parameters*
   Rapid identification of the real causes of a problem within a supply chain can only occur if all participants are using the same performance measurement criteria. As end user satisfaction should drive the marketing process, then clearly all participants need to base their internal control systems on metrics determined by the final end user. Hence, in the case of the photocopier system, issues such as product operating specifications, variety of model choice, acceptable prices and delivery times can all be translated into metrics which can be adopted by the supply chain members.

2 *Final customer-driven 'real time' integrated information systems*
   Managing the process of effectively fulfilling final customer needs can only be achieved if all parties are cognisant of how changes in customer needs (e.g. overall photocopier sales, model purchase patterns) will influence future demand. By the creation of linked data bases and adoption of common production management software systems such as MRP II, all organizations within the system are then able to interact instantly with each other over discussions concerning planning future output and the timing of production schedules.

3 *Final customer-driven 'real time' logistics systems*
   Having the right finished goods on hand ready for shipment at each level within the supply chain is of little benefit unless these outputs can arrive at the next level within the system and thereby sustain agreed JIT operating parameters. Thus, in the case of the photocopier example, the various supply chain members will need to seek ways of optimizing their logistics operations by approaches such as EDI systems which permit interchange of data on expected delivery dates and rapid identification of the causes of any delays in the execution of the order-placement/product-replenishment cycle.

4 *End customer-driven innovation*
   Sustaining ongoing satisfaction of end user needs can only be achieved if knowledge of gaps between actual and desired product performance can, through product and/or service innovation, be translated into the timely launch of new and/or improved products. In the case of the photocopier example, this should involve all members of the supply chain in the sharing of data generated from end user market research which then permits the knowledge to be exploited in the determination of appropriate product innovation plans.

5   *Organizational compatibility*
    Given the need for integration of decisions and actions at all levels across
    the supply system, then clearly it is necessary to ensure that differences in
    intra-organizational management processes do not place obstacles in the
    path of responding to end user needs. There is a tendency for some acad-
    emics to argue that supply chains should always be constituted of flat,
    empowered organizations. This perspective in some cases clearly flies in
    the face of reality (e.g. the classic Fordist, hierarchical structures found
    within many of the highly productive Korean manufacturing firms).
    Hence it is probably safer to suggest only that marketers comprehend the
    nature of the managerial philosophies which exist across their market
    system and then endeavour to ensure inter-organizational interfaces are
    constructed in a form which optimizes inter-organizational trading
    activities.

The wider perspectives and broader role demanded of marketers operating in network-based, business-to-business markets clearly places major
burdens on these individuals when contrasted with the circumstances confronting their counterparts in the more classical active supplier–passive
buyer, transactional markets (e.g. production of primary commodity
materials such as steel girders, or standard-specification engineering components such as flow valves for gas pipelines). Hence, in attempting to
justify the superiority of adopting a network, relationship orientated
approach to the business-to-business marketing management process, it is
probably worth noting that this philosophy is seen as the reason some US
corporations have retained their world-class standing even in the face of
increasingly fierce competition from Pacific Rim organizations (Moskal
1990).

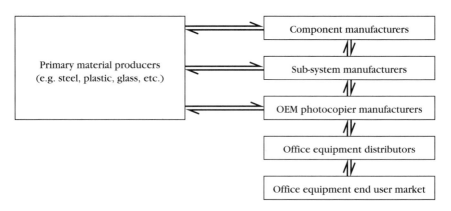

Figure 7.4   **A photocopier supply chain system**

Institutional Marketing

Having survived the mud of Flanders or the arid lunar landscape of the Dardanelles during the 1914–1918 war, army conscripts in Britain were promised by their politicians that they would be returning home to a 'world fit for heroes'. The subsequent poverty and unemployment which they experienced in the 1920s and 1930s clearly demonstrated the hollow nature of these political promises. Hence, at the end of the Second World War, returning troops overtly insisted that their politicians must construct more equitable and caring socio-economic environments. Responding to these demands led many of the Western European nations to create a new world in which the welfare state promised 'care from the cradle to the grave' delivered through the medium of social services such as free education, free healthcare and, for the unemployed, state-funded benefits. Additionally, in many of the European nations, to protect individuals from exploitation by management, many core industries, such as railways, utilities and coal mining, were nationalized.

Although many of the national leaders of this massive change in socio-economic systems acted with the best of humanitarian motives, it has since become apparent that many politicians were also acting out of the fear that maintenance of an unbalanced capitalistic economic system could result in their electorates turning to communism as an alternative route to achieving social equality. In the golden years following the Second World War, tax flows in Western Europe generated by global economic growth were sufficient to support an ever-increasing expansion of the welfare state and at the same time to allow the managerial inefficiencies which were beginning to appear within most nationalized industries to be ignored. Furthermore, because these latter organizations were essentially operating monopolistic business environments, marketing was rarely perceived as a relevant business function.

In the 1970s, the impact of the OPEC energy crisis, the growing power of public sector unions, and the sustaining by governments of full employment through ever-increasing deficit spending, all combined to spark off a massive inflationary spiral within many Western nation economies. By the 1980s some electorates, battered by the impact of inflation eroding the value of personal incomes and lengthy strikes disrupting the delivery of public sector services, were prepared to vote for political parties who offered monetarist-type solutions for rebuilding ailing economies.

The election of Margaret Thatcher in the UK provides one of the most widely known examples of political change. This government espoused the concept of creating an 'enterprise culture' in which public sector organizations would be made more effective by exposing them to 'market forces'. Their policy involved the dual strategy of returning industries such as telecommunications and utilities to the private sector and at the same time attempting to engender a more competitive environment in those areas of the economy such as education and healthcare which apparently could not be privatized.

Newly privatized companies such as British Airways and British Telecom immediately moved towards embracing the various managerial concepts associated with effective marketing such as advertising, sales promotions and customer care programmes. Those organizations which remained within the public sector domain were also persuaded by the consultancy firms hired by the government that marketing was a relevant discipline through which to respond to the external environments now confronting them. In the late 1980s and early 1990s, nurses were sent on courses to learn that patients should be referred to as customers, teachers were shown the Boston Consulting Matrix as a route to building new educational portfolios, and local councils spent a significant proportion of tax receipts on glossy brochures claiming the creation of a new exciting world in which the 'customer comes first'.

With hindsight it is now clear that the public sector was making the same mistake that service firms had earlier made in unquestioningly assuming the validity of adopting classic f.m.c.g. marketing practices as a path by which to build customer loyalty. This mistake was to assume that marketing concepts can be transferred from one sector to the next without too many concerns about the real relevance of the different context in which these theories are being applied.

In the case of institutional marketing, senior managers were rarely willing to risk incurring the wrath of their political masters by openly expressing the view that classic marketing theory probably had little relevance in the sectors in which they were operating. The reason classicist theories of marketing proved to have little relevance was that, in virtually every case, the welfare state model in most developed nation economies faces the need to address a much more fundamental problem – that the 'aging' of their populations, linked to declining economic performance, means that funding the delivery of a full range of completely free services is no longer a realistic option.

Underlying these problems was the unfortunate phenomenon that, until very recently, few politicians were willing to put their chances of re-election in jeopardy by openly admitting it was no longer economically feasible to offer 'free services to all'. Nor were they prepared to tell their electorates that society will need to accept that, over time, private citizens with sufficient personal incomes will have to take greater personal responsibility for funding their own consumption of services such as healthcare, education and pensions.

One of the first proponents of a mixed private / public sector welfare economy was the New Zealand politician, Roger Douglas (Walker 1989). His views have subsequently been adopted by other 'new socialists' such as the UK Prime Minister, Tony Blair. Fortunately, such individuals have been willing to risk personal unpopularity by initiating the debate over the future inadequacy of public sector resources and the requirement of the private citizen to finance some of the free services previously provided by the state.

The rediscovery of integrity by some of the politicians responsible for determining welfare state operating policies now provides the institutional marketer with the environment in which it becomes feasible to evolve appropriate models for managing the marketing process within this sector of a nation's economy. The starting point in the new world of institutional marketing is to assess realistically the scale of future demand and then to determine the degree to which it can be met by available public sector resources. Clearly, for the institutional marketer to effectively do this will require governments to mount marketing campaigns to educate the general public to revise life-long consumption patterns in order to fund personally the costs of services previously provided by the public sector (e.g. persuading young people to allocate a greater proportion of earnings from the first day of entering the workforce to the funding of personal pensions).

A common obstacle facing the marketer in many public organizations is that senior management are continuing to specify no change in service quality targets even though it is quite apparent that declining availability of resources makes achievement of these targets completely unrealistic (e.g. specifying a maximum wait time of ten minutes in the casualty department of a hospital while at the same time making nurses redundant because of a budget crisis). Having persuaded these senior managers to base their strategic thinking upon a realistic assessment of the degree to which demand can be met by available resources, institutional marketers can then begin to craft marketing plans which ensure that internal intra- and inter-departmental customer management processes within their organizations can be orchestrated in a way which most effectively fulfils external customer expectations.

Fortunately for marketers embarking on reframing the marketing process with their institutions, it is possible to draw upon the techniques and lessons already learned in other sectors. Tools such as the service industry SERVQUAL model can be applied to determine the cause of gaps which may exist between customer perceptions and expectations (Chaston 1994a, 1994b). Process re-engineering and industrial network mapping techniques can be utilized to determine the actors, resources and activities which comprise the institutional service delivery process. These data can then be exploited in the development of recommendations concerning the re-design of staff roles, incorporating new technologies and revising operating policies such that real customer satisfaction can be achieved. For example, the marketer in a hospital facing bed-capacity constraints might become involved in leading a multi-disciplinary team examining how the adoption of new surgical procedures and the concurrent training of nursing staff to take greater responsibility for post-operative procedures could result in shortening patient stay times.

Over the next few years, it is reasonable to expect that institutional marketing will truly come of age. As this occurs, no doubt this sector will evolve new operating paradigms which marketers can then transfer into other sectors of their economies. The speed with which this occurs, however, will be critically influenced by the degree to which electorates are willing to accept a short-term decline in their personal living standards while they strive to redirect part of their income flow from immediate consumption to saving for their retirement, and/or directly contributing a greater amount towards the costs associated with educating their children. Such a fundamental change will be a massive task, at times often likely to be frustrated by an unwillingness to make sacrifices today in order to create the fundable mixed private/public sector welfare systems of the future (e.g. the social unrest in France in 1997 as politicians strove to restructure their economy in order to qualify for membership of the European Monetary Union; or the adverse reaction of parents and students to the 1997 Dearing Commission Report on higher education in the UK which proposed that students make a contribution to their university fees through payment of an 'education tax' once they enter the workforce).

References

Chaston, I. (1994a) 'A comparative study of customer management practices within service sector firms and the N.H.S.', *Journal of Advanced Nursing*, 19: 57–68.

Chaston, I. (1994b) 'Internal customer management and service gaps within the N.H.S.', *International Journal of Nursing Studies*, 31(4): 19–27.

Corey, E.R. (1991) *Industrial Marketing Cases and Concepts*, 4th edn, Englewood Cliffs, NJ: Prentice-Hall.

Ford, D. (1980) 'The development of buyer–seller relationships in industrial markets', *European Journal of Marketing*, 14(5): 339–54.

Ford, D. (1990) *Understanding Business Markets: Interaction, Relationships and Networks*, London: Academic Press.

Hakansson, H. (1987) *Industrial Technologies Development: A Network Approach*, London: Croom Helm.

Hakansson H. and Ostberg, C. (1975) 'Industrial marketing – an organisational problem?', *Industrial Marketing Management*, 4: 113–23.

Hakansson, H., Johanson, J. and Wootz, B. (1976) 'Influence tactics in the buyer–seller processes', *Industrial Marketing Management*, 4(6): 316–32.

Jackson, B.B. (1985) *Winning and Keeping Customers: The Dynamics of Customer Relationships*, Lexington, MA: Lexington Books.

Lee, H.L. and Billington, C. (1992) 'Managing supply chain inventory: pitfalls and opportunities', *Sloan Management Review*, Spring: 65–73.

Moskal, B.S. (1990) 'Logistics gets some respect', *Industry Week*, 18, June: 14–22.

Powers, T.L. (1991) *Modern Business Marketing: A Strategic Planning Approach to Business and Industrial Markets*, St Paul, MN: West Publishing.

Rangan, V.K., Shapiro, B.P. and Moriarty, R.T. (1995) *Business Marketing Strategy: Concepts and Applications*, Chicago: R. Irwin.

Schonberger, R.J. (1990) *Building a Chain of Customers: Linking Business Functions to Create the World Class Company*, London: Hutchinson Business Books.

Sheth, J. (1973) 'A model of industrial buying behaviour', *Journal of Marketing*, 37: 50–6.

Solberg, C.A. (1995) 'Defining the role of the representative and the exporter in international industrial markets', *Proceedings 11th IMP Group Conference: Interactions, Relationships and Networks*, Manchester: Manchester Business School, pp. 1077–99.

Walker, S. (1989) *Rogernomics: Reshaping New Zealand's Economy*, Auckland: GP Books.

Webster F. and Wind, Y. (1972) 'A general model for understanding organizational buying behaviour', *Journal of Marketing*, 36: 12–19.

8 Service Marketing

The service sector in many developed nations makes a significant contribution to GNP and provides the majority of available jobs. This growing importance of service industries has stimulated research to discover how the marketing process may need to be modified to suit specific circumstances facing these types of organization.

Only in certain cases has it proved feasible to transfer classic, transactional goods marketing philosophies into service sector firms. One of the barriers to transfer has been that service businesses have the unique characteristics that goods are often intangible, production and consumption inseparable, customers exhibit wide need variation, and output is often highly perishable. It is also often the case that employees across the entire organization are engaged in activities which all have direct impact on customer satisfaction. It has been proposed that this scenario suggests a need for a three-way marketing philosophy involving external, interactive and internal marketing.

Quality of service is a critical influencer of customer satisfaction and there is therefore a requirement to identify carefully any gaps in performance. The widely adopted SERVQUAL tool provides a mechanism through which to examine potential gaps in relation to the variables of reliability, tangibles, responsiveness, assurance and empathy.

There has been widespread debate about appropriate organizational structures for service organizations. Some people favour highly mechanistic structures, while others argue strongly for organic organizations and empowered workforces. The dynamic nature of service environments has also prompted the emergence of new, dispersed organizational structures linked together using computer technology.

Introduction

A characteristic of twentieth-century Western nation economies has been the increasing importance of service industries as a proportion of Gross National Product (GNP) and as a source of employment. Various factors have contributed to the growth of the service sector. In consumer markets, higher levels of affluence have enabled people to afford more expensive holidays, participate in leisure pursuits and delegate many household functions such as cleaning and repairs to external providers. They are also, along with industrial sector firms, purchasing technologically more complex products, which have spawned a whole new sector of industry offering specialist high-tech support services in areas such as design, installation, maintenance and training.

Initially, as service markets became more competitive, many organizations, having recognized the need to modernize their marketing philosophies, employed transactionalist orientated managers from f.m.c.g. companies such as Procter & Gamble, General Foods and Nestlé. These individuals persuaded their new employers to adopt a classic, transactionalist orientation towards marketing. This resulted in a major expansion of expenditure on various forms of mass marketing activity (e.g. Western world retail banks in the 1970s and 1980s investing in large-scale television campaigns and offering sales promotions to attract new customers and/or persuade existing customers to purchase a broader range of services).

In some cases, these purist f.m.c.g. approaches were extremely successful (e.g. the global expansion of fast food chains such as Burger King, Pizza Hut and Kentucky Fried Chicken). Other areas of the service sector, however, were not similarly rewarded. UK banks in the late 1980s, for example, having spent millions on television advertising found that (a) the proportion of total available consumers opening current accounts remained virtually unchanged and (b) many of their new customers were individuals who, dissatisfied with their previous supplier, switched loyalties but continued to complain about the costs and/or quality of services being delivered by their new bank.

This mixture of success and failure within the service sector prompted both academics and practitioners to revisit marketing theory. As a result, it became widely accepted that the marketing of services probably demands a whole new range of both theoretical paradigms and organizational operating principles (Cowell 1984). Initially many of the new writings in this area focused on purist service marketing in sectors such as financial services and retailing. More recently, however, there has been a growing recognition that in many manufacturing sectors, firms gain competitive advantage not by the provision of a tangible core product, but through augmenting their offering with a portfolio of value-added services.

Quinn et al. (1990), for example, have described how many of the firms at the top end of the pharmaceutical market rely upon the use of added-value services to survive in the face of competitive threats from price orientated, generic drug producers. Firms such as Glaxo and Merck are presented as achieving added value through service activities such as R&D, constructing legal and patent defences, rapidly progressing new drugs through the clinical clearances demanded by regulatory bodies, supporting clinicians in their use of new treatments and offering advisory support on optimizing the provision of healthcare by their customers such as large hospitals and health authorities. These authors also argue that as manufacturing becomes universally more automated, then added value does not come from converting raw materials into finished goods, but in areas of service such as styling, perceived quality, product customization,

JIT distribution and post-purchase maintenance and repair services. They, in fact, would argue that the bastion of f.m.c.g. marketing, Procter & Gamble, is in fact a $15 billion service corporation which has achieved success by taking specific service skills in core areas of R&D and manufacturing and linking these to a superb marketing–distribution operation.

The Growing Importance of Service

The relative importance of the factors within the mix of activities required to achieve customer satisfaction have been extensively researched by Humble and Shingles (1991) in a study sponsored by the electronics giant, Digital Equipment Corporation. The data in Table 8.1, summarizing the views of 4,000 executives in 19 countries spanning three continents concerning the importance of factors influencing customer purchase behaviour and areas for improvement, demonstrate the critical role service plays in delivering customer satisfaction. Furthermore, in all countries respondents felt that service over the last five years has become more important to customers, and they believe it will be even more important in the future. This perspective is given added weight by the results in Table 8.2 which show that the most compelling external factor influencing future performance is the ability to use service to differentiate the organization from competitors.

Table 8.1   *Factors and priorities*

Factor	Ratings of factors influencing purchase decision*			
	Europe	USA	Japan	UK
Quality	4.4	4.3	4.5	4.3
Reliability	4.2	4.1	4.6	4.1
Problem-solving	3.7	3.7	4.3	3.5
Price	3.4	2.6	4.1	3.5
Speed of delivery	3.4	3.7	3.7	3.4
Courtesy	3.1	3.8	4.3	3.4
After-sales service	3.4	3.3	3.9	3.3
Design	2.7	2.6	3.4	2.9
Guarantees	2.7	2.1	3.8	2.4
Packaging	2.2	2.3	2.9	2.1
Room for improvement*				
Quality	3.1	3.2	3.1	3.3
Speed of delivery	3.0	3.2	2.3	3.1
Courtesy	2.6	2.9	3.6	2.9
Problem-solving	3.0	3.2	3.3	2.8
Reliability	2.6	2.8	3.2	2.8
After-sales service	2.7	3.1	3.1	2.7
Price	2.2	2.6	3.0	2.3
Design	2.1	2.6	2.8	2.2
Packaging	1.9	2.3	2.3	1.9
Guarantees	1.6	2.1	2.6	1.5

*Scale: 5 = most important, 0 = least important
Source: Humble and Shingles 1991

Table 8.2   *Importance of external pressures*

	Compelling reasons for improving customer service*			
Factor	Europe	USA	Japan	UK
Service is most important as a differentiator	4.3	4.4	4.6	4.4
Competition is fiercer	4.1	4.3	4.6	4.3
Customers are more demanding	3.9	4.0	4.5	4.1
Development of advanced information technology	3.2	3.3	4.2	3.2
Shortening of life cycles for both products and services	2.7	2.7	3.7	2.7

*Scale: 5 = most important, 0 = least important
Source: Humble and Shingles 1991

The other interesting aspect of this study is that, as shown in Table 8.3, pure service companies actually receive lower ratings for service than their counterparts in the f.m.c.g. sector. Additionally, the poorest providers of adequate service quality are companies in the transportation sector (presumably reflecting respondents' experiences of delayed flights and/or train departures) and, perhaps not surprisingly, public sector organizations.

Table 8.3   *Analysis of service by sector*

Business Sector*	Europe	USA	Japan	UK
Consumer goods companies	3.2	3.2	3.5	3.2
Retailers	3.1	2.9	3.3	3.1
Industrial goods companies	3.1	3.0	3.0	2.9
Financial institutions	3.1	2.8	3.1	2.5
Transport companies	2.8	2.7	3.1	2.5
Public sector organizations	1.2	1.3	1.9	1.4

* Scale: 5 = high, 0 = low
Source: Humble and Shingles 1991

The Characteristics of Service Goods

Given the widespread presence of service activities within most organizational product portfolios, possibly one of the safest definitions of services is that provided by Kotler (1997: 347) – 'a service is any act or performance that one party can offer to another that is essentially intangible and does not result in the ownership of anything. Its production may or may not be tied to a physical product.'

One way of illustrating this definition is to plot the degree of intangibility against proportion of revenue generated by the provision of services. As can be seen from this approach in Figure 8.1, at one extreme (Point A), the offering is purely tangible and no services accompany the product (e.g. a commodity product such as salt). Point B represents an offering comprised of a goods with a high proportion of tangibility accompanied by some services (e.g. a washing machine which is offered with free installation and three years free repair and maintenance). A product at Point C offers equal amounts of tangibility and intangibility (e.g. a full-service restaurant). Beyond point C in Figure 8.1, service becomes the major component of the offering (e.g. the preparation of a firm's annual accounts by an external auditor) and at Point D the product is a pure service (e.g. a session at an aromatherapy clinic).

The characteristic of intangibility does mean that services, unlike physical products, cannot be seen, tasted, felt, heard or smelled before purchase. To reduce customer uncertainty, marketers frequently concentrate on providing tangible evidence of service quality. Some of the multitude of mechanisms available to the organization for achieving this goal include:

Place – the physical environment within which the provision of services are delivered (e.g. British Airways, 1997 £60 million external and internal facelift to their entire fleet of aircraft to emphasize their positioning as the 'world's favourite airline').

People – those involved in working with the customer/organization interface (e.g. well-trained, uniformed employees encountered at the check-in desks of car rental firms).

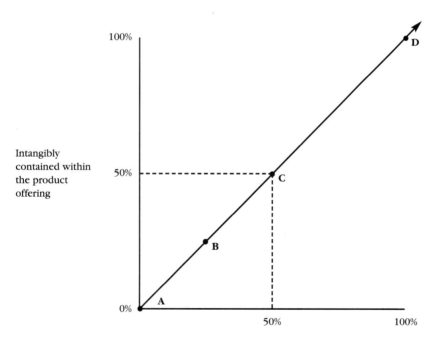

Proportion of total revenues generated by the
provision of service

Figure 8.1 **A conceptualization of the influence of service provision on the degree of product offering intangibility**

Equipment – should be of the necessary standard to help rapidly and effi-
    ciently in the service provision process (e.g. the on-line client management
    systems used by tele-sales staff in mail-order clothing operations such as
    Hawkshead and Lands End).
Communication systems – composed of a diversity of channel flows and asso-
    ciated materials which effectively promote the organization's desired
    market position as a service provider (e.g. the glossy brochures issued by
    multi-national accountancy practices featuring their partners and range of
    available client services).

A second characteristic of services is inseparability, that is, many services are
simultaneously produced and consumed. The implication of this is that for
many service outcomes to occur, both the provider and the customer must be
able to interact with each other. Thus, for example, if an organization needing urgent advice on a product liability claim approaches a small law firm and
the partner with appropriate specialist knowledge is unavailable, then the
potential client may be lost to another practice who can provide immediate
guidance.

The third characteristic of services is their variability, which is caused both
by differing customer needs and by the capabilities of employees within the
provider organization. Thus, for example, most customers entering a bank
seeking information may just need help opening a simple savings or current
account. A small minority may also require guidance on complex money
transactions involving decisions concerning a whole range of sophisticated
investment instruments. Hence, in order to manage these types of variability,
front-line bank staff will need training (a) to handle simple enquiries efficiently and (b) to ensure that customers with more complex service needs are
smoothly handed on to an appropriately qualified investment advisor within
the organization.

Unlike manufactured goods, which can be produced and inventoried for
later use, a fourth characteristic of services is that they are highly perishable.
For example, failure to sell all seats on a departing airline flight means that a
proportion of total revenue on this occasion has been lost forever. Sasser
(1976) has proposed a number of marketing strategies for responding to the
perishability problem which involve actions for more effectively matching
supply and demand. These include:

Differential pricing to move demand away from peak to off-peak periods (e.g.
    a cocktail bar offering 'buy one, get one free' during their early evening
    'happy hour').
Alternative service provision to meet the varying needs of customers during
    peak periods (e.g. a bank opening 'business only pay-in' windows at
    lunchtimes so that other customers do not have to wait while bank staff
    are checking the large amounts of cash being deposited by local firms).
Service modification to ensure that during peak periods the needs of major
    purchasers receive priority (e.g. a wine bar not permitting the clientele to

occupy tables in their restaurant area in the evenings unless they are planning to order a meal).

Demand management systems which permit the service provider (a) to identify rapidly current available capacity and (b) to propose alternative solutions (e.g. a hotel group's on-line, global reservation system which can immediately identify whether a specific hotel is full and, where necessary, offer alternative accommodation in the immediate vicinity).

Temporary capacity expansion whereby the provider can increase their ability to respond to customer needs during peak periods (e.g. a theme park hiring temporary staff during the holiday season).

Service sharing where a number of organizations work together and are willing to cross-refer customers (e.g. a group of small accountants forming a marketing network to offer a broader range of specialist services to potential clients).

Customer participation in which customers are encouraged to become self-providers (e.g. a business hotel offering a buffet breakfast service so their guests can obtain food rapidly, thereby avoiding the wait associated with a hotel employee taking their order).

Internal Marketing and Service Gap Theory

Responding to the specific characteristics of service markets described above does mean that, unlike many tangible goods situations, it is extremely difficult to separate marketing activities from all the other functions being undertaken within the firm. Furthermore the nature of the buyer–seller interaction which occurs at the production/consumption interface can have a significant impact on the customer's repeat buying decisions (e.g. if a customer arrives at a hotel to discover that a mistake has been made over a reservation and the room is no longer available, the way in which the receptionist handles this problem will have a significant influence on whether the customer can be placated or is 'lost forever' as a future guest).

Eigler and Langeard (1977) have proposed three main categories of resource involved in the buyer–seller interaction:

Contact personnel, who interact directly with the customer.
Physical resources, which comprise the human and technical resources used by the organization in undertaking the production, delivery and consumption of the service offering.
The customer, who is the person forming a purchase, loyalty decision based on the quality of service received to date.

Gronroos (1984) has proposed that management of these three variables is a marketing task which differs from traditional f.m.c.g marketing because it involves assets not usually part of the of the mainstream marketing operation, but instead is drawn from across the entire cost-generating production resources within the organization. As illustrated in Figure 8.2, Gronroos has proposed that in service firms there exist three marketing tasks. He describes these as 'external marketing' (i.e. the normal formal processes associated with the management of the 4Ps), interactive marketing (i.e. the activities which occur at the buyer–seller interface) and internal marketing. This latter variable is concerned with all of the activities associated with ensuring every employee is (a) customer-conscious and (b) committed to the philosophy that every aspect of their personal role must be orientated towards achieving total customer satisfaction.

The suggestion that internal marketing is a holistic process which integrates the multiple functions of the organization by ensuring employees understand all relevant aspects of organizational operations and are motivated to act in a service-orientated manner, creates the very difficult problem of how one measures the effectiveness of the customer–organization interaction. Although a number of writers have suggested that the objective of service satisfaction is to minimize the gap between customers' desires and actual experience, developing feasible techniques for the measurement of expectations and perceptions has proved somewhat more problematical.

One of the most important contributions to measuring these variables has been made by Parasuraman, Zeithmal and Berry (1985, 1988; Zeithmal, Parasuraman and Berry, 1990) who from 1983 onwards have implemented a carefully sequenced research project aimed at delivering an effective model for assessing the effectiveness and quality of the service provision process. The first stage of their research was to identify some common variables which could be used to categorize customer expectations. By the use of focus groups they identified the following five variables:

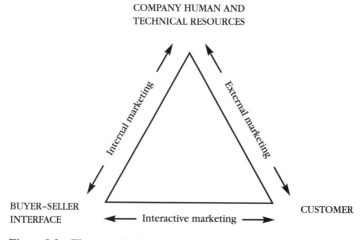

Figure 8.2 **Three marketing forms within the service provision process**

1 *Reliability* – the ability to perform the promised service dependably and accurately.
2 *Tangibles* – the images created by the appearance of physical facilities, equipment, personnel and communication materials.
3 *Responsiveness* – the willingness to help customers and provide prompt service.
4 *Assurance* – the process by which the knowledge, ability and courtesy of employees engenders customer trust and confidence in the service provider.
5 *Empathy* – created by the caring, individualized attention which employees offer the customer.

Having identified these expectations, Parasuraman and his colleagues then went on to create the SERVQUAL model which defined the following types of gap which could exist between expectations and perceptions:

Gap 1 which exists between the customer's expectations and the organization's perceptions of customer need.
Gap 2 which exists between the organization's perceptions and the definition of appropriate standards for the quality of service to be delivered.
Gap 3 which exists between the specified standards of service and the actual performance of the service provision process undertaken by the organization's employees.
Gap 4 which exists between actual service delivered and the nature of the service promise made in any communications with the customer.
Gap 5 which represents the overall gap between customer expectations and perceptions created by the combined influence of Gaps 1 through 4.

The magnitude and influence of the five service gaps can be measured using these authors' SERVQUAL tool. The technique involves surveying customers to determine their expectations and perceptions by asking them to compare their perspectives of desired service with experience of actual service received. Other gap dimensions are measured by surveying employee attitudes about various aspects of operations within their organization (e.g. the existence of quality standards, or mechanisms established for integrating all aspects of the service delivery process across the entire organization).

Application of the SERVQUAL tool can be illustrated by research undertaken to determine the underlying causes influencing SME owner-managers' poor view of the quality of services being provided by UK banks (Chaston 1994). The existence of type-1 service gaps was identified because surveys of owner-managers and bank employees revealed differing perspectives about the critical factors influencing customer expectations. Service gap type-2 situations were found to exist because bank managers and their small business clients had very differing views about which formal standards were important in terms of monitoring customer satisfaction. Bank employee data suggested that the banks, by investing in schemes to optimize service provision, such as

Actions to enhance SME customer perceptions/confidence

Gap 5 Action
Resolution of problems in Gaps 1–4.

Gap 4 Action
Immediate action to close major gap by revising promotional campaigns, delegating authority downwards to customer interface; in addition, reduce levels of management and increase face-to-face discussion to improve internal communications.

Gap 3 Action
Continue to strive for improvement in allocation of resources, upgrading operating systems, exploiting automation and further developing service provision skills of staff.

Gap 2 Action
Seek convergence of opinion between customer and bank on actual achievements over meeting specified service goals.

Gap 1 Action
Immediate action to revise bank specification of service goal priorities in SME sector provision process.

Gaps in service provision process

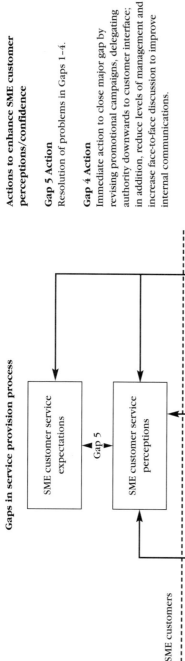

SME customers

Banks as service providers

Figure 8.3   **Actions required by UK bankers to close SME sector service quality gaps** (Chaston 1994)

computerization of money-handling facilities, were to a large degree effectively avoiding the occurrence of type-3 service gaps. Nevertheless, employees' concerns about the degree of 'over-promise' in national advertising campaigns and the unwillingness of corporate offices to speed up responsiveness to customers by delegating more decisions to local branches, indicated the probable existence of type-4 service gaps.

Analysis of these data permitted the formulation of possible actions which might be considered by banks wishing to build a stronger reputation for service provision among members of the UK small business community. Summarized in Figure 8.3, the results suggested that priority should be given to two areas, namely bankers revising (i) their perceptions of the factors which constitute customers' perceptions of need and (ii) the promotional strategies being used to communicate the exact nature of the financial services being offered to SME sector firms.

Ensuring Customer Satisfaction

Given that errors at either the buyer–seller interface and/or during the execution of the internal processes associated with service delivery can both adversely impact customer satisfaction, there has been widespread debate on how best to manage the role of the employees within service sector organizations. In two classic articles, Levitt (1972, 1976) eloquently argued for the adoption of a manufacturing orientation in the management of services. He believed that this approach was required because it allowed for (i) simplification of tasks, (ii) clear division of labour, (iii) substitution of equipment and systems for employees and (iv) minimal decision-making being required of the employees.

Many fast food chains demonstrate the validity of Levitt's proposals. Operatives are taught how to greet the customer and ask for their order in a scripted way designed to suggest the purchase of additional items. Clearly defined procedures are laid down for assembling the order, placing it on the tray, positioning the tray on the counter and collecting the money. Meanwhile, in the 'back room', other operatives are executing tasks, developed through the application of time and motion studies, designed to produce rapidly and efficiently food of uniform quality. The net result is that this production line approach permits the operation of an efficient, low-cost, high-volume food service operation which concurrently also delivers customer satisfaction.

The concept of the industrialization of service operations has not been without its critics who argue that the approach is not only dehumanizing, but also results in an inability to respond to heterogeneous customer needs because employees are forced to respond to all situations by adhering to the rigid guidelines laid down in the organization's operating policy manual. Zemke and Schaaf (1989) would argue that service excellence is more likely to be achieved by 'empowerment', which involves encouraging and rewarding employees to exercise initiative and imagination. Similar views are expressed by Jan Carlzon (1987: 183) the chief executive credited with the successful turnaround of Scandinavian Airlines. He stated that 'to free someone from the rigorous control by instructions, policies and orders, and to give that person freedom to take responsibility for his ideas, decisions and actions, is to release hidden resources that would otherwise remain inaccessible to both the individuals and the organization'.

Bowen and Lawler (1992) have presented a somewhat more balanced view of the industrialisation versus employee empowerment service delivery debate. They point to the contrasting examples of two very successful American firms in the international package delivery business, Federal Express and United Parcel Service (UPS). The Federal Express company motto of 'people, service and profits' is the foundation stone for an organization built around self-managed teams and empowered employees as the mechanism through which to offer a flexible and creative service to customers with varying needs. In contrast, UPS, with a philosophy of 'best service at low rates', uses controls, rules, a detailed union contract and rigidly defined operational guidelines to guarantee customers will receive a reliable, low-cost service.

Bowen and Lawler state that appropriateness of a service philosophy is a contingency issue; that is, that an industrialization or empowerment orientation will be dependent upon the market in which the firm operates and the influence of overall corporate strategy on the selection of appropriate internal organizational processes. By building upon their views it is possible, as shown in Table 8.4, to define factors which might help to determine which are likely to be the most effective service products and/or delivery processes for achieving the goal of customer satisfaction.

Table 8.4   *Factors influencing the service style decision*

Factor	Range of response to factors	
Customer orientation	Transactional	Relationship
Service product need	Standard solutions	New, innovative solutions
Business environment	Predictable, stable	Changing, unstable
Service delivery technology	Simple	Complex
Firm's closeness to customer orientation	Low	High
Firm's service solution orientation	Established, well known	Applying new approaches
Average skills of workforce	Adequate for executing standard tasks	Capable of executing complex tasks
Managerial orientation	Directive	Delegators

Applying the factors of influence in Table 8.4 permits the suggestion that there are probably four alternative management styles which can be utilized by service organizations. These are:

1   *Conservative-transactional service organizations* which operate in stable

markets where the customer desires to obtain standard solutions without forming close relationships with the provider. Required services can usually be delivered by a relatively unskilled workforce and without resorting to the application of complex technologies (e.g. a car-wash business).

2 *Conservative-relationship service organizations* which operate in a changing market where the customer seeks to form a close relationship with the provider as a way of obtaining standard solutions somewhat modified to suit their specific needs. Customization may demand application of complex technologies and/or involve creative inputs from a highly skilled workforce (e.g. a distributor of IBM-specification PCs who offers customized computer installation, maintenance and IT training services).

3 *Entrepreneurial-transactional service organizations* which operate in rapidly changing market where the customer, although facing unique problems demanding a completely new solution, does not wish to form a strong close relationship with any one, single provider. Solutions will demand application of complex technologies and/or involve creative inputs from highly skilled specialists (e.g. many of the major consulting firms who develop and then market concepts such as process re-engineering which require carefully researched new approaches in order to be suitable in a client-specific situation).

4 *Entrepreneurial-relationship service organizations* which operate in rapidly changing markets where the customer, seeking to resolve a unique problem demanding a completely new solution, does so by forming a strong, close relationship with a preferred service provider. Solutions will demand application of complex technologies and/or involve creative inputs from highly skilled specialists working in collaborative partnership with the client's own workforce (e.g. computer software designers developing new risk-management systems for international financial institutions involved in global currency and/or share trading).

It is proposed in Figure 8.4 that there are two empowerment dimensions associated with the four alternative styles. One dimension is the degree to which employees are empowered to use creativity to revise the nature of the service delivery process. The other dimension is the degree to which employees are empowered to exercise imagination in the formulation of totally new forms of service. In the case of the conservative-transactional firm, employees are permitted little freedom in modifying either the form of service or the service delivery process. Customers of conservative-relationship firms are usually interested in their service providers optimizing the service delivery process by being prepared to customize some aspects of what essentially is a standardized service (e.g. a delivery service willing to modifying the routing of their transportation fleet to ensure successful delivery of urgently needed spare parts to a remote location). Thus, to achieve this goal, the service provider employees should be permitted to exhibit personal initiative in overcoming any problems which might be encountered.

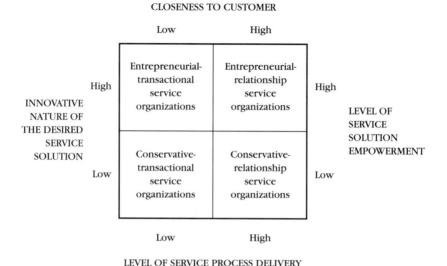

Figure 8.4   **Alternative service styles**

Entrepreneurial-transactional firms have clients who face a major problem, resolution of which will probably require a new, radical approach. This can only be achieved if the provider is willing to delegate authority to employees, who are charged with the development of an appropriately innovative solution. As most contracts of this type contain fixed penalties for failure, the provider will, however, demand that staff adhere to clearly defined guidelines concerning all aspects of the project management process. This can be contrasted with the situations often confronting the entrepreneurial-relationship service firm. Here the client and the provider fully realize that collaborative 'blue sky' thinking by the employees of both is probably the only route to evolving a feasible solution. Hence the provider will seek to instil an attitude of employee empowerment in relation both to the generation, and to delivery of, the most effective service solution which can be developed in the time available.

New Organizational Forms

In an excellent review of the myths surrounding the management of services, Zeithmal and Bitner (1996) have proposed that, contrary to popular belief, it is feasible to deliver lower-cost outputs while at the same time maximizing personalization and customization of customer services. Achievement of these joint goals, however, demands both the creative use of leading-edge technologies and acceptance of new organizational configurations.

Quinn and Paquette (1990) argue it is incorrect to assume that between low cost and high flexibility are mutually exclusive goals in service sector scenarios. In their view the secret lies in (a) designing service systems as micro-units located close to the customer (e.g. the insurance advisor using a laptop-based project-costing system to do an on-site review of a manufacturing firm's needs for coverage appropriate to current trading circumstances) and (b) using technology to permit inexperienced people to perform very sophisticated tasks (e.g. front-line staff in a travel agency using on-line reservations systems to create complex, customized holiday packages). In the process of achieving these goals, the organization will probably recognize that new organizational forms are now demanded in order to optimize employee productivity.

Computer-based information systems appear to mean that there is virtually no limit to the span of control between supervisor and operatives. This means that service organizations can safely consider moving to create 'infinitely flat' organizations in which authority is delegated to the lowest possible level and all employees empowered to make the best possible decision to satisfy changing customer needs. Federal Express, for example, has over 42,000 employees in more than 300 cities worldwide, but has a maximum of only five organizational layers between operatives and senior management. Co-ordination of service provision activities is achieved by permitting all employees to have access to the organization's DADS and COSMOS computerized MIS.

As large international organizations such as accounting and consultancy firms offering complex client-specific services act to sustain localized customer contact by opening offices around the world, the problems of up-dating staff on technological advances, and thereby sustaining leading-edge service quality, increase. Fortunately the advent of technologies such as Lotus Notes and video-conferencing has permitted these organizations to re-orientate themselves into networked structures which use electronic media to ensure the dispersed nodes of their service operation can continually remain in touch with each other. Quinn and Paquette (1990) have, for example, described the structure of a leading consulting firm, Arthur Anderson & Company, which uses the latest available technology to link together its 40,000 staff in over 200 different countries. One of the major benefits of their system is that an individual facing a difficult client problem can now use the organization's electronic bulletin board to discover if anybody elsewhere in the world may have already evolved an effective solution.

Service firms in the small business sector have traditionally faced the problem that they often lack sufficient breadth of expertise to compete with larger firms who can offer a complete service portfolio solution. Hence one of the real attractions of structured networking is that these small firms can enter into collaborative relationships with other like-minded organizations within their sector as a path by which to expand the range of services which they can offer to their clients. An example of this philosophy is provided by a recently formed small business network, WEAR I.T., based in north-east England. The six small specialist IT firms who constitute this network are Omnicom who offer Local Area Networks (LANs) consultancy, TGE who specialize in automated data protection, CIA who deliver specialist training across a broad range of commercial software systems, Treepax who offer client/server computing consultancy, RSD who develop PC-based business solutions, and QIS who have developed an interface management system. Although each has had some success in their respective market sectors, the new business network now permits them to enter the international market offering a unique 'one-stop-shop' IT design, installation and operations service to large, multi-national manufacturing and service organizations.

References

Bowen, D.E. and Lawler, E.E. (1992) 'The empowerment of service workers: what, why, how and when', *Sloan Management Review*, Spring: 31–9.

Carlzon, J. (1987) *Moments of Truth*, New York: Ballinger.

Chaston, I. (1994) 'Rebuilding small business confidence by identifying and closing service gaps in the bank/SME client relationship', *International Small Business Journal*, 13(1): 54 -62.

Cowell, D. (1984) *The Marketing of Services*, London: Heinemann.

Eigler, P. and Langeard, E. (1977) 'Services as systems: marketing implications', in P. Eigler and E. Langeard (eds), *Marketing Consumer Services*, Cambridge, MA: Marketing Science Institute, pp. 89–91.

Gronroos, C. (1984) 'A service quality model and its marketing implications', *European Journal of Marketing*, 18(4): 36–44.

Humble, J. and Shingles, G. (1991) *Service: The New Competitive Edge*, Reading, Berkshire: Digital Equipment Company.

Kotler, P. (1997) *Marketing Management: Analysis, Planning, Implementation and Control*, 9th edn, Upper Saddle River, NJ: Prentice-Hall.

Levitt, T. (1972) 'Production-line approach to service', *Harvard Business Review*, Sept.–Oct.: 41–52.

Levitt, T. (1976) 'Industrialisation of services', *Harvard Business Review*, Sept.–Oct.: 63–74.

Parasuraman, A., Zeithmal, V.A. and Berry, L.L. (1985) 'SERVQUAL: a multiple item scale for measuring consumer perceptions of service quality', *Journal of Retailing*, 64(1): 12–23.

Parasuraman, A., Zeithmal, V.A. and Berry, L.L. (1988) 'A conceptual model of service quality and its implications for future research', *Journal of Marketing*, 49, Autumn: 34–45.

Quinn, J.B. and Paquette, P.C. (1990) 'Technology in services: creating organizational revolutions', *Sloan Management Review*, Winter: 67–78.

Quinn, J.B., Doorley, T.L. and Paquette, P.C. (1990) 'Technology in services: rethinking strategic focus', *Sloan Management Review*, Winter: 79–87.

Sasser, W.E. (1976) 'Match supply and demand in service industries', *Harvard Business Review*, Nov.–Dec.: 133–40.

Zeithmal, V.A. and Bitner, M.J. (1996) *Services Marketing*, New York: McGraw-Hill.

Zeithmal, V.A., Parasuraman, A. and Berry, L.L. (1990) *Delivering Quality Service: Balancing Customer Perceptions and Expectations*, New York: The Free Press.

Zemke, R. and Schaaf, M. (1989) *The Service Edge: 101 Companies that Profit from Customer Care*, New York: New American Library.

9 New Product and Innovation Management

New product success is influenced by factors which include product superiority, economic value to user, overall project fit, technological complexity and familiarity to firm. The standard approach to optimizing success is a sequential process of idea generation, idea screening, concept development, business planning, prototype development, market test and launch. Launch will involve deciding between a phased roll-out to optimize fund flow versus entry into all markets to avoid pre-emption by competitors.

Poor performance by Western nation firms in the area of new product development may reflect excessive emphasis on profit maximization and risk avoidance. Research on UK managers in Japanese corporations proves that they can acquire a longer-term perspective if employed by organizations who perceive innovation has a critical role in achieving trading objectives.

Attention has recently begun to be focused on reducing time-to-market through mechanisms such as concurrent product development, use of IT-based modelling systems and implanting more entrepreneurial cultures. The latter issue is illustrated by 3M Corporation which has adopted strategies such as the requirement that new products must represent at least 25 per cent of product mix, establishing small, autonomous business units and providing staff with 'thinking time'.

Marketing style may also influence the nature of a firm's approach to innovation. Entrepreneurial firms are more likely to be involved in new products early in the product life cycle. As products move into maturity these firms may decide that as innovation focus shifts towards process technology, this phase of the life cycle may be more effectively exploited by conservatively orientated organizations. Increasing technological complexity in many sectors of industry also means that relationship orientated firms working in partnership with other like-minded organizations may gain competitive advantage over transactionally orientated competitors.

Factors of Influence

During the twentieth century technological advances have massively impacted on both individuals and entire industries. In the home, we now take for granted products such as the refrigerator, television and microwave oven. At work, few employees have remained untouched by the influence of the computer. In some cases, the outcome has been that their jobs have disappeared completely (e.g. bank counter staff being replaced by automatic teller machines). Given this situation, it must be concluded that even the world's most successful firms cannot expect to survive into the twenty-first century unless they find ways to achieve excellence in the critical areas of new products and process innovation management.

A number of authors have undertaken research to identify factors influencing the success and failure of new products. One of the most prolific writers in this area, Professor Cooper (1975, 1986, 1988, 1990), has conducted numerous cross-sectional and longitudinal studies of Canadian firms. Application of factor analysis has permitted the development of his Newprod computer-based evaluation tool. The factors which form the basis of the Newprod predictive assessment of probable performance of a new product are:

Product superiority/quality in relation to the issue of how product features, benefits, uniqueness and/or overall quality contribute to competitive advantage.

Economic value in terms of offering greater value than existing product(s).

Overall fit in terms of the product development project being compatible with the organization's existing areas of production and marketing expertise.

Technological compatibility in terms of the product being compatible with the organization's existing areas of technological capability.

Familiarity to firm in terms of whether the firm can draw upon existing expertise or will be forced to learn completely new operational skills.

Market opportunity in terms of nature of market need, size of market and market growth trend.

Competitive situation in terms of how easy it will be to penetrate the market and cope with any competitive threats.

Defined opportunity in relation to whether the product fits into a well-defined category as opposed to being a truly innovative idea providing the basis for a completely new market sector.

Project definition in terms of how well the product development project is defined and understood within the organization.

A similar project (Rothwell 1976, 1979) revealed there were a number of common causes for failure within UK firms. These were either market related (e.g. no market existed, there was insufficient information on the market/competition, marketing skills were inadequate, and product did not offer any real benefit) or of a technical/managerial nature (e.g. poor overall management, limited resources, poor R&D and inadequate communication/control systems).

A New Product Process Management Model

As recently demonstrated by the problems associated with Unilever's reformulation of their Persil brand (which apparently led to a 'new, improved' detergent which had the potential to damage certain fabrics during the wash cycle) even highly experienced firms can make minor new product development mistakes which adversely influence sales revenue. Clearly, therefore, a major market failure will have a devastating impact on the future of an organization. An example is provided by the post-war UK aircraft industry. Having failed in the first generation, civilian jet aircraft market because of

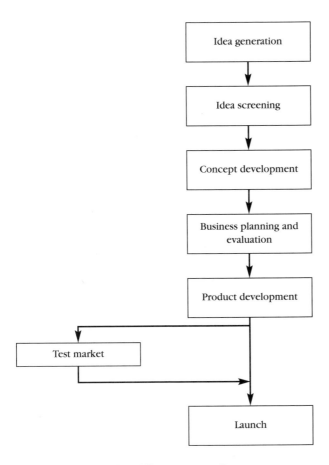

Figure 9.1 **A traditional linear new product process management model**

unforeseen metal fatigue problems with the Comet, the industry in the UK, in the unfounded belief that speed rather than cost of travel would be the key market influencer, turned its attention to developing the Concorde. The commercial failure of this aircraft can be contrasted with the success of the Boeing Corporation who, having achieved market dominance with their 707, subsequently went on to develop their world-beating 747 Jumbo Jet. Despite some latter-day success as a member of the European Airbus consortium, the UK aerospace industry will probably never totally recover from the ground lost by launching not one, but two, new product failures.

Growing recognition of the costs of failure has resulted in the development of various systems to manage the new product development process. Traditionally these systems have been of a sequential nature of the type illustrated in Figure 9.1. The starting point for this type of process is idea-generation, with the ultimate aim being to launch only those products for which success is guaranteed. Hence, as the organization moves through the process, at each stage the question is posed about whether the product under development should be continued with or terminated.

As the costs associated with development increase at an exponential rate while the product is being developed through to launch, then clearly the earlier the firm reaches a project termination decision, the greater will be the savings made. It is, however, critical that the firm does not make a 'drop error' resulting in an idea not being supported which could have generated significant revenues if progression through to launch had occurred (e.g. IBM apparently declining the offer to become involved in the photocopying technology which subsequently formed the basis for the creation of the Xerox Corporation).

Idea-Generation and Screening

The objective of the idea-generation stage is to maximize the number of ideas available for consideration. Traditionally this is achieved by involving sources such as the customer, intermediaries, the sales force, employees from all areas of the organization, competitors' products, the R&D department and suppliers. Those organizations which operate in a market where customer and/or suppliers are relationship orientated are also able to draw on these external sources for additional ideas. This is in contrast to organizations operating in transactionally orientated market sectors, which are often forced to develop products with limited assistance from other members of their market system.

Organizations may seek to broaden their search for ideas by exploiting sources such as markets in other countries, forming links with research institutions, and monitoring scientific breakthroughs in areas outside of the mainstream technology being utilized within their industrial sector. Such practices are probably most prevalent in sectors of industry where long-term success is critically dependent upon making a major technological advance and then protecting this new knowledge with patents (e.g. biotechnology and telecommunications).

In recent years, writers such as Buzan (1993) have cautioned that the logical, positivist education which most people receive in Western nations may be causing the excessive production of 'left-brain thinkers'. This type of person typically favours systematic investigation of problems and the formulation of a solution through a step-by-step analysis of a situation. It is argued that what is required within many organizations is more intuitive or 'right-brain' thinkers', who use an open-minded, often multi-faceted, exploratory problem-solving approach. This view of alternative thinking styles has, over recent years, resulted in the introduction of a range of techniques for enhancing employee creativity (e.g. mind mapping, lateral thinking and brainstorming) (Buzan 1993).

At the idea-screening stage, the objective is only to pursue those ideas which appear to have genuine potential for success. Given that originators of ideas may develop an emotional attachment to their proposal which can reduce their objective thinking abilities, some organizations use highly structured systems for evaluating ideas. Typically these are based around some form of scoring system in which all ideas are rated against factors such as market size, market growth trends, impact on the existing product portfolios, opportunity for market diversification, intensity of competition, ability to produce goods/services, financial resources and availability of key raw materials. More recently, as organizations have increasingly been confronted by legislation addressing the need to take a more responsible attitude as custodians of Planet Earth, idea assessment activities are now often extended to cover matters such as the ability to use only sustainable resources and/or minimize the risks of creating adverse environmental impact during both the manufacturing and/or product usage phases.

Concept Testing and Business Planning

New ideas are usually framed around phrases and descriptions used by individuals within an industrial sector, many of which are often not understood by the customer. Hence the first step in the concept development phase is to redefine ideas into customer-orientated benefit and product attribute statements. The resulting concept statements can then be tested with possible target audiences using techniques such as focus group meetings and one-to-one interviews.

As in many cases the product does not yet physically exist, this type of research is often undertaken using surrogates such as the storyboard of a possible television campaign, the layout for a print advertisement, or a mock-up of the product packaging. Data from focus groups and interviews enable the researcher to assess purchase probability, appeal of product benefit and customer price expectations.

Purchase probability information provides the basis from which to forecast sales and then to evolve a business plan for the new product. The sales forecast, when linked with estimates for cost of goods, marketing expenditure, operating overheads and fixed asset requirements, permits estimation of expected profits and Return On Investment (ROI) for the project. These profitability figures are usually assessed against the minimum new product financial performance standards which have been established by the organization. Only if the plan can demonstrate that the minimum performance standards will be exceeded, should approval be given to proceed to the product development phase.

Product Development and Market Testing

Understanding of specified customer benefits identified during the concept development stage, when linked to forecasted production costs in the business plan, permit the creation of a detailed specification for use by the R&D department during the product development phase. Once prototypes have been produced, market research to determine whether the actual product is capable of fulfilling customer needs can begin. In consumer goods markets, this research is often based on activities such as side-by-side comparisons and in-home placement tests. In industrial markets, firms often involve the potential customer in the evaluation activity through a technique known as Beta-site testing. In this situation, the customer is kept closely involved in all aspects of the prototype development programme and, through usage of the test product in their organization, can provide detailed feedback which is used to identify possible significant modifications for improving the final product.

Advantages of Beta-site testing are that 'in-use' problems are recognized before launch, the usage experience offered to participants often causes them to be the first purchasers of the new product, and these organizations also often act as part-time marketers promoting the item to their contacts within their market sector. An example of an organization which relies heavily on Beta-site testing is Microsoft. In the case of their office, multi-tasking product, Windows 95, they were apparently able to use the technique to identify most (but unfortunately not all) of the new software's operating problems prior to implementing their largest ever global product launch.

In industrial markets the small number of customers, the high unit value of purchase per customer and the use of one-to-one personal selling as the primary promotional vehicle usually means that, following successful completion of the prototype development phase, the new product can immediately be launched. Virtually none of the market research undertaken during all of the new product development phases will, however, answer the question of whether a new product will survive in the self-service environment characteristic of many consumer goods markets or provide data on how the product will respond to different levels of promotional spending. This means that, prior to the launch decision, many consumer goods are further evaluated through the medium of a test market. The objectives of the test market are to assess in a geographically restricted area, the performance of the product when placed alongside competitive offerings in end user outlets. During the test, research studies are undertaken to measure variables such as product awareness, trial rate, repeat purchase rate, market share attainment, achieved level of in-store distribution and behaviour of competition. Measurement of this latter variable is necessary in order to determine whether competitors are behaving normally or mounting a specific response to the test market which they would never duplicate in a national situation (e.g. doubling promotional spend or offering 'buy one, get one free' sales promotions).

In relation to customer response there are four possible outcomes for a test market, as shown in Figure 9.2, each of which has different implications. The Case 1 high trial/high repeat outcome would usually mean the test market has been successful and the product should be launched immediately. Case 2 of low trial/high repeat rate would require further investigation. Given that the repeat rate is high and, presumably, the product appeal was positive during both concept and prototype development phase evaluations, then the most likely cause of observed low trial rate is inadequate awareness and/or poor achieved level of in-store distribution. Both of these matters can usually be remedied through increased consumer and trade promotional activity. Thus all that requires assessment is whether the increased expenditure associated with required activities would still permit the product to exceed the organization's minimum financial performance standards.

Case 3 of high trial/low repeat is a little more worrying because it usually implies that, having tried the product, consumers remain unconvinced of the merits of adding the item to their 'shopping basket' of regularly purchased goods. Typically, further investigation of this situation will reveal that due to unforeseen manufacturing problems the product evaluated at the prototype development stage is no longer the formulation being used upon scaling up production to supply the test market. Hence, unless the manufacturing department can find a way of overcoming this problem and thereby begin to duplicate the prototype product specification, the decision will probably have

TRIAL RATE	REPEAT RATE
(1) High	High
(2) Low	High
(3) High	Low
(4) Low	Low

Figure 9.2　**Possible test market outcomes**

to be that of terminating the product launch plan.

Finally, the worst scenario is Case 4 where both trial and repeat rates are low. Here one must assume fundamental problems exist and, therefore, serious questions need to be posed of the project team to find out what exactly has been going on at all stages within the new product development process. A very usual outcome is that the post-mortem will reveal the need to make major changes in either the staff or the project management processes being used by the organization.

Product Launch

Once a launch decision has been reached, the next question confronting the marketer is whether the product should be introduced on a national or a phased, market-by-market, basis. The financial attraction of this latter scenario is that investment in new production facilities can be spread over a longer period of time and revenue from one market can be used to fund the introduction into the next market area. These gains have to be weighed, however, against the drawback that competitors may develop an equivalent product which they then launch into those geographic market areas which the firm has not yet occupied. Global firms in the same situation face the even greater problem of how to fund a multi-country launch if they wish to avoid being pre-empted by competitors in key markets around the world.

In view of the pre-emption risks associated with phased versus national launch and the even larger financial burdens facing the global firm, some organizations might decide that the safest options are (a) to wait until another firm has launched a new product and then enter the market with an equivalent proposition at a later date and (b) to not even consider the issue of entering overseas markets when developing new products. The available research evidence would tend to indicate, however, that neither of these are commercially wise decisions.

Robinson and Fornell's (1985) study of mature markets, for example, concluded that if market pioneers implement an effective marketing strategy based on a new product offering genuine customer benefit, then they will usually achieve a market share higher than that of competitors who enter the market at a later date. Cooper and Kleinschmidt (1990) examined the implications for industrial markets of designing new products solely for domestic market use versus an innovation orientation of wishing to use the new product to enter overseas markets. They found that products designed for international markets tended to be significantly more successful both at home and abroad. The conclusion from this study is that an international new product orientation results in the firm taking much more care to avoid mistakes in the product development process and sets much higher standards in relation to issues such as design, selection of raw materials, specification of product benefit, marketing planning and market research.

Western Nation Malaise

In view of the importance of continually adding new products to an organization's portfolio of customer offerings, it must be of major concern to observe that in markets such as consumer electronics, office equipment and machine tools, virtually all of the most successful ideas are spawned by Pacific Rim organizations.

An important reason for many Western nation firms performing so poorly in the race to launch new products over the last two decades is that this area of the marketing management process can be both risky and expensive. By the end of the 1970s, when marketers were often promoted on the basis of their skills both at controlling expenses and at manipulating balance sheets to sustain a high ROI, it was perhaps not surprising to find most new product programmes emphasized cost reduction as a path by which to extend the life of existing products. Evidence of this frightening trend was provided by the research undertaken by the consulting firm Booz Allen Hamilton (see Table 9.1), which found that most new product development effort in US corporations was directed towards improving the profitability of existing products.

Table 9.1   *New product resource allocation within US industry*

Nature of project activity	Proportion of resources (%)
Cost reduction for existing products	11
Repositioning of existing products	7
Improving the performance of existing products	26
Product line extensions for existing products	26
Products new to the firm	20
Products new to the world	20

Source: New Products for the 80s (1982), New York: Booz, Allen & Hamilton

At the beginning of the 1980s, the growing success of Japanese and Taiwanese companies using new products to build global market share should have set off warning bells in Western nation board rooms. Even towards the end of the decade, however, research comparing the European operations of American, Japanese and UK firms demonstrated that huge cultural differences still existed concerning the management of innovation (Wong et al. 1988). Their study measured the attitudes of British managers working for American, Japanese and UK-owned corporations. As evidenced by the data in Table 9.2, managers in UK firms are expected to focus on short-term profit generation, concentrate on cost reduction and operate in the bottom, price-orientated, end of a market. In contrast, their counterparts in Japanese firms are expected to take a much longer-term outlook, build share through superior product performance and operate in the middle/top end of the market.

Table 9.2   *A comparison of attitudes of firms operating in the UK*

	% of firms responding to a specific management issue		
	UK	US	Japanese
Issue 1: Primary objective is good short-term profits			
	87	80	27
Issue 2: Primary focus of market share strategy			
Prevent share decline	27	7	3
Defend share	17	3	0
Maintain share	23	17	0
Achieve steady share growth	13	23	17
Aggressively grow share	13	33	57
Dominate market	7	17	23
Issue 3: Description of strategic focus (multiple response)			
Enter new market sectors	40	50	77
Beat existing competition	53	73	83
Stimulate overall sector demand	40	83	67
Reduce operating costs	83	70	43
Issue 4: Technological capabilities			
Advanced product R&D capabilities	33	63	68
High level of process R&D capability	30	60	77
Issue 5: Product performance relative to competition			
Quality is superior	47	77	93
Wider product line	43	27	43
Superior product performance	54	61	69
Issue 6: Product positioning			
Down-market	20	3	0
Middle market	43	27	43
Up-market	37	70	57
Issue 7: Management style			
Non-hierarchical	17	43	65
Informal internal communications bias	40	47	69
Flexible, ad hoc job roles	33	30	73
Strong team orientation	50	63	73
Issue 8: Budget criteria important to senior management			
Profitability	60	87	7
Cash flow	40	33	7
Total sales	47	33	65
Share of market	27	67	67

Source: Wong et al. 1988

Accelerating the Innovation Management Process

Only after an organization accepts that innovation should be driven by the need to meet customer aspirations rather than the financial community's demand for profitability, does it become possible to evolve a more effective innovation management philosophy. A probable starting point in this re-orientation is to revisit the classic stage gate process illustrated in Figure 6.1 and to recognize that this is essentially a linear system which can lead to rigid and inflexible decision-making within the organization.

Cooper (1994) has proposed that greater creativity within the stage gate process can be achieved by permitting progression to the next stage in the development even though certain issues may still require further investigation. Essentially what drives Cooper's new vision is a fact repeatedly validated by Japanese corporations, namely that the organization must find ways of reducing the time taken from idea-generation through to product launch. In an increasingly competitive world, managers seeking to reduce 'time-to-market' will have to balance the risks of not proceeding to the next phase until key information becomes available against being pre-empted by a more entrepreneurially orientated competitor.

An example of adopting an entrepreneurial attitude is provided by Honda who, in the 1980s, managed to produce a new generation of vehicles in less than three years while some Western nation producers still required five to seven years to move from concept through to market launch. An extremely important tool in reducing development times in the process is concurrent engineering (Hartley 1992). This involves cross-functional teams using available information to initiate parallel activities, possibly even while the concept is still at the preliminary idea stage (e.g. the manufacturing department begins to design a new production line; suppliers commence work on the development of machine tools to manufacture components that will be required by the new product; the advertising agency begins to evolve an appropriate promotional campaign).

Although concurrent engineering is an intuitively appealing concept, effective implementation is often found to be extremely difficult. Dickson (1995), in a study of high-growth, high-profit companies, concluded that senior managers often felt that they had not effectively managed the transition from sequential to concurrent engineering. Identified problems included testing the validity of the manufacturing process prior to adoption, accurate cost estimation and waiting too long before involving suppliers and/or customers in the development process.

The modern computer has had an immeasurable impact on accelerating time-to-market. Designers can now use computer-aided-design (CAD) systems to develop and evaluate virtual reality prototypes. By linking these systems to computer-aided-manufacturing (CAM) systems, engineers can often assess the feasibility of manufacturing a new product idea prior to construction of a new production line. Furthermore, if the manufacturer is willing to overcome reservations about project confidentiality, the firm can provide suppliers with real-time data links thereby keeping suppliers totally informed about all new product projects as they progress from idea through to manufacture of early prototypes.

Boeing Corporation, for example, adopted a philosophy of linking customers and suppliers into their internal data systems to optimize the development of their new generation wide-body jet – the 777. The company used a three-dimensional CAD system to design the aircraft and shared the output from the system with their sub-contractors. Customers such as British Airways and United Airlines also participated in the on-line design process by being permitted to engage in debates over the implications of alternative cabin layouts suited to their specific operating needs. During prototype construction, sub-contractors located anywhere in the world could gain access to the Boeing CAM system to obtain project progress up-dates and/or to gain immediate, real-time approval for specification changes when experience of actual manufacturing processes revealed a need to alter component specifications.

Attitude Shifts

An extremely important issue in enhancing the innovation management process is to optimize the organizational structure and lines of authority for managing the new product development process. Until very recently, the traditional model found in many f.m.c.g. companies was for newly promoted brand managers to be responsible for the management of new products. After some months on this assignment, the individual was typically rewarded for his or her endeavours by being moved to an existing brand with a much larger marketing budget which was at the maturity stage on the product life cycle curve.

It is now recognized that this managerial approach has significant drawbacks. First, assigning the least experienced managers to new products might be interpreted by other departments as a clear message that existing brands are more important than new products. Second, the very young managers put in charge of new products, often lacked the experience required to overcome any major problems which might emerge during the product development process. Third, by assigning the role of new product management to the marketing operation, other departments often concluded that they were not perceived as being important contributors to the innovation management process.

As a result of the poor track record for innovation within the f.m.c.g sector, many firms have revised their processes for managing new products. In some cases this has resulted in the creation of a new department to manage major product innovation projects. Staffed with highly experienced managers, the new department is typically independent of the established products marketing operation, acquires access to resources across the entire organization by the creation of cross-functional teams and reports directly to the main board of the company.

An important impact of this alternative approach is that new products are no longer seen to be aligned with any single department, but are now the responsibility of all employees within the organization. This increases the breadth of sources from which ideas can be drawn and avoids development delays because all departments are recognized as having a critical role to play in the management of innovation. Furthermore, because emphasis is placed on effective inter-departmental communication, inappropriate decisions are avoided which might cause problems at a later date (e.g. designers work in partnership with manufacturing to overcome potential product assembly problems; procurement validates the availability of key raw materials; the views of service engineers are sought to avoid design features that would cause maintenance problems when the product is on-site at a customer location).

Once an organization has accepted that the goal of 'delighting the customer' should drive the innovation process, then the next step is to abandon the classic 'not invented here' syndrome and widen the search for ideas to encompass sources from outside the firm. Relationship orientated firms have the advantage over their transactional counterparts because the former can turn to suppliers and/or customers to identify new opportunities for innovation.

Unfortunately, in both types of firm mergers and acquisitions often remain the preserve of managing or finance directors who take the myopic view that the primary goal of such activities is to strengthen the balance sheet. At the extreme, this philosophy can lead the organization down the very dangerous road of growth through acquisitions which offer the opportunity for asset stripping and/or the issuance of junk bonds. Under these circumstances, the organization can soon lose sight of the fact that acquisitions and mergers are extremely effective mechanisms through which to gain access to new markets or new knowledge which can provide the basis for enhancing the management of innovation.

Possibly the most effective practitioners of this policy are the Japanese, for when they recognize a lack of capability within their domestic industry, firms within the sector often embark on the acquisition of overseas operations as part of a strategy to achieve global dominance. In the semiconductor industry, for example, the US Government's blocking of Fujitsu's attempt to purchase Fairchild in 1987 did not prevent the subsequent purchase by the Japanese of about 30 other US companies involved in the semiconductor business (Forester 1993). When a complete takeover was not desirable or possible, Japanese companies would offer joint-venture partnerships or strategic alliances as another route to gaining access to the specialist skills which exist in Silicon Valley, California.

Innovative Culture

Over the last 20 years, as more research has been undertaken on the factors influencing the performance of firms, some theorists have suggested that senior managers need to pay greater attention to the nature of the prevailing culture within their organizations. Unfortunately these various writers rarely appear to agree on exactly what they mean by the concept of culture. Hence, for the purposes of the following discussion, it is assumed that culture is a reflection of the dominant attitudes and values exhibited by the majority of the workforce.

The survival of large multi-national f.m.c.g companies is often dependent upon their ability to offer superior value, standardized goods across a diverse range of transactionally orientated markets around the world. It is perhaps understandable, therefore, that many of these firms find that the most effective management culture is that based on closely defined employee job roles, permitting minimal variation in personnel policies between departments and using detailed, performance indicator-type monitoring systems to rapidly identify financial variances.

The risk with highly regimented internal environments is that employees cease to exhibit creativity and flexibility in responding to new situations. This is not a problem as long as the organization is able to sustain growth while retaining a conservative-transactional marketing style. Many firms have found, however, that as markets have become more competitive, there is a need to become more entrepreneurial and that implementing a culture shift of this magnitude is no easy task.

Perhaps one way of comprehending the scale of change required to become a truly entrepreneurial organization is to observe prevailing practices within the Minnesota Mining and Manufacturing Corporation (Chaston 1993). More commonly known as 3M Corporation, this firm has an amazingly diverse product portfolio ranging across market sectors which include anti-static videotape, translucent dental braces, synthetic ligaments for damaged knees, reflective coatings for warning signs, industrial abrasives and heart–lung machines. In 1988, 32 per cent of 3M's $10.6 billion annual turnover came from products which it had introduced since 1982.

The cornerstone of their success is to strive to retain an entrepreneurial culture directed towards new ways of delivering customer satisfaction. Rigid operating policies are kept to a minimum, salaries are tied to the success of new products and employees are encouraged to be inventive. The 25 per cent rule requires that a quarter of a division's sales must come from products introduced within the last five years. Meeting the 25 per cent rule is a crucial yardstick at bonus time, so managers are forced to take innovation seriously. Any barriers to success such as turf fights between departments are kept to a minimum and the 'not invented here' syndrome is actively discouraged. Divisions are kept small, on average about $200 million turnover, and there are now more than 40 divisions within the corporation.

At 3M, staying close to the customer is an ingrained cultural trait. Researchers, marketers and manufacturing personnel are actively encouraged to spend time in the field, and customers are routinely invited to join brainstorming sessions organized by 3M. Once an employee comes up with an idea, he or she is encouraged to form a multi-disciplinary action team to progress the new concept through to market launch. The success of a product is accompanied by promotion for the originator. At the $5 million sales level, the individual becomes a project manager, at $20–30 million sales a department manager and a division manager once annual sales approach $75 million. To give people thinking time, there is a 15 per cent rule which permits virtually anybody to spend up to 15 per cent of their working week engaged in an activity of their choosing as long as this is associated with product development or improvement.

In 1983 some employees complained that worthwhile projects were going unnoticed because guaranteed free time did not also mean necessary resources would be made available. To overcome this criticism, 3M created the Genesis Grant which gives inventors up to $50,000 in funding to progress projects beyond the idea identification stage. A panel of experts reviews the grant applications and, on average, over 100 new projects are funded every year. In total, 3M's investment in R&D regularly exceeds 6 per cent of sales, which is twice the level of spending among the other top 50 corporations in America.

Despite 3M's divisional structure, the company seeks to encourage interchange of technology. Experts on abrasives, for example, co-operated with technologists from the non-woven fibres group to create the Scot-Brite scrubbing sponge. This type of inter-divisional co-operation, when linked to all of the other elements associated with creating an entrepreneurial culture, is the reason why 3M has created a trading entity which continues to excel in delivering customer satisfaction based upon 'out-innovating' competition on a global scale.

Marketing Style and the Focus of Innovation

Major new-to-the world innovation typically occurs because a highly entrepreneurial individual or organization decides to break free from existing customer satisfaction conventions and offer a radically new solution. This type of innovation is somewhat difficult to achieve in large firms serving established markets because internal orientation is towards discovering new ways of improving the quality/value mix for existing products through emphasis on process-orientated innovation. In view of this situation, therefore, it is critical for a firm to understand whether their marketing style is compatible with their innovation management aspirations.

As illustrated by the Innovation Ownership Matrix in Figure 9.3, once a new-to-the world concept has been launched, there are two possible outcomes which can occur. Which outcome becomes a dominant influence within an industrial sector will be determined by the two factors of product technology complexity and market penetration. In those cases where the technological complexity is relatively low (e.g. most consumer non-durable goods and service markets), as the product gains acceptance within a market, the originating entrepreneurial-transactional firm(s) usually faces the choice of (i) retaining ownership through the late growth/maturity stages of the product life cycle by revising their corporate operational style or (ii) accepting that over time, product ownership will shift into the hands of conservative-transactional firms which are more competent at producing standardized products offering a superior price/quality/value combination. Whether the new product originator changes style or ownership moves to other firms, the focus of innovation within the market sector will tend to shift away from product performance towards being focused on using upgraded process technologies to further enhance product value (e.g. exploiting economies of scale to drive down prices; simplifying manufacturing processes to reduce costs; offering customers greater choice by expanding the breadth of the product line).

In many of today's industrial markets, once a scientific breakthrough has been made, the complexity of technology is of a scale that to be successful the entrepreneurial originator will need to form partnerships with other organizations. This step is necessary in order to gain access to the additional expertise required to create a product which offers genuine performance benefits to the customer. A recent example of this scenario is the Internet which, originally created as a data-interchange system for American scientists, only became a truly commercial proposition following the involvement of specialist software firms in Silicon Valley, California. Here again, however, as demonstrated by Netscape and Microsoft's growing dominance of the Internet software market, once a new product begins to achieve high market

PRODUCT TECHNOLOGY COMPLEXITY

	Low	High	
PRODUCT	Entrepreneurial-transactional style New-to-world innovation • → Path 2a Path 1a	Entrepreneurial-relationship style • Path 2b	Low
PROCESS	↓ • Path 3a	↓ Path 3b •	High
	Conservative-transactional style	Conservative-relationship style	

FOCUS OF INNOVATION

MARKET PENETRATION

Figure 9.3   **Innovation ownership matrix**

penetration, the entrepreneurial-relationship orientated developers will have to change style or accept loss of ownership to firms more able to deliver standardized, low-cost product propositions.

Once a product has entered the late growth/maturity phase of the life cycle, as shown in Figure 9.3, effective process innovation may involve switching between transactional and relationship marketing styles. It is posited that Path 3a may occur because members of a supply chain recognize that to exploit new technologies it is necessary to work in much closer partnership with others. Japanese car manufacturers, seeking to improve further the performance of their products have, for example, demonstrated the benefits of forming R&D partnerships with their component suppliers.

It is also suggested by Path 3b in Figure 9.3 that once a technology is widely understood and price becomes the dominant influencer in the purchase decision, firms which are extremely competent at conservative-transactional process innovation may become the major players in a market sector (e.g. certain French pharmaceutical companies operating in the European public sector health provision sector who specialize in the manufacture of generic drugs which can be produced at a much lower price because the original patents have now lapsed).

References

Buzan, T. (1993) *The Mindmap Book*, London: BBC Publications.

Chaston, I. (1993) *Customer-focused Marketing*, Maidenhead: McGraw-Hill.

Cooper, R.G. (1975) 'Why new industrial products fail', *Industrial Marketing Management*, 4: 315–26.

Cooper, R.G. (1986) *Winning at New Products*, MA.: Wesley, Reading.

Cooper, R.G. (1988) 'The new product process: a decision guide for managers', *Journal of Marketing Management*, 3(3): 255–85.

Cooper, R.G. (1990) 'Stage-gate systems: a new tool for managing new products', *Business Horizons*, 33(3): 44–54.

Cooper, R.G. (1994) 'Third-generation new product processes', *Journal of Product Innovation Management*, 11: 3–14.

Cooper, R.G. and Kleinschmidt, E.J. (1990) *New Products: The Key Factors of Success*, Chicago: American Marketing Association.

Dickson, P. (1995) 'Managing design in small high-growth companies', *Journal of Product Innovation Management*, 12: 406–14.

Forester, T. (1993) *Silicon Samurai: How Japan Conquered the World's I.T. Industry*, MA: Blackwell, Cambridge.

Hartley, J.R. (1992) *Concurrent Engineering: Shortening Lead Times, Raising Quality and Lowering Costs*, Cambridge, MA.: Productivity Press.

Robinson, W.T. and Fornell, C. (1985) 'Sources of market pioneer advantage in consumer goods industries', *Journal of Marketing Research*, August: 305–17.

Rothwell, R. (1976) 'Marketing – a success factor in industrial innovation', *Management Decision*, 14(1): 43–54.

Rothwell, R. (1979) 'The characteristics of successful innovation and technically progressive firms', *R&D Management*, 17(3): 191–206.

Wong, V., Saunders, J. and Doyle, P. (1988) 'The quality of British marketing', *Marketing Management*, 4: 32–46.

10   Flexi-Promotion

The role of promotion is the provision of information to assist customers throughout the process of product selection and post-purchase usage. The marketer has access to a wide array of techniques such as advertising, direct marketing, personal selling and sales promotion. Experience of service markets has necessitated the broadening of promotional management philosophies to encompass the activities of the entire workforce within the supplier organization.

Promotional strategies are influenced by a number of factors. Customer understanding during different phases of the Product Life Cycle can influence the nature of the promotional message. Another influence is market structure, with industrial markets permitting a cost-effective reliance upon personal selling, whereas the typically more diffuse consumer goods markets will usually use some form of advertising to communicate information.

Promotional strategies must be compatible with the overall marketing strategy. Furthermore, given that promotion usually represents a significant proportion of total expenditure, effective diagnostic control systems must be in place. The advent of integrated IT systems has greatly helped in the creation of more effective control over promotional processes. As firms move closer to a relationship orientation with customers, however, this is frequently accompanied by more contact between the customer and individuals throughout the supplier organization. To manage this situation effectively, the firm will need to create information systems which ensure all interested parties know what has been discussed with the customer.

Small firms often face the constraint that they are unable to fund the required level of promotional effort. One effective way to overcome this obstacle is to form promotional networks with other organizations and by sharing costs (e.g. of a sales person), this type of co-operation can greatly enhance the effectiveness of small-firm promotional activity.

Definition of Process

The traditional view of promotion is that it comprises all the activities associated with communicating information about a product or service. The aim of these activities is to provide the information which leads the customer to buy the product. Marketers have a variety of information delivery systems available to them which can be used to construct an appropriate 'promotional mix strategy'. These include (Kotler 1997):

Advertising which permits the delivery of a non-personal message through the action of renting time and/or space within an advertising channel (e.g. radio, television, cinema, newspapers, magazines and billboards).

Collateral promotion which covers a variety of message-delivery approaches including brochures, packaging, merchandizing materials, logos/company information on delivery vehicles, layout of office areas where service providers have contact with the customer, and the corporate clothing worn by company personnel.

Direct marketing which exploits advances in technology to create an ever-increasing portfolio of techniques to interact with the customer (e.g. mail shots, tele-marketing, e-mail, fax, voice mail and Internet home pages).

Personal selling which involves one-to-one interaction between the customer and the producer's sales force (or the sales staff of intermediaries) within the marketing channel.

Public relations and publicity which is constituted of a broad range of activities designed to promote the organization and the organization's products (e.g. an article about the organization in a trade magazine, or sponsorship of a popular sporting event such as a round-the-world yacht race).

Sales promotions which involve activities that offer the customer some form of temporary, increased value (e.g. a coupon usable on next purchase, or the chance to participate in a competition offering an overseas holiday as the prize).

Up until the late 1970s/early 1980s, service organizations were usually thought to face the same marketing problems as those confronting the f.m.c.g.'s sector. Hence, it was frequently the case that service firms such as banks or supermarkets would adopt a consumer goods, transactional marketing orientation and invest in a major television advertising campaign when seeking to build market share. However, as academics and practitioners began to realize the important influence of service quality in influencing customer loyalty, views about the nature and the selection of appropriate promotional techniques began to change.

Banks, for example, found that factors such as the friendliness and efficiency of their counter staff probably has more influence over customer purchase decisions than benefit claims communicated in television commercials. Airlines realized that messages such as 'fly the friendly skies' or the 'world's most popular airline' can do little to sustain repeat purchase if, during their travels, passengers encounter problems such as delayed flights, overbooking or baggage being lost. Hence, in an increasingly competitive world, where in many cases there is insufficient tangible difference between products to support advertising campaigns based on meaningful, impactful, benefit messages, marketers realized that all contacts between the organization and the customer should be considered critical elements within the promotional process.

Recognition of the potential negative impact on the organization's market image caused by employees 'behaving badly' has resulted in the promotion process now being perceived as any activity associated with the provision of information that may influence the customer at any time during the purchase behaviour process cycle – starting with initial customer need recognition and ending with the final phase of post-purchase evaluation. Furthermore, marketers also realized that the nature of promotional information which might influence customer perceptions can be that which has been communicated directly (e.g. an answer provided by a sales person), or indirectly in terms of an outcome which is the customer's own interpretation of organizational capability (e.g. the dissatisfaction caused by a service department promising that a spare part will be dispatched as an overnight, air freight delivery, but which actually arrives some days later by mail).

Given the nature of this broader definition of promotion, it should be apparent that although planning a promotional strategy may remain the responsibility of a marketing department, implementation of process will involve every employee within the organization (Garvin 1987; Peters 1987). Unfortunately it appears that some marketers have been slow to respond to this changing situation. Senior management's growing frustration over the marketing department's failure to respond proactively to a changing world, has frequently resulted in actions, such as launching customer care programmes and enhancing employees customer-interaction skills through training, being implemented by others from within the organization (e.g. HRM department) or by appointing an external service quality consultant.

Promotion and the Product Life Cycle

The nature of customer behaviour in relation to (a) the diffusion of innovation curve and (b) the growing importance of price as customers gain knowledge through usage of the product over time, does mean that the role of promotion should be expected to change depending upon the product's position on the PLC curve (Wasson 1978). The implications of this situation are summarized in Table 10.1.

As can be seen from Table 10.1, in the early stages of the PLC promotional activity is directed at educating the customer about the new product and seeking to build market awareness. As the product enters the growth phase, promotional activity, although still aimed at generating trial among the early majority type of customer, now also has a concurrent role of stimulating repeat purchase. Maturity is typically the most competitive period during the life of the product, and promotional activity is very much concerned with defending the product against competition. Typically this will require a

Table 10.1 *Marketing mix and the product life cycle*

	Introduction	Growth	Maturity	Decline
Sales	Low	Rising	Maximum	Falling
Marketing objectives	Trial and awareness	Ongoing trial and initiate repeat purchase behaviour	Maximize sales by defending market share	Sustain required sales volume
Product strategy	Offer basic product proposition	Increase variety by product line expansion	Maximize by choice of available product types	Scale down breadth of product line
Pricing strategy	Price to meet innovator value expectations	Price to increase market penetration	Price to support chosen product positioning	Reduce price to sustain sales
Generic promotion strategy	Educate potential customers and build market awareness	Expand awareness and stimulate repeat purchase	Communicate product benefit superiority claim	Reduce to minimum level to sustain loyalty
Sales promotion strategy	Stimulate trial	Stimulate repeat purchase	Use to defend against competitor activities and price competition	Use as an alternative to price reductions
Distribution strategy	Selective, restricted to full service intermediary outlets	Enter new outlets to expand market coverage	Act to maximize market coverage	Return to selective distribution

promotional strategy stressing the nature of the benefit superiority offered to the customer. Once the product enters the decline phase, price usually becomes the dominant factor influencing demand and, therefore, promotional activity is drastically reduced.

Sales promotion is an activity designed to offer higher temporary value to the customer (e.g. price pack or money-off coupons). Sales promotion management, therefore, is as much concerned with providing a tool to supplement the product pricing strategy, as it is a mechanism for communicating information to customers. In most cases, price becomes a more dominant influencer of customer purchase behaviour the further one progresses through the PLC. Consequently as shown in Table 10.1, sales promotion only begins to really dominate the promotional mix during the late maturity and decline phases of the PLC.

Promotional Mix and Market Structure

It is proposed that, as illustrated in Figure 10.1, promotion can be considered as a process whereby information about the organization's product or service is encoded into a promotional message for delivery to the customer (Ray 1982; Crowley and Hoyer, 1994). The diagram suggests that upon message delivery there are two possible feedback responses which may be initiated by the customer. First, in those cases in which reaching the product purchase decision and/or subsequent usage of the product requires a high level of knowledge, it is very probable that the customer will seek more information from the supplier. As dialogue is possibly the most effective form of communication, it is likely that in these types of situation the supplier will rely heavily upon the use of a sales force to deliver the major part of the promotional message.

Unfortunately, personal selling is possibly the most expensive method per customer contact to deliver information to the market (Anderson 1994). Hence, although all firms would probably like to include a large sales force in their promotional portfolio, it only becomes cost effective where the average unit cost of purchase per customer is very high. Consequently one tends to find that personal selling dominates the promotional mix in industrial markets, but that it is replaced with lower-cost customer delivery systems such as advertising (a) in industrial markets where the value of the unit purchase per customer is quite low (e.g. office supplies such as staples or paper clips) and (b) in the majority of consumer goods markets.

In those cases where the knowledge required by the customer to select and/or use a product is relatively low, then the customer will have fewer questions of the supplier. Their need for a limited amount of additional information can usually be met through mass communication media such as magazine advertising or an instruction manual supplied with the product.

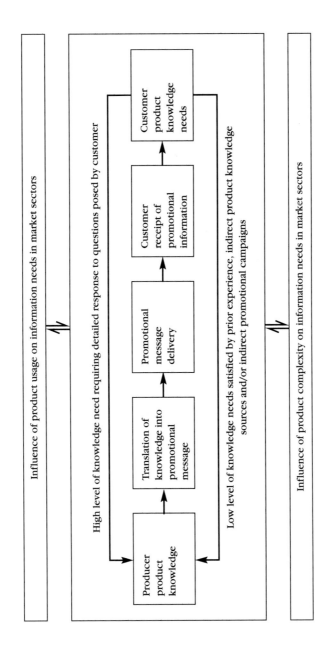

Figure 10.1 **Producer/customer information needs and information flows**

Another way of visualising the interaction of choice between one-to-one selling versus other less direct promotional tools is to plot importance of alternative promotional processes against market structure. Using this approach generates the proposition, shown in Figure 10.2, that as one moves from a highly concentrated market containing few customers each buying a large proportion of the organization's total output towards a diffuse market constituted of numerous customers each purchasing a very limited percentage of output, personal selling is gradually replaced by other information delivery systems.

Given that normally the objective of an organization is to minimize the costs associated with the delivery of information to the customer, it is critical to recognize that promotional planning must be a dynamic process which is continually being adapted to suit identified changing circumstances in the external market environment. One change factor is the reduction in information needs as product complexity is reduced in an industrial sector where customers have moved from purchasing unique, tailored solutions to accepting products produced using standardized process technologies, operating systems and components. Thus, for example, only a few years ago a computer manufacturer in the business-to-business market would probably have to rely heavily on the firm's sales force, and/or the activities of an intermediary's sales staff, to guide the customer through the product selection process. Now that the computer industry has finally gone down the route of seeking to use the same components, operating systems and software tools in order to achieve inter-system compatibility, many customers now make their purchase decisions by responding to the promotional claims made by direct marketing campaigns such as mail shots or tele-sales canvassing. As customers gain experience through usage of a product, their need for information will also usually decline. If an organization recognizes this trend ahead of competition,

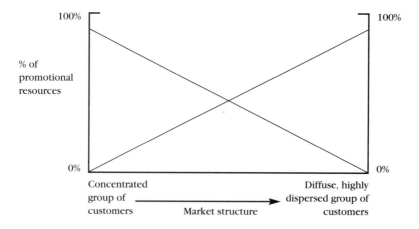

Figure 10.2   **A conceptual presentation of the allocation of promotional resources depending on market structure**

it can provide an opportunity for gaining competitive advantage. A classic example of this scenario has occurred in the UK car insurance market. Traditionally, car owners had one-to-one contact with the employees of an insurance company or staff at the office of an insurance intermediary. Direct Line Insurance recognized that as most customers only really have one question, namely 'What is the price upon renewal of the policy?', they moved to replace one-to-one selling with a centralized tele-sales operation. The impact of this initiative was that the firm went from nowhere to market leaders in just two to three years. Furthermore, having validated the benefits of the approach, the firm has subsequently diversified into offering other tele-marketed insurance products (e.g. house insurance). More recently, the company has entered other areas of the financial services market which were previously the sole preserve of the UK's high street banks and building societies.

The Direct Line example demonstrates the powerful capability which advances in IT can offer the proactive marketer. Fundamental to the viability of this type of promotional activity have been the concurrent trends of the ever-decreasing data-storage costs and increasing speed of data-processing capability offered by the modern microchip. Firms in the financial services sector (e.g. American Express) which realized the immense potential for exploiting computers as a mechanism for working more closely with their customers, have gained a significant lead over other service providers who were less certain of the benefits of continually upgrading their data-processing capabilities.

Until recently, one of the greatest constraints in direct marketing was the ability to further enhance service response by finding cost-effective ways of capturing data on individual customer buying behaviour. This obstacle has now been overcome by the advent of the 'smart card', because companies who provide their customers with these cards now have the ability to use the encoded information as the basis for developing highly targeted, promotional campaigns. It was knowledge from this source, for example, which recently enabled the UK supermarket chain, Sainsbury's, to create their 'Pets' scheme, which is a club for customers offering tips and information on how best to care for their animals. Similarly, another UK supermarket chain, Tesco, has recently created clubs targeted at specific customer groups (e.g. pensioners or mothers with very young children).

Possibly the prime objective in incorporating new technologies into the promotional process is to create 'real-time', interactive customer links. One of the critical catalysts for this was the arrival upon the marketing scene of the Internet, initially created as an information interchange system for scientists in the US defence industry. As advances in microchip technology and software began to lower both the cost and ease of electronic data transmission, entrepreneurial marketers, often based in smaller firms, began to realize that by establishing a home page on the Internet they could create 'electronic shopfronts'. Initially the complexity of the software tools available for building home pages meant that early shopfronts were really on an electronic version of the organization's existing sales brochure. More recently, however, as it has become technically much easier to add 'live buttons' to home pages, firms can now permit their customers to access more information, place product orders and, via bulletin boards, interact both with the organization's employees and other like-minded customers. Exploitation of the Internet and other technological advances such as e-mail, have been labelled by Schultz et al. (1993) as 'integrated marketing communications' (or IMC).

Promotional Planning and Programme Implementation

The various stages associated with the promotional planning process are summarized in Figure 10.3. The usual starting point in the process is to review the market situation to determine the effectiveness of the current promotional activities relative to both the organization's marketing objectives and the promotional activities of competition. As the purpose of promotion is to communicate information about the organization's product or service portfolio, it is critical that the situation review be accompanied by an assessment of compatability between the organization's overall marketing plan and the current promotional strategy.

Issues covered in the determination of future aims and objectives typically include quantitative goals for customer awareness, product trial/repeat purchase rates, product distribution targets and definitions of cost of information delivery per customer for each area of promotional activity. These aims and objectives can then be used in the preparation of future promotional budgets using techniques such as task quantification (e.g. calculation of the optimal size for the sales force by analysing data on the number of customers, required call frequency per customer and known acceptable workload per sales person) or the construction of multivariate equations which express sales as a function of customer usage rates, promotional activity, pricing and distribution.

It is frequently the case that early budget calculations generate expenditure levels incompatible with overall financial forecasts for future performance. This will often cause the marketer to re-examine promotional targets and/or proposed promotional processes for delivering information to customers. For example, a pharmaceuticals company might find that the operating costs for an optimally sized sales force are far too high. Hence it might be necessary to revise promotional aims and objectives or examine alternative promotional mechanisms (e.g. replacing part of the field sales team by the appointment of a distributor who will be responsible for managing all sales calls on small, independent pharmacies).

The budget having been determined, the next promotional management phases are the concurrent activities of planning promotional campaigns and selecting appropriate channels through which to deliver information to the market. Some of this work may be done in-house (e.g. determining the sales techniques to be used by the sales force and the selection of customer target groups), while other elements may be delegated to an external supplier (e.g. assigning to an advertising agency the responsibility for developing advertising campaigns and recommending appropriate media channels for message delivery).

Having completed campaign development and channel selection, the marketer will then supervise programme implementation, followed immediately by the initiation of processes to monitor actual achievements against plan and, where appropriate, take effective remedial action. Thus, for example, our pharmaceutical company, on launching a new prescription drug, might discover that the sales force is unable to gain the level of product adoption by the medical profession specified in the marketing plan. This outcome would probably result in use of the sales force call-reporting system to undertake a situation assessment review. The objective of the review would be to determine whether the variance in actual sales versus forecast could be explained by factors such as an inadequate number of calls, a failure to convert calls into orders or a failure to negotiate large orders from key medical profession customers.

Marketers, as most line managers in any organization, normally prefer to

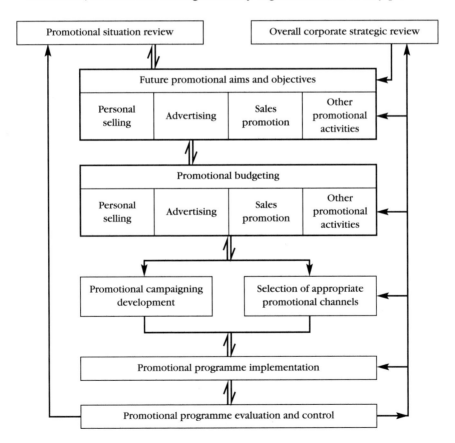

Figure 10.3 **A promotional planning and programme implementation model**

minimize the number of control systems used to monitor actual performance versus plan (Chaston 1993). Hence, in the past there has been a strong tendency to adopt control systems which provide an infrequent assessment of actual events (e.g. an annual survey to assess awareness and recall for an advertising campaign just prior to the drafting of the following year's marketing plan; a quarterly review of sales by product category; an annual report on the trend in the number of customers redeeming on-pack, money-off coupons). The fundamental flaw in this approach is that by the time a problem has been identified, several months have passed before any form of effective remedial action can be taken.

Those organizations that realize the importance of responding to adverse situations before they develop into problems of scale that can severely impact corporate performance, tend to adopt the view that all areas of their operations can benefit from regular, frequent monitoring of events (Peters 1987). In the case of promotional controls, some companies have moved to attempting to capture data on virtually an hour-by-hour basis. The multi-national computer firm Hewlett-Packard, for example, in the mid-1990s found they were encountering problems because of slowing industry growth, increasing competition, complex products becoming harder to sell and rising promotional costs per order generated (Nash 1994). As part of the solution to these problems the company reviewed how IT might assist in the more effective execution and control of promotional activities. They upgraded their direct marketing operation by creating a customer data base which linked enquiries from mailings, advertising and other awareness-building activities directly with their sales order entry and product shipping systems. The sales force can now use their laptop computers from anywhere in the world to gain access to the company's centralized data base to obtain information on potential or existing customers, and also communicate with employees elsewhere within this global organization. The marketing department can also use the customer data base to analyse markets, determine why orders are won or lost, evaluate the effectiveness of promotions and generate revised sales forecasts (Nash 1994). The impact of this integrated promotional management system is demonstrated by the fact that Hewlett-Packard have:

- Reduced overall direct marketing costs by 10 per cent.
- Sales staff now discard only 15 per cent of generated leads compared to 75 per cent of potential new business leads in the past.
- Sales volume dealt with by the tele-sales operation has risen by 15 per cent.
- Knowledge of customers has increased by 100 per cent.
- Promotional costs per customer order have decreased by 10 per cent.

The Hewlett-Packard scenario is no longer a rare example of promotional practices within the world of direct marketing. Many other organizations now use similar 'real-time' control systems for monitoring the impact of promotional activity and use this knowledge to gain competitive advantage.

By tracking customer order patterns and collecting data on which promotional device prompted customer response, these firms are in a position to assess rapidly both the effectiveness of the various promotional activities in relation to specific customer target groups and to forecast future near-term demand patterns for each of the many items which constitute their entire, often highly diversified, product portfolio.

Trends in Information Interchange

In the case of organizations operating in classic transactional-conservative marketing environments, the customer is typically seeking to purchase the lowest priced, standardized goods which can fulfil their well-defined product usage parameters. Configuration of information interchange channels in this type of environment is likely to be of a highly formalized nature. Furthermore, the active involvement of parties in the data exchange is often tightly controlled by the marketing department in the supplier organization and the procurement group within the customer organization (Van de Ven 1976).

In business-to-business markets, as organizations move towards a relationship marketing orientation, the tendency is for the number of inter-organizational contact sources to increase as both parties promote the concept of maximizing the number of communications links between employees in both organizations. Typically, this change in the nature of the organizational relationship is accompanied by a sharp rise in the overall volume of data exchange. As shown in Figure 10.4, a move from a transactional to a relationship orientation is initially reflected by establishment of department-to-department contacts. Over time, however, as both parties gain confidence that even in the most open of relationships commercial confidentialities can be preserved, then the next phase is to move towards a far more complex web of information exchange between the two organizations.

We can expect to find patterns similar to those described in Figure 10.4 in consumer markets, except that on the buyer side there usually remains only one person who is the prime recipient of information. Thus the more usual pattern in these markets is for the supplier to 'open up' their organization and make it easier for the customer to make immediate contact with the relevant department who can service their needs for information at specific points in the purchase decision and usage cycle. Again, as in other areas of promotional management, computer technology has made a major contribution to more complex information interchange than was even thought possible only a few years ago.

Many firms offer an automated routing system by which, upon making an initial telephone contact, the customer is instructed to press one of numerous number combinations to reach the department they wish to contact. Accompanying the front-end system is a 'behind the scenes' on-line response

A Transactional-Conservative Market Environment

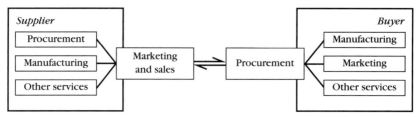

B Transition towards a Relationship Orientated Environment

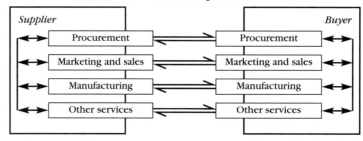

C Integrated Relationship Orientated Environment

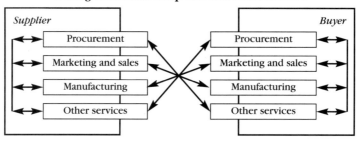

Figure 10.4 **Evolution of information interchange systems**

system. This latter element is critical to ensure the consumer receives an appropriate response. It is usually based on an integrated, computerized, customer data base system which permits the responding employee both to validate the background of the customer and to record actions which have been initiated in response to each enquiry.

Although building multi-faceted links of the type described in Figure 10.4 between the supplier and the customer can help to strengthen the marketing relationship, there exists a clear risk that problems can arise because not everybody is kept up-to-date about the latest information exchanged or decisions reached. For example, the sales department may exchange e-mails with a key account customer about bringing forward the timing of a sales promotion to meet the latter's need to revise their in-store merchandizing activities. Unfortunately, because the supplier's manufacturing department are unaware of this decision, they fail to revise the production schedule and this leads to insufficient inventory being on hand to cover an unexpected upswing in order size from the customer. Meanwhile on the customer side, their distribution centre, also unaware of changing events, has not yet allocated an inventory slot in their computerized warehouse management systems for the 'deal pack' which carries a unique Universal Product Code. This situation causes further confusion when the supplier attempts to deliver the promotional pack to the customer's warehouses around the country.

Not surprisingly, these sorts of problem cause some managers to question whether relationship marketing and the expansion of the number of communication channels which accompanies this new operating philosophy will result in a strengthening of customer loyalty. Their understandable concern is that if inter-organizational and/or intra-organizational communications are poorly managed, the 'left hand will not know what the right hand is doing', and mistakes will occur that can lead to massive customer dissatisfaction. In fact it is not unusual for some marketers to argue for a return to a more disciplined approach in which all promotional communications between their organization and the customer must be channelled through their department. However, in those market sectors where customers perceive significant value-added benefits from developing closer relationships with their suppliers, a move to return to centralized, autocratic control of information flows would probably be a very retrograde step.

A more effective solution is to recognize that IT permits a quantum leap in the volume of data interchange, if operating systems are correctly designed. Additionally, the technology can be used to ensure that all parties are kept completely informed about all issues that may influence employees' effective execution of assigned responsibilities. For this to be achieved, however, does mean that in the design of promotional communication systems, information flows must be carefully analysed to ensure all parties receive data they require, but are not overwhelmed by receiving data which are not relevant to their role.

Resolution of this type of problem has been made easier because many companies are now using (a) EDI systems to permit on-line communication between a supplier's and a customer's computer (e.g. a supermarket can link its store-level, stock movement analyser to driving an order replenishment computer system which communicates product requirements to a supplier's ordering and production scheduling systems), or (b) Intranet groupware systems such as Lotus Notes which can be programmed to copy automatically all individuals who might wish to be up-dated on any changes in supplier–buyer decisions initiated by an individual working elsewhere in their respective organizations. An example of the benefits of creating an integrated, groupware system is provided by McVities, a division of the UK company United Biscuits (Nash 1994). Having moved to a flatter structure in order to create an organization more able to respond rapidly to customer needs, they realized that their existing electronic information systems were a potential barrier in the management of information critical to optimizing their marketing activities. Their solution was to use the METAPHOR system, an integrated data-interpretation system that was a spin-off from Xerox Corporation's late 1970s research on advanced relational data bases. The new system linked 180 users into a network and thereby ensured a rapid flow of key information between sales, marketing, manufacturing and finance. The inclusion of a sales forecasting model resulted in enhancing manufacturing efficiency because stock levels now more accurately reflected real market need. Brand managers could be held accountable for the effects of promotional programmes, key account management teams could keep everybody up-dated on promotional events agreed with their respective national accounts, and management reports from the six brand managers, which previously took two weeks to prepare, could now be made available in only a matter of hours when requested by the Board. The system also had a customer service ratings facility which at an account, brand and/or factory-producing level permitted measurement of order fulfilment rates and provided information, when 100 per cent customer service levels were not achieved, on why this situation had occurred.

Promotional Delivery through Networks

A common constraint facing many smaller firms is their inability to fund promotional activity of a scale sufficient to achieve parity with other, often larger, competitors. One way of overcoming this obstacle is to form an alliance with other firms through the formation of a business network. At one end of the promotional continuum, one is increasingly encountering small firms coming together in a network to achieve greater promotional impact in a domestic market (e.g. a group of small, independent hotels in south-west England pooling their limited marketing budgets to launch a national campaign built around the common theme of promoting the beauties of their coastal, rural environment). Meanwhile, at other end of the continuum very large firms are building formal alliances with other organizations in the same industrial sector to expand their coverage of global markets (e.g. the international joint venture formed between the Swedish freight forwarding firm, ASG, and the West German firm, Schenker, to support their entry into the rapidly growing Far East air and sea freight markets (Hertz 1996)).

Having formed promotional networks, many of the participants rapidly encounter the problem of having to manage information flows, not just with customers, but now also with other members within the new collaborative trading entity. This problem is clearly exacerbated in those cases where the network members, in their previous incarnation as independent organizations, have tended (a) to seek to retain absolute control over internal information in order to protect themselves from competitive threats and (b) to adopt a somewhat transactional orientation in the execution of promotional activities.

As shown in Table 10.2, for owner-managers in SME sector firms to enter

Table 10.2 *Changing processes accompanying the move from autonomous to network-based promotional activities*

Managerial processes	Autonomous small firm	Network organization
Structure and lines of managerial control	Functional departmental roles driven by marketing and/or sales department	Structure determined by information acquisition and flow processes; tendency to move towards flatter, more organic structures
Employee involvement	Sales and marketing staff	Individuals from across all areas of the member firms and/or the customer organizations
Promotional objective	Maximizing the number of successful sales transactions	Building strong inter-organizational bonds with the ultimate aim of maximizing customer loyalty
Promotional claims	Based on communicating superiority across areas of perceived customer need	Based upon confirming the network's ability to fulfil the needs and expectations communicated by customers
Communication process	Primarily one-way from supplier to customer	Emphasis on two-way interactive dialogue both between network members and customer groups
Advertising media	Preference for using mass-marketing approaches and/or media channels seen as traditionally appropriate within sector	Adoption of diverse, customer-specific messages delivered by a multiplicity of different, innovative media channels
Use of IT	Restricted to monitoring of financial performance and possibly order entry activities	Recognized as providing the only effective way through which to manage network member and customer information flow interactions and thereby differentiating the network from competition

Note: Data acquired by author during observations and analysis of small business networks in Australia, Europe and New Zealand.

and then operate successfully within networks designed to upgrade promotional programme effectiveness, pressure begins to grow for a whole range of fundamental shifts in operating philosophies and practices. Typically the first phase in this process shift will be in the area of revising promotional claims and adding to the diversity of media channels used to communicate with customers. As the network members begin to recognize the benefits of sharing information both between themselves and with their customers, more open relationships start to develop and all parties begin to perceive that there are genuinely mutual advantages in working more closely together. This outcome causes a rapid expansion both of the volume of information interchange and of the number of individuals involved in the promotional process. In the face of this exponential rise in the volume of inter-organizational communication, the network will typically begin to move towards adopting flatter, more organic structures, at the same time investigating how investment in IT can further enhance the strength of relationship within the network and with the network's customers.

References

Anderson, R. (1994) *Essentials of Personal Selling: The New Professionalism*, Englewood Cliffs, NJ: Prentice-Hall.

Chaston, I. (1993) *Customer-focused Marketing*, Maidenhead: McGraw-Hill.

Crowley, A.E. and Hoyer, W.D. (1994) 'An integrative framework for understanding two-sided persuasion', *Journal of Consumer Research*, March: 44–55.

Garvin, D.A. (1987) 'Competing on the eight dimensions of quality', *Harvard Business Review*, Nov.–Dec.: 101–9.

Hertz, S. (1996) 'Drifting closer and drifting away in networks', in D. Icacobucci (ed.), *Networks in Marketing*, Thousand Oaks, CA: Sage, pp. 179–204.

Kotler, P. (1997) *Marketing Management: Analysis, Planning, Implementation and Control*, 9th edn, Upper Saddle River, NJ: Prentice-Hall.

Nash, E.L. (1995) *Direct Marketing: Strategy, Planning, Execution*, 3rd edn, New York: McGraw-Hill.

Nash, R. (1994) *How to Transform Marketing through IT*, London: Management Today Publications.

Peters, T. (1987) *Thriving on Chaos*, New York: Alfred Knopf.

Ray, M.L. (1982) *Advertising and Communications Management*, Upper Saddle River, NJ: Prentice-Hall.

Schultz, D.E., Tannenbaum, S.I. and Lauterborn, R.F. (1993) *Integrated Marketing Communications*, Lincolnwood, IL: NTC Business Books.

Van de Ven, A. (1976) 'On the nature, formation and maintenance of relations among organizations', *Academy of Management Review*, October, 24–36.

Wasson, C.R. (1978) *Dynamic Competitive Strategy and Product Life Cycles*, Austin, TX: Austin Press.

11 Flexi-Pricing and Distribution

The economist's view that price is an issue of determining the intersection point on demand and supply curves has proved a somewhat questionable concept in seeking to manage real world scenarios. Other factors are often found to influence an organization's pricing strategy. Customers may change attitude to price during periods of economic downturn and/or expect price declines as they gain experience of goods or services. Transactional customers will probably expect lower prices than customers who seek a close relationship with suppliers. Internally, price decisions may also be influenced by the views of other departments, and externally by prevailing industry circumstances (e.g. the outbreak of a price war during periods of excess production capacity within an industrial sector).

Distribution is the process of linking supplier to final customer in order to complete the delivery of offered goods or services. Marketers are increasingly aware that distribution management, treated for many years as merely a matter of logistics, can offer a path to new competitive advantage – for example by exploiting JIT to increase speed of response or offer greater product choice.

Possibly the greatest recent influencer of distribution theory is the advent of IT systems (e.g. the introduction of home banking in the financial services industry). Additionally some suppliers are now evolving hybrid distribution systems to more effectively service variation in customer delivery needs.

As in the case of promotional activity, firms are increasingly perceiving the benefits associated with the formation of distribution networks. The effective operation of such networks is critically influenced, however, by the degree to which participants have accepted the need to adopt a relationship orientation when working with others in their channel system.

Pricing Management

At first glance, pricing would appear to be the simplest of the marketing management tasks. Economists have clearly validated the concepts of (a) the

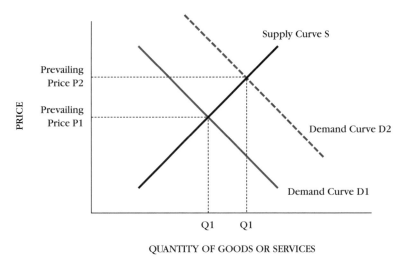

Figure 11.1 **A classic supply–demand scenario**

demand curve, which posits that for most goods as prices decline customers purchase more, and (b) the supply curve, which posits that as prices rise suppliers are willing to increase output. Hence by combining these two curves as shown in Figure 11.1, in a perfectly competitive market where both customers and suppliers are provided with all available information, the point of intersection of the two curves will determine the prevailing price P1. Furthermore, if another aspect of the marketing mix such as advertising causes the demand curve to shift up and to the right (D2 in Figure 11.1), assuming no change in the supply curve, then prevailing price (P2) and quantity sold (Q2) will both increase.

Unfortunately there are some very critical assumptions which have been made in order for the model of the type shown in Figure 11.1 to be applicable to the real world. First it is assumed that all parties are fully informed. However, in many markets the customers may have very limited access to the data required to reach a 'fully informed' decision. Second it is assumed that there are no tangible differences between goods offered by suppliers. Third it is assumed that all the suppliers (a) are physically capable of expanding supplies as prices rise and (b) desire to expand capacity. The fourth assumption in the model is that suppliers all share the same views and have already reached similar decisions concerning other strategic issues such as advertising and distribution.

Hence although over the years economists have provided some extremely useful management paradigms, when it comes to price it is necessary to accept that 'real life' pricing is often a very much more complex affair than that illustrated in Figure 11.1. Possibly a safer approach is to accept that illustrated in Figure 11.2 – namely that actual market price is an outcome heavily influenced by complex interactions between prevailing industrial, organizational and customer circumstances.

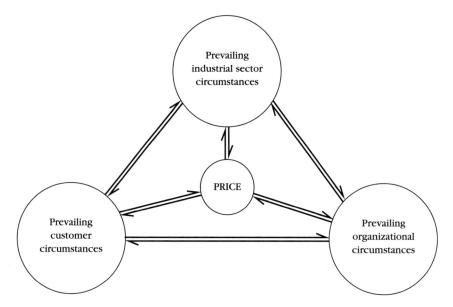

Figure 11.2   **Factors influencing price**

Customer Circumstances

Two fundamental driving forces influencing customer pricing expectations are prevailing economic circumstances and product usage experience. In relation to economic circumstances, if customers in consumer goods markets feel economically insecure (e.g. as a response to rising unemployment rates accompanied by banks charging a high level of interest on borrowings), then typically this will be reflected by a desire to pay a lower price. The same attitude will also prevail in an industrial market where firms perceive a further worsening in future trading conditions. Under these circumstances, suppliers should expect customer price resistance unless they are able to offer alternative, lower-cost offerings. For example during the severe UK recession of the early 1990s, the major UK package holiday firms were forced to heavily discount prices in order to sustain revenue.

The reverse scenario is, however, also valid; namely, rising optimism among customers is reflected in a willingness to pay a higher price. Thus the 1997 response of UK consumers receiving free shares associated with the change in status of building societies was for many to spend their 'windfalls' on overseas holidays which meant these same UK package holiday companies encountered little resistance to the full price for even the most expensive of offerings in their product portfolio.

In relation to usage experience, product life cycle theory contends that prices tend to fall as the market approaches maturity (Day 1981). An underlying force affecting this situation is that as the product matures, customer learning derived from usage is reflected in an expectation that generic category prices will decline. For companies wishing to sustain a high price, typically this will only be achieved if customers perceive that through improvements in product and/or product services, they are being offered greater value than is available from the standard core product which constitutes the generic market sector.

In the past, major brands in consumer goods markets were able to sustain a high price because apparently many customers perceived greater added value from purchasing branded goods than the equivalent own-label brands offered by the major supermarkets. In the 1990s, however, we have seen a major shift in Western nation consumer willingness to purchase branded goods. A leading proponent of challenging the value offering of branded goods companies has been Dave Nichols, the President of the Canadian supermarket chain Loblaw's. Having validated the benefits of offering excellent value through his President's Choice / Master Choice ranges of own-label brands in Canada, he then licensed the concept to a number of US supermarket chains. Among the earliest casualities in the move were Coca Cola and Pepsi Cola who found that their in-store sales were adversely impacted by the arrival of Master Choice Cola (Rapp and Collins 1994). Similar success was achieved subsequently by the British entrepreneur Richard Branson who adopted the same philosophy in his very successful introduction of Virgin Coke into the UK market.

The implications for the marketer is that in determining the price acceptable to customers, it is clearly necessary to determine the product value expectations of the customer. One way of approaching this analysis is to create a value map to determine interactions between customer requirements and price (Rangan et al. 1992). Typically, the vertical dimension in value maps is the price customers are willing to pay for the core product. Customers who seek a 'no frills' product will be willing to pay a low price, whereas customers who require that the product be augmented in some way are usually willing to pay a higher price (e.g. an airline offering special check-in facilities and rapid baggage handling to business travellers). One possible horizontal axis for a value map is the degree to which the customer seeks a relationship with the supplier.

As shown in Figure 11.3, these two dimensions generate four alternative pricing scenarios depending on price and closeness of relationship. Conservative-transactionally orientated customers seeking to pay a low price will accept a standard product and have minimal expectations of the supplier being prepared to become involved in activities such as adding pre- and post-support services (e.g. no expectations concerning the availability of a 24-hour telephone hotline for arranging repairs).

Conservative-relationship orientated customers also expect to pay a low price for the core product. In this case, however, if the supplier is able to offer additional, value-added services (e.g. JIT delivery; customizing certain product features), then this type of customer is willing to pay a higher price for an augmented product offering in those cases where they seek to build long-term relationships with suppliers. The supplier must recognize that in some cases, however, especially where there is intense competition between

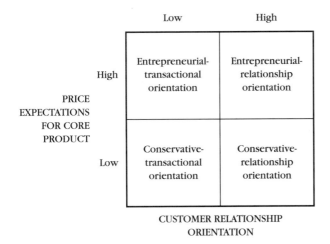

Figure 11.3   **A price-relationship customer value map**

suppliers, the customer will expect an augmented product offering, but will not tolerate being charged a higher price (e.g. some Western nation car manufacturers in the 1980s faced competition with higher-quality Japanese cars which were more reliable and therefore repair bills over the life of the vehicle tended to be lower).

In an entrepreneurial-transactionally orientated market sector, the supplier will exploit innovation to offer new, truly superior products, and because (a) competitors are unable to match the offering and/or (b) customers are not expecting service augmentation from the supplier, a high price can be commanded for the core product. This is in contrast with the entrepreneurial-relationship orientated sector, where although customers are willing to pay a high price, they also expect the supplier to work closely with them through offering augmented propositions such as collaborative R&D programmes and supplier participation in joint marketing programmes.

Company Circumstances

Price is a variable which should not be considered in isolation from other organizational issues. For, as shown in Figure 11.4, the organization, in addition to bearing in mind customer price expectations, will also need to consider price as an element within a hierarchical interaction of decision variables. The overall guiding influence should be the organization's aims and objectives. If the aim is market leadership, then the organization may perceive price as a weapon through which to achieve this objective. Alternatively, if the organization is in a business consolidation phase, then it may be more appropriate to be a price follower, only being willing to adjust prices in response to changes in generic pricing levels within their market sector.

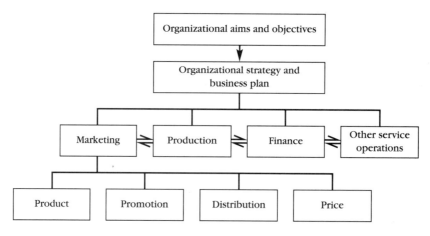

Figure 11.4 **Hierarchical interactions in determination of pricing strategy**

Price must also reflect, and thereby support, strategy. As shown in Figure 11.5, there are a number of pricing alternatives depending upon which strategic position the organization wishes to adopt within a market sector. Organizations which are positioned on the basis of offering superior product performance, have three alternative pricing strategies which might be considered.

Premium pricing involves charging a high price to support the claim that the customer is being offered the highest possible product performance (e.g. the cost of a ticket on British Airways supersonic Concorde aircraft). Penetration pricing is used by firms wishing to build market share rapidly through aggressive pricing. Successful application of this strategy usually involves being able to explain to the customer why the price is below that normally offered for this level of product performance – for example, gaining high market share over the longer term enables the supplier to reduce costs by exploiting economies of scale (e.g. Texas Instruments offering a competitively priced new generation of microchips, because if many customers can be attracted by

RELATIVE PRICE

	High	Average	Low	
PRODUCT PERFORMANCE POSITIONING	Premium price	Penetration pricing	Challenging convention	High
	Skimming	Average price	Sale price	Average
	Zero customer loyalty	Limited customer loyalty	Economy pricing	Low

Figure 11.5 **Alternative product/price positioning strategies**

the new offering, the high costs associated with R&D and manufacturing plant investment can be spread across a high volume of subsequent output).

Offering a low price on a superior product usually involves the risk that the customer, assuming that 'you get what you pay for', is suspicious of the validity of the performance claim. Hence offering superior quality goods at low price requires that customers trust the firm. A recent example of this is provided by Toyota who apparently 'broke the rules' in the luxury car market by launching their Lexus at a price significantly lower than that of competitors such as BMW and Cadillac. Their subsequent achievement of market leadership clearly demonstrates that customers are prepared to accept a value claim from a Japanese firm but may reject this proposition when evaluating equivalent offerings from Western nation car manufacturers.

A skimming strategy involves customers deciding there is benefit in paying a high price for what they clearly recognize are only average quality goods. Camera manufacturers, for example, have found that price is no obstacle for photography enthusiasts, in return for the privilege of being the first to own the latest advance in product technology. Hence these firms often launch a new model at a high price and then, after 12–18 months, reduce prices before seeking to enter mass markets. Average pricing is used by firms who service the needs of the majority of customers who are seeking average performance from products purchased. Sale pricing is used by firms (e.g. discount retailers) serving the needs of the more price-sensitive customer seeking to purchase average performance goods.

A policy of low quality and high price rarely sustains any degree of long-term customer loyalty. Those organizations which use this strategy can usually only survive if customers who are lost after a single purchase are easily replaced by new buyers entering the market segment. Similarly, organizations using a low performance/average price strategy only survive in those markets in which customers who change their loyalty after two to three purchases are regularly replaced by an influx of new, less informed, customers.

Economy pricing involves offering low, but acceptable, quality goods at highly competitive prices to customers whose price sensitivity is usually a reflection of limited financial means. It can be an extremely successful market position, but the low margin per unit of sale does mean the supplier has to sustain a very high level of customer transactions in order to achieve an adequate level of overall profit. The other potential problem is that, should changing circumstances enable the customers to pay higher prices, they are likely to change their loyalty, move upmarket and begin to purchase goods from average or premium price suppliers. This scenario occurred in the UK retail industry in the mid-1980s and forced firms such as the Asda supermarket chain to attempt to reposition itself from an economy to an average/premium price position. Unfortunately, the downturn in the economy at the end of the decade caused many customers to return to an economy orientated buying behaviour, and perceiving Asda as having become an average price/quality supermarket, some customers switched their loyalties to more price-competitive retailers such as the Aldi store group.

Additional Considerations

Although the marketing department is usually assigned the responsibility for managing price, it must be aware that other groups within the organization also have a vested interest in any pricing decisions. Manufacturing departments, for example, tend to prefer low prices because this will maximize plant throughput and thereby ensure absorption of overhead costs. In a period of financial stability, an organization's accountants will tend to favour high margins and often are prepared to forgo revenue if higher prices generate a percentage net profit margin on sales higher than the industry average. Alternatively, in periods of adverse fund flow, these same individuals will urge price cutting to reduce inventories, and exhibit little sympathy for marketers who are concerned that such actions may damage long-term brand image.

Assuming the marketer is able to work in harmony with other departments over price, there is then the issue of balancing price with other elements within the marketing mix to optimize overall performance. These deliberations will involve both determining the price/value attitudes of the customer and deciding whether these can be best met through aggressive pricing or by revisions in product performance, advertising and/or distribution strategies.

Industry Circumstances

Other than in monopolistic circumstances, organizations cannot make pricing decisions without considering the prevailing market conditions within the sector in which they operate. It is proposed in Figure 11.6 that there are

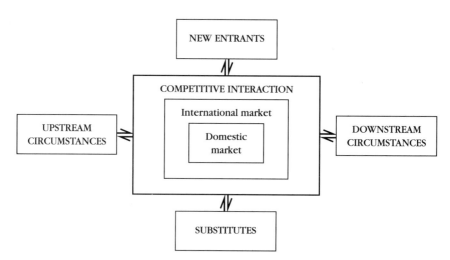

Figure 11.6   **Industrial sector price interaction factors**

a number of industrial sector factors which may affect prevailing prices. Within a domestic market, organizations will usually be surrounded by competitors who may or may not share a common view over the degree to which price should feature as a lead variable within the marketing mix.

Garda and Marn (1993), for example, believe that using price wars to achieve business growth is a destructive philosophy which rarely results in a satisfactory outcome for the supplier. They feel the approach should be avoided because as profits are extremely sensitive to price falls, any advantage gained is usually short-lived and the activity can distort customer expectations. Marshall (1997), in reporting on the prevailing pricing strategies within the UK soft drinks market, concluded that with raw material prices increasing by 10 per cent per annum, any increase in consumption generated through ongoing further price reductions could not be expected to be accompanied by any improvement in profitability. In his view, a more practical approach for the industry would be for the major companies to focus on building stronger brands by improving customer service and investing in product innovation.

Few firms can expect to survive by merely responding to the pricing activities of domestic competitors. In most industrial sectors, the marketer will need to take note of trends in other countries because eventually these can be expected to impact trading conditions in markets all around the world. Thus, for example, most European manufacturers of televisions and video equipment have been forced to find ways of producing lower-cost goods in the face of the aggressive pricing strategies used by Pacific Rim producers seeking to build market share within the European Community.

In some sectors, prevailing prices may be affected by new entrants. Until recently in Western Europe, for example, organic farmers had few problems commanding premium prices for their crops. Recently, however, farmers from former Eastern Bloc countries such as Poland, who in the past could not afford to use modern chemical fertilizers to improve crop productivity, are now finding their 'old technology approach' to agriculture means that their produce can be labelled as organic. Recognition of this new opportunity has permitted them to offer their produce at extremely competitive prices within European Union markets.

As with new entrants, substitute goods usually also threaten price stability for existing products because these goods usually gain market share by being offered as a low-price alternative (e.g. the discovery of large natural gas fields around the world in recent years, the output from which can be offered to power stations as a low-cost alternative to the oil-fired generation of electricity).

Whether upstream and/or downstream circumstances will influence prevailing prices will, to a large degree, depend upon the power which these groups can exert within a specific market system. If, for example, upstream producers wish to generate higher absolute revenue by increasing total output, the creation of a 'supply glut' may subsequently be followed by a period of falling prices. Alternatively, if these same producers wish to obtain a higher price per unit of sale, they may decide to withhold supplies from the market with the result that scarcity is reflected by an upward movement in prices. One of the most widely known examples is the attempt of the OPEC nations to control world crude oil prices over the last 25 years.

In those markets in which a small number of downstream market system members have strong control over the flow of goods and/or services, their behaviour may have a dominant influence on prices within a market sector. This situation, for example, has prevailed for many years within the UK supermarket sector where four major chains control almost 80 per cent of all grocery products sold in Great Britain. Thus if these four retailers decide to compete with each other on a price platform, their scale of purchasing often permits them to demand that their suppliers be prepared to reduce prices or offer higher value sales promotions (e.g. replacing the standard 30 day 10 per cent price discount with a 30 day 50 per cent price discount offer).

Distribution Management

For many years, marketers have considered 'place' to be the most boring of marketing mix variables because essentially it was perceived as being concerned with minimizing the cost of moving goods from the producer to the point of final consumption within a market system. Traditionally distribution systems are presented as vertical systems in which responsibility for goods is transferred from one layer to the next (Figure 11.7).

The supplier has the choice of working directly with customers or, alternatively, involving one or more distributors. Direct supplier–customer distribution tends to occur where each end user purchases a large proportion of total output, or where goods are highly perishable, or where the complex nature of the goods requires a close working relationship between supplier

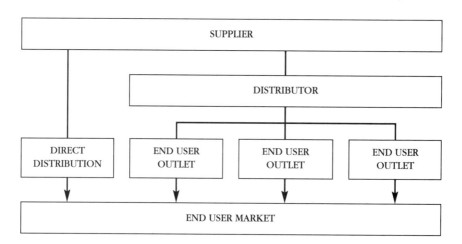

Figure 11.7   **Traditional direct versus indirect distribution system**

and final customer. This latter scenario still prevails, for example, in large capital goods markets such as the shipbuilding and aerospace industries.

In those markets in which an indirect distribution system is perceived as being more cost effective, then one or more distributors will become involved in the distribution process. These distributors will typically receive a truckload-sized shipment which they break down into smaller lot sizes. These are sold to an end user outlet who will be responsible for managing both the purchase transaction and any customer post-purchase service needs.

Multi-layered distribution systems were a feature of Western nation consumer goods markets in the nineteenth century. They remain the predominant system in most developing nations and also in many of the Pacific Rim tiger nation economies. Japan, for example, is often characterized as having long, complicated multi-level networks serving numerous retail outlets. The existence of these systems is, in fact, often seen as a major obstacle to Western firms seeking to enter this market (Min 1996).

A common occurrence in Western world economies during the twentieth century has been that of retailers perceiving scale benefits in purchasing directly from suppliers. In these cases, the outcome is usually that of cutting out the middleman, with the retailers establishing vertically integrated procurement, warehousing, distribution and retailing operations. Exploitation of this opportunity provided the basis for the successful establishment of trading dynasties such as Sears Roebuck in America and Marks & Spencer in the UK.

An orientation towards selecting distribution systems on the basis of cost minimization is reflected in many of the earlier writings on the marketing management process. Authors presented models showing how intermediaries, by consolidating purchases from a number of sources, could reduce the number of transactions and at the same time increase the variety of choice offered to customers within a market system. In many of these writings, marketers were warned about the possibility of power imbalances within indirect distribution systems which could be to their disadvantage during pricing negotiations. Another commonly described scenario requiring caution on behalf of the marketer is the emergence of a new force within a distribution channel. The risk in this situation is that suppliers may lose sales because they do not move rapidly to develop a relationship with this new dominant force within the distribution system (e.g. UK out-of-town warehouse operations which, in the 1970s, replaced department stores as the primary outlet for soft furnishings such as carpets).

The Changing Face of Distribution

A potential error in many of the early theories concerning channel management was that in seeking to minimize distribution costs, suppliers appeared to be advised not to worry about the critical issue of sustaining customer satisfaction. During the 1980s, however, the more far-sighted organizations began to rediscover the fact that effective management of distribution channels can actually provide additional opportunities to gain advantage over competition.

As in the earlier discussions about marketers' lack of involvement in the Total Quality Management movement, the discovery of the concept of satisfying customers through effective channel management was in many cases prompted by moves of management groups from other areas within the organization such as manufacturing and data processing. One of the very important influencing factors was the concept of Just In Time, because as organizations made smarter decisions about effective management of raw materials on-hand, work-in-progress and finished goods inventories, they began to realize that an important side-effect was an enhanced ability to respond more rapidly to changing customer needs.

In the world of manufacturing, the adoption of the principles of JIT and the application of robotic systems to automate production processes further, rapidly led to the recognition of the benefits of flexible (or 'lean') manufacturing systems. As McKenna (1991: 72) eloquently noted, 'in a world of mass manufacturing, the counterpart is mass marketing. In a world of flexible manufacturing, the counterpart is flexible marketing. The technology comes first, the ability to market follows. The technology embodies adaptability, programmability and customability; now comes marketing that delivers on those qualities.'

Certain members of the automobile industry such as Toyota and Honda rapidly realized that the concept of flexible manufacturing offered new opportunities both to enhance manufacturing productivity and to reduce time-to-market for the development and launch of new models. Some European manufacturers then identified the fact that by exploiting the latest advances in IT, responsiveness to customer needs could be improved through the mechanism of linking lean manufacturing with the concept of 'lean distribution' (Wade 1996). Traditionally car distribution has worked on a 'stock-push' principle with dealers ordering cars from the factory in line with agreed allocations and budget targets set for them by the manufacturer. This often led to high stocks of the wrong cars being held on dealer forecourts, and the customer was required to wait several weeks because the manufacturer had not yet scheduled production of the model specification which they required. In the UK an interim solution has been to take stock out of the hands of the dealers and to hold the vehicles in central distribution centres. By 1994 for those companies operating distribution centres, only 20 per cent of cars were supplied from dealer stock, while 51 per cent came from central stock and 'build to order' was up to 29 per cent. Currently the waiting time between placing and receiving a build-to-order car in the UK is in the region of six weeks. Within the next few years it is expected that ongoing improvements in the effective management of fully integrated supply chains will reduce this figure to within two to three weeks.

In the meantime, the lateral thinkers within the Korean Corporation

Daewoo decided that an alternative approach to managing distribution channels in the UK was to remove the dealers completely from the system and replace this element of the distribution system with their own outlets. Their subsequent gain in market share in an intensely competitive market again demonstrates the critical role of effective management of the marketing channel as a mechanism through which to excel at exceeding customer expectations.

The service sector also provides examples of cases in which increasing intensity of competition is causing suppliers to re-examine how their management of distribution channels and the exploitation of advances in IT might offer new ways of delivering customer satisfaction. Howcroft (1992) posits that in the world of consumer banking, the emergence of non-branch competitors and the cost constraints caused by tighter operating margins, caused the traditional banking establishment to experiment with alternative distribution channels such as automatic teller machines (ATMs), electronic funds transfer at point of sales (EFTPoS) and home banking. In his view, the effective management of distribution channels will be the central issue in the future development of appropriate marketing management processes within the financial services industry well into the twenty-first century.

Commenting on the same issue, Austin (1994) suggested that business process re-engineering will result in a convergence of the telecoms, computing and TV/home entertainment sectors with home banking being perceived as a natural add-on to IT systems being made available to the consumer. He feels that the high street banks may fail to grasp the implications of these trends, and questions whether these latter institutions might actually die out in a world in which electronic cash has become a reality.

Another important force in the changing world of channel management has been the move by some distributors to examine how, by changing operational strategies, they can also acquire competitive advantage. Massey (1992) has examined how, in the world of computers, sales channels are changing as a result of falling prices and changes in customer attitudes. Some dealers, in recognition both of the complexity of their clients' sector-specific problems and of the tendency of some larger manufacturers to sustain a mass-marketing approach of offering low-price, standard solutions to all, have become value-added resellers (VARs) by acting as systems integrators bringing together appropriate hardware and software from various sources to satisfy market need. Other dealers, having adopted the more classic role of acting as the link between supplier and customer, are facing problems surviving in the face of an ever-expanding number of direct marketing operations. What must be extremely galling to these distributors is that, in many cases, these direct marketers are the same manufacturers from whom they purchase products for stocking in their end user outlets.

Rangan et al. (1993), in reviewing the future strategic implications of new approaches to channel management, have suggested that the marketer must now view the flow of goods and services in relation to the question of whether channels can serve to create competitive entry barriers, enhance product differentiation and enable greater customer intimacy. Their proposal is that it is now necessary to 'unbundle' the channel functions of information provision, order generation, physical distribution and after-sales service. The next step is to determine how customer needs can best be met by channel members working together as a team of channel partners, each performing those tasks in which they excel.

Moriarty and Moran (1990) have referred to these new, more customer orientated, approaches to channel management as 'hybrid marketing systems'. They present the example of IBM which, over the years, has moved from a single channel based on their own sales force, to expanding into a hybrid operation involving dealers, VARs, a catalogue-selling operation, direct mail and tele-marketing. In the last 10 years, this has been reflected in a doubling of the size of their own sales force and the opening of 18 new channels to serve the highly diverse nature of customer needs. Moriarty and Moran's view is that the two forces driving this type of change have been the need to expand market coverage and the concurrent requirement to contain costs by improving the efficiency of channel members.

Distribution Networks

The growing recognition of the potential benefits of moving from an adversarial to a co-operative orientation in the management of the flow of goods from supplier to final customer has prompted a number of writers to promote the advantages of creating vertical distribution networks. A significant influence on this area of marketing theory was Williamson's (1975) work on markets and hierarchies in which he used a transaction cost-analysis approach to analyse buyer–seller relationships. He concluded that new interdependent organizational forms were necessary if firms were to remain able to sustain a flexible response to rapidly changing customer needs.

Although the post-Fordist landscapes painted by writers such as Piore and Sabel (1984) of relationship orientated suppliers and downstream channel members working together in complete harmony to achieve the joint aim of absolute customer satisfaction are aesthetically pleasing, it can be argued that these idyllic scenarios may reflect a lack of appreciation of real-world circumstances. For as demonstrated by researchers such as Ford (1990) and Hakansson (1982), the marketer would be well advised to analyse carefully the orientation of the various parties who are members of a specific channel prior to opting for involvement in a vertical network.

Vertical distribution networks are usually only likely to be an outcome in those cases in which both supplier and downstream channel members perceive mutual advantage in the creation of this type of relationship as the most effective basis for linking final customer with sources of supply. In reality, the nature of supply relationships will be heavily influenced by whether the supplier and/or channel members are directive monopolists (i.e. can exhibit absolute control over a significant proportion of goods or services, thereby enabling them to dictate terms to others within the system), transactionalists or relationship orientated organizations.

The implied outcomes of variation in orientation are summarized in Figure 11.8. In four cases, differences in orientation could result in an impasse because suppliers and downstream channel members will never reach a mutually satisfactory solution until one or more of the participants are willing to change their negotiating position radically. In the case of the supplier and downstream member both being directive monopolists (e.g. multi-national f.m.c.g. companies working with large supermarket chains), then both parties may be able to exert equality of power to reach a negotiated, mutually acceptable compromise.

In the case of a transactionalist supplier and a dominant downstream member (e.g. component firms selling to large OEMs), it is likely the latter will be able to exploit their scale of purchase advantage, specify price and thereby create a 'buyers' market'. The reversal of this situation will mean power remains in the hands of a monopolist supplier and therefore a 'sellers' market' will prevail because they can dictate pricing terms to customers desperate to obtain supplies (e.g. in the golfing industry, where the organizers of an international championship are forced to revise the scale of the prizes offered in order to persuade leading players to participate in their tournament).

Where a market system is constituted of transactionally orientated organizations, it is probable that all parties will be keen to attract final customers by offering competitive prices. In these situations (e.g. commodity markets such as the fresh fish industry which contains both numerous suppliers and distributors), the final customer can expect to be offered extremely keenly priced goods or services. As can be seen from Figure 11.8, only in the somewhat rare

SUPPLIER ORIENTATION

	Directive monopolists	Transactional orientation	Relationship orientation	
Directive monopolists	*Outcome* Negotiated compromise	*Outcome* Buyers' market	*Outcome* Potential impasse	
Transactional orientation	*Outcome* Sellers' market	*Outcome* Price-competitive market	*Outcome* Potential impasse	
Relationship orientation	*Outcome* Potential impasse	*Outcome* Potential impasse	*Outcome* Distribution network market	

DOWNSTREAM CHANNEL MEMBER(S) ORIENTATION

Figure 11.8   **Influence of orientation on distribution channel outcomes**

case of suppliers and downstream channel members both adopting a relationship orientation, can one expect to encounter the emergence of supply systems constituted in the form of collaborative business networks (e.g. the manufacturer–retailer network created by the international furniture firm IKEA).

References

Austin, D. (1994) 'Get interactive: new delivery systems in retail banking', *Banking Technology*, 11 September: 58–60.

Day, G.S. (1981) 'The product life cycle: analysis and applications issues', *Journal of Marketing*, 45, Autumn: 60–70.

Ford, I.D. (1990) *Understanding Business Markets*, San Diego, CA: Academic Press.

Garda, R.A. and Marn, M.V. (1993) 'Price wars', *The McKinsey Quarterly*, 3: 83.

Hakansson, H. (1982) *International Marketing and Purchasing of Industrial Goods*, New York: Wiley.

Howcroft, B. (1992) 'Contemporary issues in UK bank delivery systems', *International Journal of Service Industry Management*, 3(1): 39–51.

McKenna, R. (1991) 'Marketing is everything', *Harvard Business Review*, Jan.–Feb.: 65–79.

Marshall, S. (1997) 'Price wars could take the fizz out of soft drink sales', *Marketing*, 7 March: 75.

Massey, J. (1992) 'Distribution: changing channels', *Computer Weekly*, 28 May: 28–31.

Min, H. (1996) 'Distribution channels in Japan: challenge and opportunities for the Japanese market entry', *International Journal of Physical Distribution and Logistics Management*, 26(10): 13–24.

Moriarty, R.W. and Moran, U. (1990) 'Managing hybrid marketing systems', *Harvard Business Review*, Nov.–Dec.: 146–55.

Piore, M. and Sabel, C. (1984) *The Second Industrial Divide*, New York: Basic Books.

Rangan, V.K., Moriarty, R.T. and Swartz, G. (1992) 'Segmenting customers in mature industrial markets', *Journal of Marketing*, 56, October: 72–82.

Rangan, V.K., Moriarty, R.T. and Swartz, G. (1993) 'Transaction cost theory: inferences from field research on downstream vertical integration', *Organization Science*, 4(3): 454–77.

Rapp, S. and Collins, T.L. (1994) *Beyond MaxiMarketing: The New Power of Caring and Sharing*, New York: McGraw-Hill.

Wade, P. (1996) 'Market intelligence in the vehicle supply chain', in U. Schonberg (ed.), *Research Methodologies for the New Marketing*, Esomar, Amsterdam: Esomar/Emac Symposium, pp. 299–312.

Williamson, O. (1975) *Markets and Hierarchies*, New York: Free Press.

12 From International to Borderless World Marketing

Classical transactionalist marketing proposes that international marketing is a natural extension of activity for a firm which has already established a strong position in a domestic market. In determining an overseas market entry strategy there are a number of alternative choices ranging from exporting through to establishing new greenfield manufacturing sites in key markets around the world.

The variation in international marketing success of different countries has caused Porter (1990) to conclude that there are some common influencing factors. These include socio-economic resources, national sectoral interactions, sectoral infrastructure and national market demand.

The trend towards the removal of trade barriers is gradually leading to the creation of a 'borderless world'. This situation means that the distinction between domestic and international marketing is becoming increasingly blurred. The New Zealand organization Tradenz (1997) has proposed that in response to this change firms should move to exploit opportunities in markets in developing nations, recognize the competitive advantage of being part of knowledge-based industries, while retaining the flexibility to respond to 'wild card' scenarios.

Developing a global perspective requires the foresight to evolve, ahead of competition, a vision based on how world markets may offer different opportunities in the future. This vision provides the foundation from which to execute the three-phase process of answering the questions 'What will be?', 'Where do we wish to be?' and 'How do we define and start the marketing journey?' A critical factor underpinning this process is comprehending what core competences will be required of the organization in the future. These will be strongly influenced by the nature of the marketing style the organization decides to adopt in the management of global opportunity.

International Marketing

As demonstrated by the empire-building activities initiated in the Middle Ages by countries such as France, Spain, Holland and Britain, expansion into overseas markets has long been accepted as a fundamental requirement in the incremental generation of national economic wealth. During the twentieth century, the accepted transactionalist approach to international marketing has been first to build a dominant position in a home market and then to exploit accumulated financial resources to expand overseas.

This philosophy is exemplified by well-known multi-national American firms operating across a diverse range of sectors, who, having achieving leadership in the US market, then sought to spread their operations throughout the rest of the world) Early 1930s exemplars are companies such as Ford and General Motors. After the Second World War they were followed by household names such as Wrigleys, Levi Strauss and Burger King. Many of these latter organizations were helped by the fact that America was perceived as the life-style model to which other nations aspired. Consequently, overseas customers avidly sought to purchase consumer goods which were presented as an integral component of the 'American Dream' in films produced by the major Hollywood studios.

Most marketing texts present international marketing as a carefully planned classicist process of developing appropriate strategies and plans aimed at generating incremental sales revenue by entering new markets. Marketers are advised to undertake extensive market research studies with the aim of acquiring knowledge on issues such as market size, expected level of resistance from incumbent competitors, household expenditures, political stability and access to appropriate distribution systems. By applying some form of factor analysis to rank market alternatives, the marketer is guided to prepare a 'hit list' of those countries which apparently offer the greatest level of immediate opportunity (e.g. Bradley 1995).

If an organization lacks experience in operating overseas this will mean that moving from a domestic to an international market can be a high-risk activity. To provide a system for balancing risk against degree of control over the marketing process, management theorists have evolved models of the type shown in Figure 12.1 for firms to use in the selection of an appropriate market entry strategy. The lowest level of risk and control is provided through indirect exporting where the distribution of goods or services into overseas markets is managed by a third party (e.g. the Japanese *shoga shona* trading companies). Should the firm decide it requires slightly more control, then it will probably become directly involved in exporting through activities such as appointing overseas agents and/or distributors (e.g. the UK earth-moving equipment company JCB, which appoints distributors to represent it in countries around the world).

Licensing is a very simple way for manufacturers to become involved in overseas markets without making any significant new investments. The UK glass manufacturer Pilkingtons, for example, used this approach to implement their strategy of persuading the world to adopt their float glass technology as the new standard manufacturing process within their industrial sector. For licensing to be effective, however, it is clearly necessary to structure the licence in a way which generates revenue for the licensor and

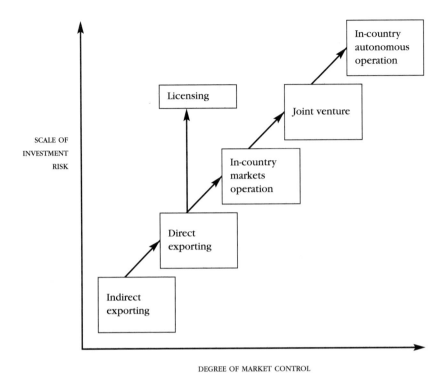

Figure 12.1   **Alternative overseas market entry strategies**

at the same time avoids the subsequent problem that has repeatedly confronted US electronics firms – namely that the new knowledge acquired by the appointed licensee permits them, at a later date, to become a new competitive threat.

   A higher-risk strategy is for the firm to establish its own marketing operation within an overseas market. This usually involves investment in activities such as establishing a sales force, constructing warehouse facilities and mounting country-specific advertising campaigns. This approach has been adopted by up-market car manufacturers such as Porsche, Ferrari and Jaguar for managing their US market operation. If a firm experiences early success, it is often the case that continuing to ship products in from their domestic plants is an obstacle to profit optimization. This problem in fact was one which confronted the North American operation of the German car manufacturer BMW in the late 1980s. In this type of situation the firm can either enter into a joint venture with another in-country producer (e.g. as is frequently the case of Western nation firms currently attempting to expand their activities in the mainland China market) or alternatively start constructing its own, autonomous production operations. (e.g. the Anglo-Dutch Unilever company's operations in North America).

International Competitive Advantage

An implication of the Classicist marketing model is that any firm which performs well in a domestic market will be sufficiently competent to succeed automatically upon entering into an overseas marketing venture. An apparent contradiction of this view, however, is provided by the fact that at any point in time certain nations appear to be more successful in international markets than others (e.g. the new Pacific Rim tiger nations when compared to many EU member states).

Porter (1990), in seeking to throw further light on this situation, instigated a very extensive comparative study of nations. The results of the project caused him to suggest that there exists a combination of factors which will influence the ability of firms to acquire and sustain an international competitive advantage. A version of Porter's international factor forces model is presented in Figure 12.2. This suggests that the following four factors have significant influence.

National Socio-economic Resources

These are those nation-specific resources which can contribute to superior performance in world markets. They might include access to certain physical resources (e.g. extensive mineral deposits), the skills of the workforce (e.g. the high educational attainments of the Singapore population) and infrastructure (e.g. the well-developed hub and spoke airfreight system which exists in North America).

National Sectoral Interactions

It is no coincidence that in many industrial sectors certain nations achieve a dominant share of world markets (e.g. the USA in the aerospace industry; Switzerland in banking; Korea in shipbuilding). One of the primary reasons for this phenomenon is that in many cases learning to survive in the face of the competitive pressures which exist between firms in a domestic market then endows these organizations with the necessary skills to overcome any new threats which might emerge upon entering world markets. Another important aspect of sectoral interaction is that as an area of industry starts to dominate a domestic economy, this is typically accompanied by an expansion of the number of highly skilled workers upon whom firms can draw to underpin a global expansion of their operations (e.g. the huge number of IT specialists in America which has permitted ongoing dominance of the world computer software market).

National Sectoral Infrastructure

Competitive advantage can rarely be achieved by a firm acting in isolation within a sectoral supply chain. Thus the evolution of an industrial sector

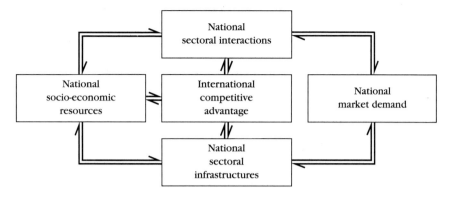

Figure 12.2 **Factor interactions influencing international competitive advantage**

within a domestic market is often critically dependent upon the creation of a support system that provides access to production process inputs such as key raw materials, machine tools and components. Italy's success in the international shoe market, for example, has been heavily influenced by access both to domestic leading-edge, leather-working machinery and to designers capable of producing new styles which can sustain the country's position as a world trend-setter for up-market fashion goods.

National Market Demand

Conditions in home markets usually have a beneficial impact through influences such as high demand permitting accumulation of wealth to fund international expansion (e.g. Boeing Corporation's sales of aircraft to the American airline industry), lessons learned being transferable to world markets (e.g. Japan's need to produce small electronic consumer goods because of the shortage of space in the average Japanese home) and/or meeting the high standards set by domestic customers (e.g. the influence on German machine tool companies of domestic OEMs demanding to be supplied with high-quality/high-reliability production equipment).

The Emergence of the Borderless World

Many of the managerial experiences which underpin the basic theories of international marketing were evolved during the Cold War in which the world was divided into two distinctly separate trading blocs, the communist and non-communist nations. At this time in world history, the non-communist nations often sought to protect their domestic industries through policies such as tariff barriers, import taxes and the procurement by public sector organizations of goods and services only from domestic suppliers. In view of this economic heritage, it is understandable that, even to this day, some marketing literature still tends to concentrate on managing the foreign customer behaviours which marketers can expect to encounter as they move into new overseas markets.

By the 1970s, the European nations had already begun to realize the economic disadvantages of continuing to retain economic independence. The solution was the creation of the European Union which involved actions such as the removal of border controls and harmonization of industrial legislation and employment laws. More recently, similar actions have occurred elsewhere in the world (e.g. NAFTA – the move by Canada, America and Mexico to create a North American free trade area; APEC – a forum of 18 Asian Pacific nations seeking to achieve open and free trade in their region by 2010; and Mercosur – a regional co-operative trade agreement between Brazil, Argentina, Paraguay and Uruguay).

Together with these actions to expand regions of free trade, another major impact on the global economy has been the post-*perestroika* dissolution of the USSR, which in turn has been followed by other communist nations such as China opening up its borders to overseas investors. In parallel with these fundamental changes in the world political map, variables such as increased international travel and satellite broadcasting have given the peoples of 'Planet Earth' much more knowledge about life-styles outside their national borders. This in turn has led consumers to express a diversity of demand for goods, from soft drinks (e.g. Coca Cola) through to electronic goods (e.g. the Sony Walkman).

For many years, the big multi-nationals have sought to exploit the scale benefits in both the production and promotion of marketing the same goods and services across the world. The removal of trade barriers and convergence in demand for the same life-style goods, such as Nike brand trainers and Nintendo computer games, means that all firms need to recognize the validity of Ohmae's (1990) claim that we now live in a 'borderless world'. It is no longer safe for smaller firms to restrict activities to only serving domestic markets, while at the same time assuming that overseas marketing can safely remain the preserve of large multi-national corporations. This 'blinkered' attitude among some small firms means they will be unable to learn first-hand of changes in customer behaviour which are occurring around the world and thus are ill-equipped to respond to new sources of competition which will inevitably occur as overseas suppliers enter their domestic markets.

Understanding World Futures

Some fascinating insights on responding to a changing world order are provided by events in New Zealand. In the 1970s and 1980s, this country was hit with the 'double whammy' of (a) Britain's membership of the EC being accompanied by withdrawal of New Zealand's favoured trading nation status for agricultural goods and (b) their government's decision to terminate policies aimed at protecting domestic manufacturers from overseas competition.

New Zealand's economy is essentially constituted of numerous small firms. Hence, assisting this sector of the economy to develop the capability to expand into new overseas markets has been the prime objective of the government's export agency, Tradenz. One key phase in their programmes was the research undertaken by Val Lindsey at the University of Auckland to understand the factors influencing the success of manufacturing firms operating in markets outside New Zealand (Tradenz 1990). This study concluded that the following factors were critical to becoming a globally effective marketing organization:

Commitment to R&D   Successful firms clearly recognize that only through investment in continuous innovation can the organization evolve unique products and/or process technologies.

Marketing strategy   Strategies must be based upon a careful assessment both of current and of probable future circumstances by drawing upon qualitative insights (e.g. information generated during on-site visits by customers) and formal structured in-country quantitative research studies. The most likely strategic position for most New Zealand firms is that of seeking to dominate global, specialist market niches through the provision of world-class products and/or services.

Market selection   Firms must avoid the classic convenient marketing approach of entering geographically nearest neighbour markets. Instead they should proactively seek to enter those markets which both maximize sales opportunities and ensure learning by confronting 'best in class' competition.

Market management   Effective market management can only be achieved by building partnerships with overseas customers and/or distribution channel members. Customer loyalty is founded on the dual platform of product superiority and treating customers as if they were close personal friends.

Active investment   The priority in the utilization of profits generated from current operations is to fund further growth programmes, expand R&D activities and ensure fixed assets are always constituted of 'state of the art' technologies. Dispersement of profits to shareholders should only be considered if this will not hamper investment plans to further upgrade future organizational performance.

Quality   A commitment to exceeding world-class standards for quality in all aspects of the business operation. This is achieved through adoption of appropriate TQM strategies which have the dual aim of both exceeding customer expectations and optimizing employee productivity.

Management style   Based on an empowered workforce operating in a flat organization where all employees are encouraged to bring entrepreneurial flair to all aspects of fulfilling their assigned job roles. Strong organizational commitment to employee development, with managers being required to lead by example and involve the workforce in all aspects of the firm's decision-making processes.

This study also revealed a profit life-cycle model through which most firms will pass on their journey to achieving dominance of global market niches. Phase 1 is where the firm first enters world markets and, because it still lacks many of the operational features of world-class firms, profits are eroded. This failure demands a period of retrenchment, rethinking and re-planning of international marketing activities. The firm having invested in an organizational development programme in order to begin to acquire world-class capabilities, Phase 2 of the cycle is a period during which profit growth ensues. Unfortunately, continued success often leads to entry into Phase 3 of the cycle where profits again downturn because the firm lacks sufficient human, financial and/or production resources to become a dominant player in world markets. At this stage, some firms are forced to retrench; whereas others acquire a new injection of equity-based capital to fund the restructuring necessary to create a truly world-class organization.

Recently, Tradenz has recognized that in addition to helping firms understand the characteristics exhibited by world-class marketing operations, the management of such firms will also need to comprehend and effectively respond to the environments likely to prevail in world markets as we enter the new millennium. Tradenz's Strategic Development Director, David Espie, has, therefore, crafted a guidance document in which he presents a fascinating view of a changing world (Tradenz 1997). For those readers who wish to obtain more information on this study, it can be accessed on the Tradenz Internet site at *http://www.tradenz.govt.nz*.

Tradenz's view of the world is that the forces of openness which have created a borderless world mean that opportunities for growth from expanded global marketing activities are almost infinite. They highlight, for example, the opportunities available as China moves to establish a developed nation economy, and India's recent moves to create a more outward-looking economy. Linked to this scenario, they point to Akamatsu's (1990) 'flying geese' pattern of industrial development in which developing nations move from labour-intensive production towards the creation of automated, capital intensive industries. It is argued that for the existing developed nations, by acting to assist these flying geese, they will find major new market opportunities for their knowledge-based industries such as computing and automated manufacturing tools.

The study also highlights the importance of not just relying on carefully crafted plans based upon detailed research, but also being willing to respond rapidly to non-forecastable, unexpected 'wild card' events. This philosophy is illustrated by the New Zealand Carter Holt Harvey Roofing Company. During a bush fire in California, the only homes in the fire zone which survived were the ones which had a roof made from the company's fire-resistant Decra Tile. By exploiting the dramatic evidence provided by aerial photographs of this and other natural disasters, the firm has been able to gain global awareness of the ability of their product to protect homes from events such as forest fires and the outbreak of fire following an earthquake.

Another aspect of the study was to note that actual manufacturing of goods or the production of core services was increasingly becoming a smaller and smaller component of the total overall product costs. This is especially the case if globalization permits the standardization of the output generation process. The leisure producer Nike is cited as an example of a firm which designs products in the USA, sub-contracts manufacturing to Pacific Rim countries and then markets output as a global brand. The advent of modern process technologies permits producers to experiment with adding value by customizing output to suit individual customer needs (e.g. Levi Strauss's in-store computer system which collects information that enables their factories to produce jeans which are individually tailored to fit the specific shape of individual customers). Linked to this picture of new millennium markets is the need to 'think global, but respond locally' by exploiting the power of computerized data bases to identify rapidly newly emerging micro-market niches and to respond with appropriately tailored products or services (e.g. a producer of yacht sails analysing weather characteristics around the globe and offering customized designs most suited to local climatic wind conditions).

As we enter the new millennium, marketers will have to be increasingly vigilant about changing power bases within their marketing channels. Traditional end user outlets may be replaced by new market entrants (e.g. retailers moving into the world of consumer banking and offering an alternative source of financial services). Component suppliers may find the horizons of their OEM customer base have to widen to encompass the new manufactures in countries such as India and Brazil.

The final issue covered in the Tradenz report is the impact of what they call 'electronic connectedness', which demands that firms recognize the growing importance of technologies such as EDI, the Internet and video-conferencing for communicating with others in their sector's supplier–customer chain. In an electronically inter-linked borderless world, only if firms desire to sink into oblivion should they resist adopting innovations such as home page sites with 'hot buttons' to be used by customers seeking more information, comparing offerings, placing orders and/or seeking post-purchase services from their suppliers.

Gaining Ownership of Futures

Hamel and Prahalad (1994) researchers into globally successful firms, have concluded that market leadership can only come from 'seeing the future' and ensuring ownership of this future ahead of competition. They propose that in existing markets this is probably achieved by seeing the future and then changing the rules (e.g. the founder of Microsoft, Bill Gates, who realized that software would replace hardware as the critical basis for gaining competitive advantage). The alternative is to see the future and invent new markets (e.g. Xerox's launch of the photocopier).

Hamel and Prahalad believe successful global players tend to exhibit the following characteristics:

(i)   Have infinite curiosity and are prepared to take on apparently impossible challenges.
(ii) Are never satisfied with their achievements and re-invest profits into new products and/or process innovation.
(iii) Are always open-minded and willing to learn from any source.

Once an organization has acquired these characteristics, they would be well advised to use materials such as those provided by the Tradenz study of the next millennium as the basis for constructing a picture of the future. During this process it is critical to recognize that few customers exhibit sufficient foresight to be able to describe their future needs (e.g. it is doubtful that 15 years ago the average consumer could have accurately described a world in which the telephone moved from being a static device to one which delivers a diverse, mobile communications system).

The first step in crafting the future is to recognize that a firm's current market vision usually only represents the 'tip of the demand iceberg'. Imagine the vast new range of opportunities available if, as suggested in Figure 12.3, the marketer does not limit thinking to merely extending known satisfaction into new markets, but is prepared to probe the issue of what forms of satisfaction have not yet even been recognized by the customer.

In some cases an examination of the 'prevailing rules of the game' may stimulate identification of a new global vision. This approach has been extensively studied by Slywotzky (1996) in his book entitled *Value Migration*, in

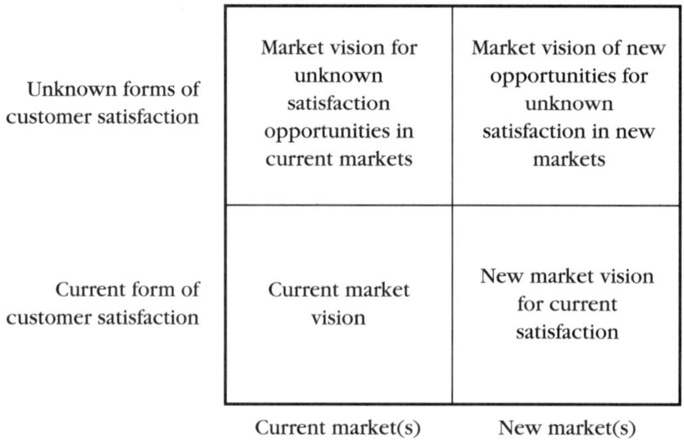

	Current market(s)	New market(s)
Unknown forms of customer satisfaction	Market vision for unknown satisfaction opportunities in current markets	Market vision of new opportunities for unknown satisfaction in new markets
Current form of customer satisfaction	Current market vision	New market vision for current satisfaction

Figure 12.3 **A futures direction matrix**

which he documents a wide diversity of examples of this approach. One case he presents is that of the US Steel Industry which in the 1950s and 1960s adopted a strategy of producing a broad line of products delivered at a competitive price through investment in high fixed-cost, high-productivity steel plants. By the mid-1960s, these massive, highly integrated plants were generating huge revenue flows and nobody in Pittsburgh was too concerned about the fact that the Japanese were gearing up to challenge the Americans through the simple process of building even more efficient steel plants. By 1971, Japanese and US output was almost equal. Then, to add to the industry's problems, some major customers such as the soft drinks industry switched from steel to aluminium as the raw material for drinks cans.

One individual, Kenneth Iverson of Nucor Corporation then developed a new vision. This involved using scrap steel instead of iron ore and building small, low-cost, highly flexible factories located near to customers as a way to supply low-cost steel delivered on a JIT basis. From this vision emerged a whole new industry know as 'mini-mills'. By the 1980s, the shareholder value of Nucor at £1 billion was almost equal to that of one of the largest and oldest steelmakers in the world, Bethlehem Steel. Importantly Iverson is not an individual who believes in a single vision. He recognized that competition from other mini-mills would eventually threaten his business. So in the late 1980s, Nucor took the high-risk strategy of building a thin-strip continuous casting plant in Indiana which permitted the firm to move into flat-rolled steel for use in appliance and automobile manufacturing.

Another perspective on effective visioning is provided by Christensen's (1997) analysis on the emergence of new technologies within industrial sectors. Again, through the use of case studies, this researcher has developed new insights on how technological visions can dramatically alter market ownership. Interestingly, he posits that great firms do not miss new technologies, but that often their existing customers are pushing them so hard to continually improve current products, that new opportunities are left to be exploited by new market players.

His documentation of the computer disc-drive market shows how, in the 1960s, mainframe computer customers demanded greater capacity from producers of 14-inch disc drives. The first generation of smaller 8-inch drives lacked capacity and were ignored. New suppliers entered the market by recognizing that a new customer group, the producers of minicomputers, were the real source of opportunity. Then along came the 5.25-inch drive and history repeated itself. In this case the minicomputer firms were not interested and a new generation of drive producers marketing their products to PC manufacturers became the dominant players. They in turn were replaced by producers of 3.5-inch drives (whose first customers were not the major PC manufacturers, but OEMs producing the early generations of laptop computers). Currently the latest technology is the 1.8-inch drive and as yet it is not clear who will be the new customer group who embraces this advance in data storage.

The above case materials provide examples of visions built upon the emergence of new solutions to old problems and the application of new technologies to improve the performance of existing products. Such approaches are, therefore, most likely to appeal to the entrepreneurial organization which likes evolving visions by extrapolating from reasonably well-documented existing scenarios. For the 'big dream' entrepreneur, however, even these situations are perceived as constraining the boundaries of opportunity. Although much rarer, such individuals are those whose visions led to the creation of completely new industries or industrial sector operating philosophies (e.g. in the past the founders of Bayer, DuPont, Ford, GE Corporation or IBM; more recently, the Intels and Virgins of this world).

Whichever scale of entrepreneurial vision is adopted by the organization, it is apparent that in the search for as yet undefined customer satisfaction opportunities, the marketer will need to go beyond standard market research techniques such as surveys or usage and attitude studies in order to gain ownership of the future. Intuitive insight or methodologies such as scenario planning, Delphi techniques or neuro-linguistic programming will need to be considered. Then, having begun to define the shape of the future, this knowledge can be used both to envision possible future markets and to pose the critical questions of:

1 What core competences will be critical to fulfilling the future needs of both existing and non-customers?
2 Which of the required competences are currently owned by the organization?
3 What new competences will need to be acquired?

Constructing the Future Global Marketing Strategy

Having acquired a vision for the future, the next stage for the organization is to define the necessary steps to acquire market ownership ahead of competition. In Figure 12.4 it is proposed that answers will need to be sought to the fundamental questions of: (a) What will be? (b) Where do we wish to be? (c) How to define and commence the journey?

In reviewing the process presented in Figure 12.4 it is critical to note that although at first glance this appears to be a classic linear, sequential planning model, as suggested by the double headed arrows, information will have to flow in two directions. The reason for this is that apparently non-resolvable issues will occur at all stages, additional data may be required before decisions can be reached and/or new information may become available which will demand that the manager revisit topics which previously had been accepted as an accurate specification of probable events.

In the first phase of 'what will be', it is suggested that focus should be on the two issues of what might be future market need and the competences that will be required by the organization to serve this market. This approach is

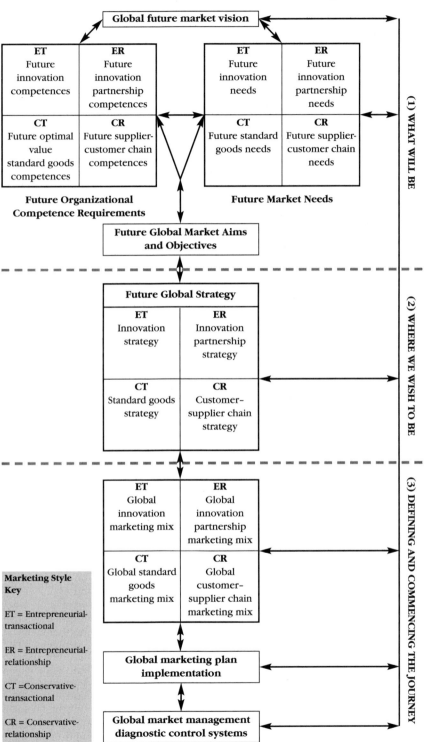

Figure 12.4 **The global strategic planning process**

somewhat different from the classicist strategic marketing approach which uses as a starting point in the planning process, the question 'Where are we now?' The reason for not examining the present in Figure 12.4 is that, to quote Prahalad (1997: 163) 'the future will not be an extrapolation of the past . . . a company has to be willing to jettison parts of its past which no longer contain the fuel and which are becoming excess baggage.'

Once some understanding of potential market need is established, the firm will need to pose the three key questions listed on p. 192 concerning what are critical core competences, which are already owned and what new competences will be needed.

During this review of future markets and competences, the specific nature of the analysis will be influenced by the marketing style adopted by the organization. Conservative-transactional firms will probably consider standard goods or services and the competences required to optimize the value of output which it proposes to produce. This can be contrasted with conservative-relationship firms which will have to consider value optimization, but in the context of the customer–supplier chain of which they might be part.

The strong level of interest in innovation will mean that entrepreneurial-transactional firms will probably embark on 'blue sky' thinking to identify opportunities. In many cases their early ideas may seem more like science fiction than real life. The entrepreneurial-relationship firms will tend to initiate similar thought processes but framed in the context of development partnerships with other like-minded organizations within their chosen market system.

Once there is a clearer understanding of 'what will be', the organization can move on to defining global aims and objectives followed by a determination of the appropriate strategy which can ensure achievement of selected performance aspirations. Here again the marketing style of the organization will have a major influence on which strategies are selected. The transactional firms will tend to favour strategies which permit achievement of goals without too much reliance upon other firms, whereas in the case of relationship orientated firms, the strategy will be driven by perceptions of the practicality of working closely with others who have similar aspirations concerning future marketing achievements.

The final phase of the process is then the specification of an appropriate marketing mix, implementing the plan and establishment of appropriate tools which can diagnose any variations from planned progress once the journey has begun.

An Example of Futures

One of the amazing features of science fiction is that the scenarios presented by writers are frequently followed by the arrival of similar environments and products in the real world (e.g. cloning of humans; computers that have an ability to think intelligently). By drawing upon such ideas it is possible to speculate on how one or more firms might adopt a global vision of exploiting advances in IT and/or robotics to automate activities which take place in the kitchen.

A conservative-transactional firm will probably concentrate on incorporating near-market technology into existing product concepts with the aim of producing new products at affordable prices. This will then permit the creation of a new global market for standard goods. Importantly, the firm would prefer to market goods through existing distribution channels, because in this way it can avoid the need to create new, closer relationships with others within their market system.

The advent of (a) in-home computers to manage domestic activities and (b) voice recognition software, might be the area which is attractive to this type of firm. Through further research, they may find they are able to launch a 'friendly toaster'. By adding a bread and waffle dispenser, this appliance can be instructed via the in-home central computer to prepare breakfast at a specified time to a specified standard. Alternatively, the householder who prefers to talk to home appliances can come down to the kitchen and verbally give the toaster the necessary instructions.

A conservative-relationship firm would also tend to focus on near-market technologies, but their relationship orientation would cause them to form a partnership with one or more other organizations. Thus, for example, an appliance manufacturer might form an allegiance with a firm which designs and installs kitchen equipment in the catering sector. Again, using advances in IT and voice recognition, together they might develop a customized hotel kitchen which contains a series of clever products such as 'thinking' ovens and refrigerators. In the case of the refrigerator, the chef can tell it what food is being considered for that night's menu. The refrigerator will review on-hand materials and if necessary automatically contact the computers at the offices of local food distributors and schedule delivery of any missing ingredients. When cooking begins, the oven can automatically come on, notify the chef when food is cooked, etc., or, if preferred, can respond to voice instructions and questions posed by the chef.

Entrepreneurial firms are likely to go beyond near-market technologies and seek solutions to problems which demand new scientific breakthroughs. Clearly a very appealing area of technology for this type of firm is the potential for introducing robots into the kitchen environment. The entrepreneurial-transactional firm will tend to favour products which can be developed and launched without the close involvement of others within the market system. This aim can probably best be achieved by concentrating on domestic environments, exploiting technology without going too far beyond the realms of product development that can be achieved in three to five years, and then to launch the goods via the Internet. One possible product could be a robot programmed for activities such as washing floors and cleaning work surfaces in the kitchen. It is likely that, having evolved this new product, the firm would rapidly diversify into robots which can execute other cleaning functions (e.g. a robot vacuum cleaner).

Robots will probably have similar appeal to an entrepreneurial-relationship firm. This organization might link with other organizations which design, build and install food preparation areas for fast food outlets. The objective of this alliance would be to build a robot capable of executing standard cooking tasks such as filling the chip fryer, flipping hamburgers and operating the automatic dishwasher.

References

Akamatsu, K. (1990) 'Flock formation of flying geese patterns of industrial development', in *Economic Development and International Trade: The Japanese Model*, translated and revised by I. Yamazawa, Honolulu, Hawaii: Resource Systems Institute East–West Centre.

Bradley, F. (1995) *Marketing Management: Providing, Communicating and Delivering Value*, London: Prentice-Hall.

Christensen, C.M. (1997) *The Innovator's Dilemma: When New Technologies Cause Great Firms to Fail*, Boston, MA.: Harvard Business School Press.

Hamel, G. and Prahalad, K.G. (1994) *Competing for the Future*, Boston, MA.: Harvard Business School Press.

Ohmae, K. (1990) *The Borderless World: Management Lessons in the New Logic of the Global Market*, London: Collins.

Porter, M. (1990) *The Competitive Advantage of Nations*, London: Macmillan Press.

Prahalad, C.K. (1997) 'Strategies for growth', in R. Gibson (ed.) *Rethinking the Future*, London: N. Brealey Publishing.

Slywotzky, A.J. (1996) *Value Migration: How to Think Several Moves Ahead of the Competition*, Boston, MA.: Harvard Business School Press.

Tradenz (1990) *Export Manufacturing – Framework for Success*, Wellington, New Zealand: Tradenz.

Tradenz (1997) *Competing in the New Millennium*, Wellington, New Zealand: Tradenz.

Index

7729671826878.